Engineering of
Pile Installations

Engineering of Pile Installations

FRANK M. FULLER

McGraw-Hill Book Company

New York St. Louis San Francisco Auckland Bogotá Hamburg
Johannesburg London Madrid Mexico Montreal New Delhi
Panama Paris São Paulo Singapore Sydney Tokyo Toronto

Library of Congress Cataloging in Publication Data
Fuller, Frank M.
  Engineering of pile installations.

  Includes index.
  1. Piling (Civil engineering) I. Title.
TA780.F85 1983   624.1'54   82-22888
ISBN 0-07-022618-0

  2 3 4 5 6 7 8 9 0 KGPKGP 8 9 8 7 6

ISBN 0-07-022618-0

The editors for this book were Joan Zseleczky and Laura Givner, the designer was Jules
Perlmutter, and the production supervisor was Thomas G. Kowalczyk. It was set in Baskerville
by Achorn Graphic Services, Inc.

Printed and bound by The Kingsport Press.

Dedicated to my mother

Contents

D.3 Records for Vibratory Pile Driving   235

D.4 Pile Inspection Reports   237

D.5 Pile Monitoring Reports   242

Preface

As pile design loads and stresses continue to increase and as the trend continues toward reducing the overall factor of safety for pile foundations by introducing design concepts involving load factors and partial safety factors, the engineering of pile installations assumes more critical significance in foundation construction. This book is more than a pile inspector's manual. It was written to assist the foundation designer in selecting piles and in preparing pile specifications in such a way as will minimize job problems. It will also help the project manager, the resident engineer, and the engineer inspector to avoid costly mistakes and to expedite problem solving and decision making. In short, this book covers all the details involved in the proper engineering of pile foundations.

Although the major emphasis of the book is on the actual pile installation process, the text describes in detail the various types of piles and the equipment and methods used to install these piles. This book starts with a description of pile types, and subsequent chapters cover pile material; the equipment, especially pile-driving hammers, used to install piles; the installation process; special types of piles; and pile load tests. Specific guidance is given for the proper engineering of pile installations under the various conditions under which piles are installed. Whenever possible, drawings and photographs illustrate such things as pile types, installation methods, and equipment operation, and examples of various types of inspection forms are also provided.

In its early stages, the manuscript was reviewed by Dr. M. T. Davisson, who offered many helpful suggestions for which the author is grateful. Appreciation is also expressed to the donors of photographs and sample inspection forms and to those who granted permission to reproduce sketches and tables. Indebtedness is acknowledged to the many authors of books and articles referenced in this text.

Frank M. Fuller

Chapter **1**

Introduction

Meaningful engineering control of pile installations can be effected only by means of competent on-site inspections. The primary purpose of inspection is to ensure that the pile foundation has been installed according to the plans and specifications and good construction practice.

Under certain conditions, the inspection or engineering control of pile installations should be very comprehensive and cover all aspects from pile material to final installation, including equipment and pile load testing. Conditions requiring complete engineering control include the installation of piles with very high design loads, the use of marginal or unique piling systems, the existence of difficult soil or installation conditions, unusual requirements such as the need to install extremely long piles, and the use of unusual installation methods. The magnitude and complexity of the project may make complete and continuous on-site inspection imperative. For each of these conditions the experience of the pile contractor could be an important element in establishing the degree of engineering control necessary. The extent of overall inspection may be dictated by the engineer, by the owner through his* engineer, or by a regulatory authority.

The term "engineer" as used in this book refers to the person or firm responsible for the foundation design. He also may have responsibilities relating to pile installation. The engineer may be represented at the jobsite by a resident engineer charged to administer the contract on behalf of the owner. The term "inspector" as used in this book refers to one of possibly several engineers working under the engineer responsible for the foundation design or the resident engineer and charged with the inspection of various construction operations. The term "inspector" may also refer to an agency or its staff hired specifically by the foundation-design engineer or the owner to inspect the work. An adequate number of inspectors must be available for the extent of inspection required. It is advisable to keep the same inspection team

*The author recognizes that women as well as men may be engineers, inspectors, consultants, etc. The pronouns "he," "him," and "his" are used in the text solely for the sake of simplicity.

1

throughout the job. Changes in inspection personnel can often lead to unnecessary delays.

Inspection is not to be confused with quality control. Quality control is the exclusive function of the contractor and is based on a quality assurance program that could be developed by the owner, the engineer, or even the contractor. The quality assurance program is a system of procedures for selecting the levels of quality required for the project to perform as intended and for assuring that these levels are attained. The quality control program is a system of procedures and standards to implement the quality assurance program.

Frequently, the need for good inspection is not given adequate consideration, and as a result, inspection budgets suffer, as does the quality and experience of inspectors. Good inspection is a worthwhile investment that can provide substantial returns. The cost of good inspection is relatively small when compared with the resulting assurance of the quality of the work obtained. Good inspection can allow more confidence in a design using advanced materials, procedures, methods, and concepts. Good inspection can expedite construction, thereby reducing costs for both the owner and the contractor. It can also control the owner's liabilities and give him what he required, called for, and paid for. In the event of construction claims, good inspection provides records to either support or discredit the claims.

The engineer, acting on behalf of the owner, provides complete plans and specifications for the project. The development of a foundation design for more important or more involved projects often involves the services of a foundation consultant or geotechnical engineer. The consultant may submit a report recommending foundation requirements based upon his analysis of subsoil conditions, the type of structure, and structure loads.

Direct responsibility for the installation of the pile foundation in accordance with the plans and specifications is usually handled by a subcontractor specializing in that type of work. Sometimes, in order to expedite the start of construction or for other reasons, the pile contractor may have a direct contractual relationship with the owner which may continue until the pile work is completed or which may be assigned to a general contractor sometime after pile installation is started. Generally, the pile contract is awarded to the pile subcontractor by the general contractor, in which case the pile subcontract is tied in many ways to the general contract. The engineer is frequently involved in the selection of the pile subcontractor.

The engineer is often responsible for the construction following the intent of the contract documents. His authority includes the right to approve the work done and to make decisions either with or without the owner. He can stop work if necessary, and he has the responsibility for final inspection and approval of payment quantities. The term "supervise" or "supervision of the work" is often found in documents defining the engineer's responsibilities. This is not intended to mean directing the work. To remove any chance of misconception, such terms should be avoided. The engineer should establish

General view of pile driving.
(*Courtesy of Raymond International Builders, Inc.*)

the type of data to be recorded during inspection, and if he is directly responsible for inspection, he should design the appropriate inspection forms.

One of the key elements in the inspection process is the qualifications of the inspector. His required qualifications are in direct proportion to his duties, responsibilities, and authority and to the complexity of the project. The role of inspector should be considered a professional service. To be designated as an inspector implies knowing what is to be inspected. The inspector must have adequate technical training and construction experience in the field of work involved. For pile foundation work, he must be familiar with the basic and special types of piles and their advantages, disadvantages, and limitations. He must have a knowledge of the equipment, methods, and techniques used for pile installation, and he should be aware of the limitations of pile installation equipment. The inspector should have a thorough understanding of the plans, specifications, and contract documents as they relate to the required pile foundation. He should be able to exercise good judgment and have the ability to work with people.

If the inspector does not have the necessary qualifications, experience, and training, the result is often an adversarial work relationship with the contractor. The inspector could create unnecessary delays, could miss noticing situations that should be brought to the attention of the engineer, and may require the contractor to do more than necessary to comply with the plans and specifications. This may lead to claims by the contractor for extra compensation. In some cases, a poorly trained and unqualified inspector could approve inferior work through ignorance.

The duties and responsibilities of a pile inspector can be very broad or quite narrow depending upon the requirements of the owner, the engineer, or the regulatory authority. These duties and responsibilities should be clearly set forth and understood by all concerned. The duties of the inspector should basically be to observe and report. He should not assume or be placed in the position of directing the work. The inspector's primary responsibility is to act on the owner's or the engineer's behalf to see that the piles are installed in accordance with the plans and specifications or subsequent approved revisions. He should call possible errors to the engineer's attention. His duties and responsibilities also involve taking measurements and recording data to establish a clear and complete record of the work performed. He should not tell the contractor what to do, and any ideas or suggestions expressed should not be considered direction or advice. All inspections should be made timely so as not to delay the contractor's work.

In addition to responsibilities and duties, the inspector should, if possible, have some degree of authority. Decisions that can be made at the job level can often eliminate substantial delays and improve relationships with the contractor. If the inspector has the necessary experience and training and knows the objectives of the plans and specifications, he can make meaningful judgments and decisions. There will, of course, be decisions that must be referred to the engineer. The limits of authority for each inspector must be clearly defined and understood by all.

For the completion of a satisfactory pile foundation, not all design and construction decisions can be made in advance. No set of construction plans and specifications is without error, and unforeseen conditions are frequently revealed as the work progresses, requiring both major and minor modifications. Major changes involve a decision-making responsibility which frequently results in substantial cost increases to the owner. Decisions based upon changed or unanticipated conditions must be made promptly to minimize construction delays, which could be quite costly to the owner in terms of both money and time. They could also lead to claims by the contractor. The responsibility for such decisions rests with the engineer and should involve the consultant. The owner must also be a part of the decision-making process, since he pays the eventual cost. Timely decisions require that current and accurate reports on the progress of the work be given to the engineer. This in turn requires continuous on-site inspection to be handled by qualified engineers.

The inspector must be furnished with copies of all plans and specifications, including general conditions, which relate to pile installation. He should also have a copy of the basic provisions of the contract governing pile installation which define the various responsibilities of the owner, the engineer, and the contractor and which may determine the payment methods. Copies of any geotechnical reports, including boring logs and the results of any field or laboratory tests, should be given to the inspector. He should have access to any soil or rock samples recovered.

Copies of all contractor submittals, including the shop drawing of the equipment, pile type, and installation methods, should be given to the inspector along with copies of any inspection or test reports or certificates relating to pile material, including the approved concrete design mix and results of concrete tests. The inspector should have a copy of all pile construction schedules, including the planned sequence of operations. Finally, the inspector should obtain copies of any referenced codes, standards, or specifications which may govern the work to be performed, such as ASTM load-test standards.

The inspector must keep clear, complete, and legible records. All original (field) notes and records must be retained, even though the information may be transcribed for reporting purposes. In addition to the prescribed inspection records and reports, it is recommended that the inspector keep a daily diary for recording the events of each construction day as they may relate to pile installation. Everything pertaining to the equipment, methods, and materials used to accomplish the work should be documented. All field reports must be prepared and submitted on a timely basis. All certificates of inspection, laboratory reports, or other documents received by the inspector must be retained and submitted with appropriate reports. Progress photographs may be part of the inspection reports.

Chapter 2

Types of Piles

Piles are columnlike structural elements driven or otherwise embedded in the ground, primarily to transfer superimposed loads down through soils of insufficient bearing capacity to soils of adequate bearing capacity. In addition to supporting structures, piles are also used to anchor structures against uplift forces and to assist structures in resisting lateral and overturning forces. Piles are generally constructed of timber, steel, concrete, or a combination of these materials. Figure 2-1 shows the basic types of piles. The inspector should be familiar with the various types of piles, their characteristics, and their methods of installation.

This chapter covers the principal characteristics and installation methods for the different types of piles which are in use in the United States. Chapter 5 covers in more detail the installation methods applicable, in general, to conventional types of piling and the necessary precautions that may have to be taken to ensure proper installation. Chapter 6 covers further considerations for special types of piles.

2.1 TIMBER PILES

Round timber piles are whole trees with the branches and bark removed (clean-peeled). They are driven with the small end down. Timber piles can also be installed with the bark either still on (unpeeled) or only partially removed (rough-peeled). The use of timber piles probably predates recorded history, and in ancient times, for practical installation reasons, very short piles, in a range of 3 to 10 ft (1 to 3 m), were used.

As indicated in Figure 2-2, timber piles are either untreated or treated with a preservative to help resist the attacks of decay, insects, and marine borers. Several different species and subspecies are used, but the principal types are shown in Figure 2-2. Most of the timber piles used today are softwood, either southern pine or Douglas fir. Red oak piles are used in areas in which red oaks grow, depending on length requirements. Sometimes exotic species such as

6

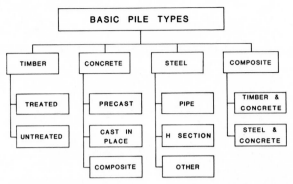

Figure 2-1 Basic pile types.

greenheart from South and Central America are used for marine structures on the basis that such timber is relatively immune to marine borer attack. However, there are known cases where severe borer attack of greenheart has been observed. Greenheart and similar species cannot be treated because of their densities and are very difficult to work with.

For round timber piles, the material specification generally referred to is ASTM D 25, *Standard Specification for Round Timber Piles.* Sawed timber could be used for piles, in which case ASTM D 25 does not apply. The material specifications for sawed-timber piles should be stricter than D 25, especially with regard to knots, and only light design loads should be permitted.

2.2 STEEL PILES

This category includes those piles for which the sole structural material is steel, such as H sections, special sections, and pipe not filled with concrete (see Figure 2-1).

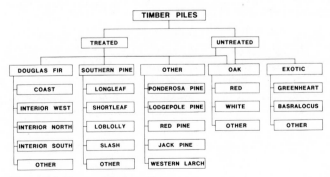

Figure 2-2 Types of timber piles.

Driving treated timber piles. (*Courtesy of Koppers Company, Inc.*)

2.2.1 H Sections. These can be either rolled (HP shapes) or built up. HP shapes are manufactured in various sizes and weights as shown in Table C-1. If the piles are built up, they should be of the H-section type, with the web and flanges of the same thickness. These piles are produced in standard mill lengths of 40 to 60 ft (12 to 18 m) but can be furnished by special order to lengths of over 100 ft. H piles can be readily spliced on the job to whatever lengths are required.

2.2.2 Pipe Piles. In this category, the pipe pile is not filled with concrete. The structural material is entirely steel. Concrete-filled pipe piles will be discussed in Section 2.3.2.3.3. Pipe used for piling is manufactured in various diameters and wall thicknesses as shown in Table C-2. In this category, pipe piles are generally driven open-ended, and the soil inside the pipe is not cleaned out.

2.2.3 Special Sections. Steel piles can be fabricated by welding together various structural shapes such as channels or steel sheet pile sections known as "box piles." These are not commonly used in the United States. Special steel piles can also be made up by welding together two or three railroad rails. Steel piles of this type are rarely used.

2.3 CONCRETE PILES

There are many types of concrete piles, as shown in Figure 2-3. The basic types are precast and cast-in-place. To this could be added composite piles, the top portion of which is concrete and the bottom portion timber or steel.

2.3.1 Precast Concrete Piles.

Precast concrete piles include those conventionally reinforced and prestressed (see Figure 2-3). Reinforced piles can be made at the jobsite or in an established plant. Prestressed piles are generally plant-manufactured. The design of precast concrete piles may vary with the manufacturer or be governed by job conditions. The design can be guided by ACI 543R[12] or by the PCI Pile Committee report.[53] Other standards are in use, such as those prepared by the Joint Committee of the American Association of State Highway and Transportation Officials (AASHTO) and the Prestressed Concrete Institute (PCI).

Conventional reinforced piles generally have a solid cross section and can be square, round, or octagonal. Prestressed piles can be of the same basic shapes, but they may have a hollow core with solid ends or be cylindrical with open ends. Prestressed concrete piles can be either pretensioned or posttensioned, and they can be bedcast, vertically cast, or centrifugally cast.

2.3.1.1 Sectional Precast Concrete Piles.

Full-length precast concrete piles can be made and driven, or sections can be assembled into full pile lengths either during or before driving. As shown in Figure 2-4, most of these sectional concrete piles are assembled during driving through the use of various basic types of joints or splicing methods. These are the sleeve splice, the dowel

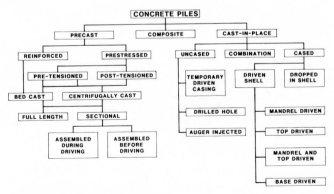

Figure 2-3 Types of concrete piles.

Driving 12-in-square precast, prestressed concrete piles. (*Courtesy of J. H. Pomeroy & Co., Inc.*)

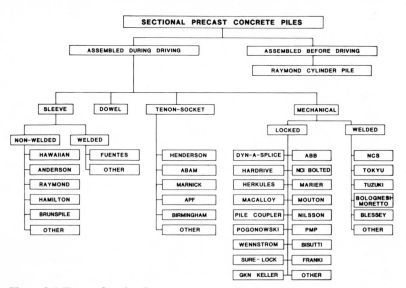

Figure 2-4 Types of sectional precast concrete piles.

10

splice, the tenon-and-socket joint, and the mechanical joint, either locked or welded.

For these basic methods, a considerable number of special systems have been used or proposed, many of which are proprietary.[59] Figures 2-5, 2-6, and 2-7 illustrate some typical special joints or splicing methods.

The Anderson splice (Figure 2-5a) consists of a simple sleeve which can be shaped to tightly fit the pile. Stops in the center of the sleeve provide for equal engagement of the pile section to be joined. A plywood pad is placed between the abutting ends. The Hawaiian sleeve splice is very similar, and usually a sheet of lead is used as a cushion between the pile sections. The Hamilton Form Company splice is of the same principle, but the sleeve consists of two semicylindrical pieces that are placed around the pile joint and bolted together. The Raymond sleeve splice was developed for repairing piles by adding sections; however, it can be used for installing sectional precast piles. It differs from the Anderson splice in that the sleeve is a loose fit, and provisions are made for grouting the annulus between the pile and the sleeve and the space between the pile sections, which are held apart by short lengths of exposed reinforcing steel or strand.

Figure 2-5b illustrates the Brunspile wedge-type sleeve splice. Steel ferrules are cast into the ends of the pile sections, which are joined together with a drive sleeve. The Fuentes splice (Figure 2-5c) is a welded sleeve joint. Steel bands are cast into the pile sections about 18 in (460 mm) from the ends. The steel sleeve is welded to these bands. Figure 2-5d shows one of several types of dowel splices. The dowels can be cast in the bottom end of the pile section to be added and grouted with cement or epoxy into holes cast or drilled into the top of the driven section. Alternatively, holes could be cast or drilled in the ends of both pile sections and the dowels inserted and grouted when the sections are joined.

The ABAM Engineers splice (Figure 2-6a) is one of several tenon-and-socket joints. Steel male and female fittings are cast into the ends of the pile sections. After the sections are joined, steel wedges are driven between the tenon and socket through holes in the socket. The wedges are welded in place. The Henderson tenon-and-socket joint is completed by inserting a steel pin through a built-in transverse sleeve and welding the ends of the pin to the socket. The APF splice is similar to the Henderson splice except that the tenon and socket are smaller, two transverse pins 90° apart may be used, and the pins are held in place with a cotter.

For the Birmingham splice, a bead on the tenon engages a matching groove in the socket when the two pile sections are driven together. The Marnick splice is a special type of tenon-and-socket joint. The tenon is a short piece of pipe that is driven into a circular slot running through the socket. The slot has an offset into which the tenon is forced by the pile hammer blows.

Figure 2-6b illustrates the Herkules joint. Machined steel fittings are cast into the ends of the pile sections. When the sections are joined, the upper

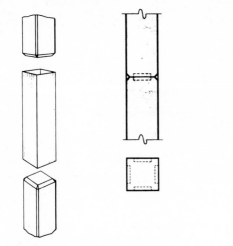

SOURCE OF INFORMATION

CONCRETE TECHNOLOGY,CORPORATION
1123 PORT OF TACOMA ROAD
TACOMA
WASHINGTON

A. ANDERSON SPLICE

SOURCE OF INFORMATION

BELDEN CONCRETE PRODUCTS, INC.
P. O. BOX 607
METAIRIE
LOUISIANA

B. BRUNSPILE SPLICE

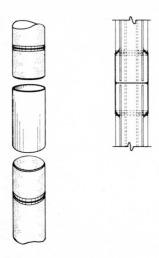

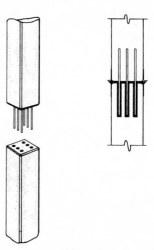

SOURCE OF INFORMATION

FUENTES CONCRETE PILE
BOX 867
BAYAMON
PUERTO RICO

C. FUENTES SPLICE

SOURCE OF INFORMATION

SOUTHERN BLOCK & PIPE CORPORATION
P. O. BOX 1778
NORFOLK
VIRGINIA

D. CEMENT–DOWEL SPLICE

Figure 2-5 Typical splicing methods for sectional precast concrete piles. (*After R. N. Bruce, Jr., and D. C. Hebert.*[59] *Reprinted with permission from the Prestressed Concrete Institute.*)

12

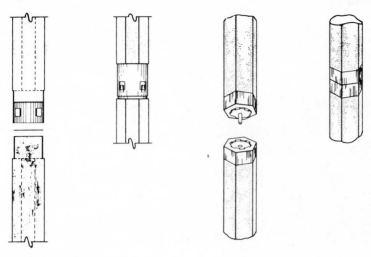

SOURCE OF INFORMATION

RAYMOND INTERNATIONAL INC.
P. O. BOX 22718
HOUSTON
TEXAS

A. ABAM SPLICE

SOURCE OF INFORMATION

AB SCANPILE
S-400 60 GOTHENBURG 6
P. O. BOX 6040
SWEDEN

B. HERKULES SPLICE

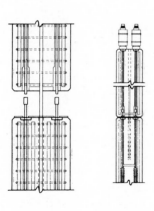

SOURCE OF INFORMATION

THE CONCRETE SOCIETY
TERMINAL HOUSE
GROSVENOR GARDENS
LONDON, ENGLAND

C. MACALLOY SPLICE

SOURCE OF INFORMATION

ELOT A. WENNSTROM
OREBRO
SWEDEN

D. WENNSTROM SPLICE

Figure 2-6 Typical splicing methods for sectional precast concrete piles. (*After R. N. Bruce, Jr., and D. C. Hebert.*[59] *Reprinted with permission from the Prestressed Concrete Institute.*)

13

Inserting the locking key for the Hardrive splice. (*Courtesy of Associated Pile & Fitting Corp.*)

section is rotated to engage the matching lugs in the male and female castings, and allen screws are tightened to hold the sections in position. The Macalloy splice (Figure 2-6c) provides for prestressing across the joint. Ducts are cast into the pile sections to contain the prestressing bars, which are screw-connected at each joint. After complete pile installation, the bars, anchored at the pile tip, are posttensioned with jacks at the pile top. The Wennstrom splice, as shown in Figure 2-6d, is typical of several joints using small keys that hold the joint together. Special steel plates are machined to take the keys and are cast into the ends of the pile sections. After the ends are joined, the wedgelike keys are driven into place to lock the pile sections together. The West's Hardrive, the Dyn-a-Splice, the Gupta PMP, and the GKN Keller methods are all similar in principle to the Wennstrom splice. The major differences are the shapes and locations of the keys. For the ABB splice, which is in this same general category, recessed lock blocks are welded to the ends of alternate longitudinal reinforcement, and the ends of opposing bars are fitted with projecting enlarged endpieces having a hole through them. When engaged, the enlarged endpieces fit into the lock blocks, and locking pins are driven through the blocks and the endpieces.

Figure 2-7a shows a typical bolted-type splice. The NCI bolted splice illustrated requires that rather elaborate fittings be cast into the ends of the pile sections. The fitting at the bottom end of the section to be added has stud bolts, and these are inserted in matching holes in the other fitting as the pile sections are joined. The Bisutti splice is another bolted joint. The fittings are recessed at each bolt hole to provide space for inserting and tightening bolts so that the plates and bolts do not project beyond the pile surfaces. The Pogonowski splice can be used to join together large-diameter cylindrical piles

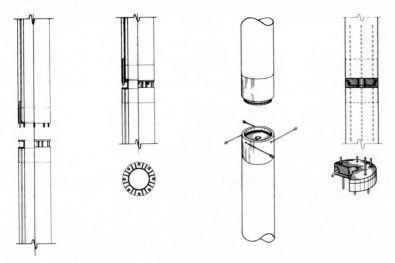

A. NCI BOLTED SPLICE

B. MARIER SPLICE

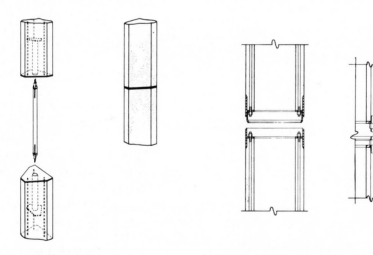

C. MOUTON SPLICE

D. TOKYU SPLICE

Figure 2-7 Typical splicing methods for sectional precast concrete piles. (*After R. N. Bruce, Jr., and D. C. Hebert.[59] Reprinted with permission from the Prestressed Concrete Institute.*)

15

that have the necessary special fittings cast in the ends. A projecting ring at the end of one pile section fits into an annulus at the end of the other section to be joined. After engagement, steel pins are driven laterally through matching holes in the fittings.

The Marier splice (Figure 2-7b) is made up of special steel caps cast into the pile ends. There are matching grooves in both the male and female caps. After the pile sections are joined, flexible steel locking pins are inserted circumferentially into the chase formed by the two grooves through holes in the female fitting. The Pile Coupler is of the same general principle except that the connecting device is a one- or two-piece steel band placed around the pile to engage the grooved edges of both the top and bottom steel joint plates cast into the ends of the pile sections. The gap (or gaps) between the band ends is closed with a field weld. The SM Sure-Lock splice is very similar to the Marier splice. To complete the joint, two square, flexible steel locking rods are driven with an air hammer into a chase formed between the male and female end fittings. The locking rods are inserted through holes that enter the chase tangentially. The locking device for the Nilsson splice is also inserted after the pile ends are joined together. The end fittings are machined so that similar raised areas on one surface match recessed areas on the other surface. The raised areas have projecting edges that can only be engaged by having one pile section offset slightly when the sections are joined and then moving the offset section laterally to engage the projecting edges. This leaves a space diametrically through the joint between the two fittings. This space is filled with a rigid steel bar to lock the joint.

Figure 2-7c illustrates the Mouton splice, which consists of a connector pin and steel fittings cast into the ends of the pile sections. The fittings have a central sleeve to accommodate the pin, which is slotted at both ends. When the pile sections are brought together, steel wedges, placed on the pin slots, expand the ends of the pin to engage the sleeves and lock the joint. The Franki splice works on the same general principle. The steel plates at the ends of the pile sections have four matching holes to accommodate the locking pins. The holes are tapered so that the bottoms are slightly larger in diameter than the tops. To make up the joint, split or slotted locking pins that have holes through their centers are set in the tapered holes. Tapered expansion pins are at each end of the locking pins. When the pile sections are driven together, the tapered pins expand the locking pins.

The Tokyu splice shown in Figure 2-7d is one of several welded joints. For this splice, the special end caps can be bolted to the pile sections. After the two pile sections are joined, the end caps are groove-welded together. The NCS splice is similar except that simple flat plates are fastened to the ends of the pile sections for groove welding. For the Bolognesi-Moretto splice, the steel plate attached to the pile section to be added is slightly smaller than the plate at the top of the driven section. This permits a simple fillet weld. The Tuzuki Cross Pile joint can also be fillet-welded because of the male-female types of

Centrifugal casing of a 16-ft-long cylinder pile section.
(*Courtesy of Raymond International Builders, Inc.*)

end fittings that are used. For the Blessey splice, the steel caps cast into the
ends of the pile sections are butt-welded.

The Raymond prestressed concrete cylinder pile is a sectional precast pile
that is assembled before driving. It is centrifugally cast in 16-ft (5-m) sections
under the combined forces of spinning, rolling, and vibration, and the concrete that is used has a slump less than zero. An extremely dense and impermeable concrete is produced which has an absorption factor 40 percent
less than that of bedcast concrete. The pile sections are placed end to end to
make up the required pile length and are posttensioned with prestressing
cables running through ducts cast in the pile wall.

2.3.2 Cast-in-Place Concrete Piles.   The principal types of cast-in-place concrete piles are shown in Figure 2-3. The basic types are uncased and cased.
These two types can be combined in a single pile.

2.3.2.1 Uncased Cast-in-Place Concrete Piles.   Uncased cast-in-place concrete piles include the drilled-hole pile, the cast-in-situ pile, and the auger-

Assembly of cylinder pile sections. (*Courtesy of Raymond International Builders, Inc.*)

grout pile. There are many other types installed outside of the United States.[75,120]

2.3.2.1.1 Drilled-Hole Pile.

This pile is constructed by drilling or otherwise excavating a hole in the ground and filling it with plain or reinforced concrete.[74,107,122] Holes can be drilled with a short-flight auger or a bucket drill. The shaft can be enlarged at the bottom by mechanical means to form a bell.

Assembled cylinder piles ready for shipment. (*Courtesy of Raymond International Builders, Inc.*)

Drilled-hole piles are known by several names, such as bored piles, drilled piers, caisson piles, and drilled shafts. When constructed in large diameters, this type of foundation is generally known as a caisson. There are varying opinions as to the diameter separating drilled-hole piles from caissons, but 36 in (1 m) seems to be a reasonable dimension.

There are three basic installation methods: (1) the dry method, (2) the casing method (often combined with a slurry), and (3) the slurry displacement method. The dry method is applicable in those soils in which the drilled hole will remain open for the placement of concrete. When caving or sloughing of the soil can occur, such as with soft soils of low shear strength or granular soils with no cohesion, the casing method is used. For this method, a temporary casing or liner is installed through the layer of unstable soil and sealed off in a stratum of impermeable soil. If the layer of unstable soil is relatively thick, it may be necessary to use a drilling mud slurry to maintain the hole until the casing can be set. If soil conditions permit, the slurry is removed with a bailing bucket after the casing has been set, and normal drilling proceeds. Concrete is placed in the dry by conventional methods. If the slurry cannot be removed, the slurry displacement method is used. For this method, a drilling mud slurry is introduced in the hole to maintain it until the concrete can be placed. The drilling mud can be formed by adding bentonite (and water if necessary) to the drill hole and mixing it by rotation of the auger, or it can be premixed before it is pumped into the hole. Under some subsoil conditions, a natural slurry can be formed with the cohesive soils being drilled. Concrete is placed by tremie or pumping methods to fill the hole from the bottom up and displace the slurry.

If the shaft is to be reinforced, the reinforcing cage is set in the hole before the concrete is placed. Generally, the shaft is reinforced along its full length, except that for the dry method, a partial cage can be used at the top of the hole.

2.3.2.1.2 *Cast-in-Situ Pile.* This type of pile is constructed by driving a temporary steel casing (or hollow mandrel), filling it with plain or reinforced concrete or grout during or after driving, and withdrawing the casing. Figure 2-8 illustrates the installation process for a typical cast-in-situ pile. The bottom of the casing can be closed with a sacrificial plate, or the casing can be driven with an internal mandrel to prevent soil from coming up inside the casing during driving. Some cast-in-situ piles can be reinforced before concrete is placed in the casing. Others are reinforced by pushing the reinforcing steel down into the unset concrete or grout column.

2.3.2.1.3 *Pressure Injected Footing.* The pressure injected footing in this category is installed with an uncased shaft. It is known by several other names, such as Franki pile, compacted concrete pile, compacted base pile, and bulb pile.

The pressure injected footing is installed by driving a steel tube to the

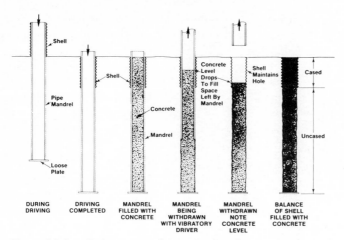

DURING DRIVING	DRIVING COMPLETED	MANDREL FILLED WITH CONCRETE	MANDREL BEING WITHDRAWN WITH VIBRATORY DRIVER	MANDREL WITHDRAWN NOTE CONCRETE LEVEL	BALANCE OF SHELL FILLED WITH CONCRETE

Figure 2-8 Installation process for cast-in-situ piles.

required bearing stratum, in which is formed an enlarged base. The tube can be bottom-driven with a drop weight operating inside the tube and impacting a very dry concrete or gravel closure plug at the bottom of the drive tube. The tube can also be top-driven with a conventional hammer, such as a diesel hammer, in which case the bottom of the drive tube is closed with an expendable steel plate.

The base is formed by driving out successive small batches of zero-slump concrete with the drop weight until a specified resistance to concrete injection has been achieved. For high-capacity piles, this would be about 20 blows with a 7000-lb (3175-kg) weight dropping 20 ft (6 m). After the base is formed, either a compacted concrete shaft or a high-slump concrete shaft is formed to the cutoff grade. For the compacted concrete shaft, successive small batches of zero-slump concrete are driven out with the drop weight as the drive tube is withdrawn. Figure 2-9 illustrates the installation process for forming the pile with an uncased compacted concrete shaft. The compacted concrete shaft is generally formed to the cutoff grade or just above and trimmed off. The shaft is usually limited in length to about 40 to 50 ft (12 to 15 m).

The compacted concrete shaft can be reinforced by inserting a steel cage in the drive tube after the base has been formed. A small batch of dry concrete is placed in the bottom of the cage and driven a short way into the base with the drop weight. If such steel is to resist uplift loads, the cage is placed before the base is completed so that the bottom of the cage will be embedded in the base. There are other methods which have been developed to make the base-to-shaft connection to resist uplift loads, such as the embedment of U-shaped stirrups in the base, with the stirrups welded to the reinforcement.

The high-slump concrete shaft is used when the shaft length is longer than about 50 ft (15 m) or when soil conditions preclude forming a compacted

Installing pressure injected footings. (*Courtesy of Franki Foundation Company.*)

shaft and do not require a cased shaft (see Section 2.3.2.2). The shaft is formed by filling the drive tube with concrete of 6- to 10-in (150- to 250-mm) slump before the tube is withdrawn.

The hole created by the drive tube should be filled with concrete to the ground surface, or the hole should be lined with a temporary steel sleeve from

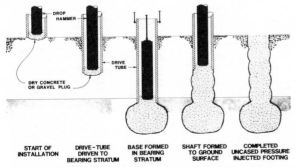

Figure 2-9 Installation process for pressure injected footings with uncased, compacted concrete shafts.

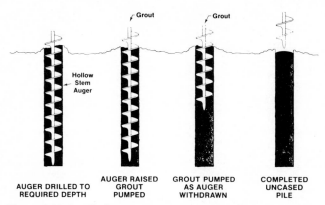

AUGER DRILLED TO
REQUIRED DEPTH

AUGER RAISED
GROUT
PUMPED

GROUT PUMPED
AS AUGER
WITHDRAWN

COMPLETED
UNCASED
PILE

Figure 2-10 Installation process for auger-grout piles.

the ground surface to just below the concrete filling. Generally, a reinforcing cage is placed in the drive tube before concrete is poured. This type of shaft is not used for uplift piles.

2.3.2.1.4 Auger-Grout Pile.

The auger-grout pile is installed by advancing a continuous-flight hollow-stem auger to the required depth and filling the hole created by the auger with grout under pressure as the auger is withdrawn. Grout is pumped with a positive-displacement piston-type pump. Figure 2-10 illustrates the basic installation process. This type of pile is also known as the Pakt-in-Place* pile, the Augercast† pile, and the auger-placed grout pile.

After the auger tip has reached the required depth, it is raised 6 to 12 in (150 to 300 mm), and grout is pumped under pressure down the hollow stem. When the grout pressure has built up sufficiently to offset hydrostatic and lateral earth pressures, the auger is advanced to the original depth. While grout is pumped, the auger is withdrawn at a smooth, steady rate so that the grouting pressure is maintained as monitored by suitable gauges. The grouting pressure is reduced to zero as the auger tip reaches the ground surface. The volume of grout being pumped is usually measured by some type of metering device.

The pile top is generally formed through a temporary steel sleeve to protect the fresh grout from contamination by surface water or sloughing soils. Alternatively, the pile is formed to the ground surface, which is above the cutoff grade, and the grout column is later trimmed off to the cutoff elevation. The top of the grout column is dipped with a strainer before the grout sets so as to remove clods or lumps of soil that may have fallen off the auger.

Within practical limits, the pile is reinforced to resist bending by pushing a cage of reinforcing steel down the unset grout column after the auger is withdrawn. Reinforcement to provide for uplift or tension loads can best be

*Intrusion-Prepakt Inc., Cleveland, Ohio.
†Lee Turzillo Contracting Company, Brecksville, Ohio.

Installing Augercast piles. Note proximity to building. (*Courtesy of Lee Turzillo Contracting Company.*)

installed by placing a single high-strength steel bar through the hollow stem of the auger before grouting. The bar must not rise with the auger as it is withdrawn. Longitudinal steel has also been placed through special ducts built into the auger.

2.3.2.2 Cased, Dropped-In-Shell, Cast-in-Place Concrete Pile.

Although it is cased, this type of pile is considered in a category separate from those cased, cast-in-place concrete piles for which a permanent steel shell or casing is driven. A permanent dropped-in shell can be inserted in almost any type of uncased, cast-in-place concrete pile except the auger-grout pile. However, the auger-grout pile has been installed with a permanent outer casing.

The most common example of this type of pile is the pressure injected footing with a cased shaft. After the base has been formed as described in Section 2.3.2.1.3, a steel pipe or corrugated steel shell is inserted in the drive tube and tamped into the base by the drop weight impacting a small charge of dry concrete placed in the shell. The drive tube is then withdrawn, and the pipe or shell is filled to the cutoff grade with conventional concrete. A reinforcing steel cage can be inserted in the shell or pipe before concrete is placed. If necessary to reestablish the lateral support of the soil, sand or grout can be washed in to fill the annular space between the shell and the soil.

Step-Taper shell sections are stockpiled along the shell assembly rack for making up the required pile lengths. (*Courtesy of Raymond International Builders, Inc.*)

2.3.2.3 Cased, Driven-Shell, Cast-in-Place Concrete Pile.   There are many varieties of this type of pile, as indicated in Figure 2-11. The piles can be mandrel-driven, top-driven, base-driven, or both mandrel- and top-driven. Mandrel-driven piles include steel pipe piles and corrugated steel shells. Top-driven piles include both pipe piles and Monotube piles. Box piles that are filled with concrete could also be considered in this category. Piles that are both top- and mandrel-driven include composite-type piles. The lower section of a composite-type pile is a top-driven pipe pile, and the upper section is a mandrel-driven shell. Pipe piles can also be base-driven.

2.3.2.3.1 Step-Taper Piles.   Step-Taper piles are manufactured and driven by Raymond International Builders, Inc. As illustrated in Figure 2-12, Raymond Step-Taper piles are installed by placing corrugated steel shells on a mandrel (see Figure 2-13), driving the mandrel and shells to the required penetration depth or resistance, withdrawing the mandrel, and filling the shells with concrete. Shells are manufactured in nominal diameters ranging from $8\frac{5}{8}$ in (220 mm) to $18\frac{3}{8}$ in (465 mm) (see Table C-3) and in standard section lengths of 4, 8, 12, and 16 ft (1.2, 2.4, 3.7, and 4.9 m). Other section lengths can be manufactured for special conditions. Shell gauges range from 10 to 18, with the heavier gauges used for the lower portions of the piles.

The shells are assembled to the required pile lengths on a horizontal rack.

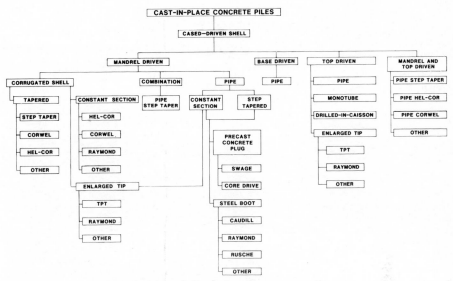

Figure 2-11 Types of cased, driven-shell, cast-in-place concrete piles.

As illustrated in Figure 2-14, the joints between shell sections are screw-connected and waterproofed with an O-ring gasket. Sometimes a heavy mastic combined with jute or burlap is used to waterproof the joint. Step-Taper shells can also be assembled on the mandrel.

The diameter of the pile increases from tip to butt at the rate of 1 in (25 mm) for each section length. Within reasonable limits, shell sections of different lengths can be combined in a single Step-Taper pile. This feature, when combined with available tip diameters ranging from $8\frac{5}{8}$ in (220 mm) to $14\frac{3}{8}$ in (365 mm), provides a wide choice of pile shapes to best accommodate soil and

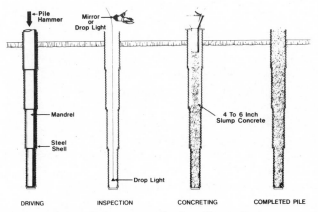

Figure 2-12 Installation process for Step-Taper piles.

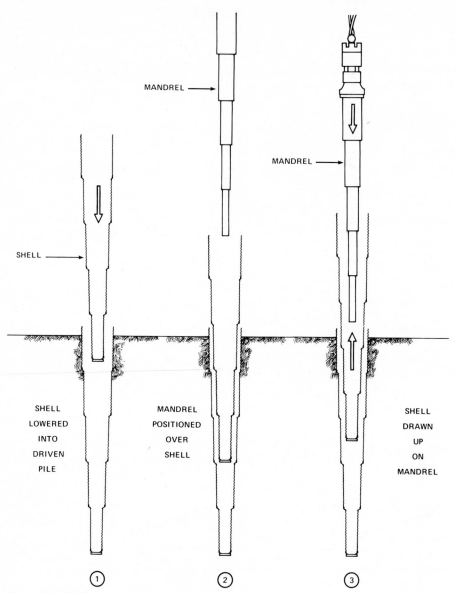

Figure 2-13 Shell-up procedure for Step-Taper piles.

loading conditions. The mandrel is a very heavy rigid steel tube shaped to fit the shells. Shoulders on the mandrel engage the drive ring at the bottom of each shell section, including the tip (see Figure 2-14). The tip is closed with a flat steel plate welded to the drive ring.

Before the shell is filled with concrete, it is inspected internally with a

Assembly of Step-Taper shells. (*Courtesy of Raymond International Builders, Inc.*)

mirror to reflect sunlight down the pile or with a powerful spotlight. Concrete is placed to the cutoff grade, and any excess shell is removed. The pile can be reinforced as necessary to resist bending, uplift, or lateral loads, in which case the reinforcing steel is placed before the concrete is poured.

Step-Taper shells can be combined with steel pipe to make up the pipe Step-Taper pile. Pipe of whatever length necessary is used for the lower portion of the pile, and Step-Taper shells make up the upper portion. Various combinations of pipe and shell diameters can be used. The mandrel can extend to the top of the pipe or partway into the pipe as a guidepoint or throughout the pipe down to the closure plate. Figure 2-14 illustrates a sleeve-type joint used between the shell and pipe. Other types of joints include welded joints and drive-sleeve joints. After being driven and inspected internally, the pipe and shell are filled with concrete.

Piles having a stepped configuration can also be formed by combining constant-section shells or pipe of different diameters. For the constant-section shells, special transition fittings are required along with a stepped mandrel.

2.3.2.3.2 Constant-Section Shell Pile. The installation sequence for this type of pile is essentially the same as for the Step-Taper pile (see Figure 2-12). The

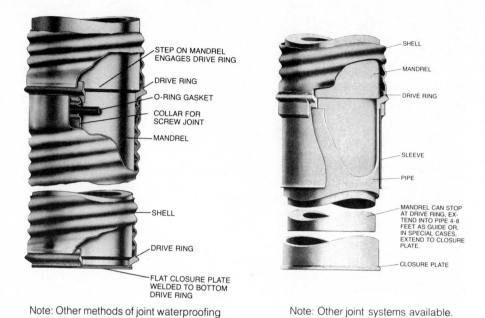

STEP ON MANDREL
ENGAGES DRIVE RING

DRIVE RING

O-RING GASKET

COLLAR FOR
SCREW JOINT

MANDREL

SHELL

DRIVE RING

FLAT CLOSURE PLATE
WELDED TO BOTTOM
DRIVE RING

SHELL

MANDREL

DRIVE RING

SLEEVE

PIPE

MANDREL CAN STOP
AT DRIVE RING, EX-
TEND INTO PIPE 4-8
FEET AS GUIDE OR,
IN SPECIAL CASES,
EXTEND TO CLOSURE
PLATE.

CLOSURE PLATE

Note: Other methods of joint waterproofing
can be used.

Note: Other joint systems available.

Step-Taper

Pipe Step-Taper

Figure 2-14 Details of Step-Taper and pipe Step-Taper piles.

corrugated pile shells are the same diameter throughout the pile length and are driven with a mandrel that can be expanded to grip the shells and contracted for insertion and withdrawal.

Various types of mandrels are used, and they are expanded by mechanical or pneumatic means. Shells are made by several manufacturers such as Armco Inc. (Hel-Cor) and Republic Steel Corporation (Corwel) in various diameters, as shown in Table C-4, and in 14, 16, and 18 gauge. Shells are made from sheet steel which is corrugated before spiral forming, whereas Step-Taper shells are corrugated after being formed into a tube. Thus for constant-section shells, the corrugations follow the helix of the spiral seam. The shells are delivered in mill lengths of 60 ft (18 m) and are butt-welded to make up the required pile length. The bottom of the shell is closed with a steel plate welded to the shell either at the manufacturing plant or at the jobsite. Constant-section shells can be combined with pipe to form a composite pile.

2.3.2.3.3 Pipe Piles. In this category, pipe piles are filled with concrete after being driven. Pipe for piling is manufactured in various diameters and wall thicknesses, as shown in Table C-2. Pipe piles can be driven either open-ended or closed-ended, in which case the bottom of the pipe is closed with a flat steel plate or a tapered point welded to the pipe.

Step-Taper shells are assembled to full pile lengths within reach of the pile rig. (*Courtesy of Raymond International Builders, Inc.*)

Driving Hel-Cor constant-section shell piles. (*Courtesy of Armco, Inc., Construction Products Division.*)

Driving Core-Drive piles. The mandrel-driven pipe is closed at the bottom with a precast concrete plug. (*Courtesy of Armco, Inc., Construction Products Division.*)

These piles can be top-driven, base-driven, or driven with a mandrel, in which case the mandrel usually engages the pipe at both the top and bottom (boot). For base-driven pipe, a drop weight operating inside the pipe impacts on a closure plug at the bottom of the pipe similar to that used for driving the tube for a pressure injected footing. Open-end pipe piles can be installed with a vibratory driver.

Pipe is delivered in single random, double random, or uniform lengths as described in Section 3.5.2. The pipe can be readily spliced to make up the required pile length; butt welds or special sleeves are used.

If pipe piles are driven open-ended, it is necessary to clean out the pipe in preparation for concrete filling. If they are mandrel-driven, the bottom end of the pipe can be closed with a precast concrete plug or a steel boot (see Figure 2-11). Within limits, different diameters can be used in the same pile to give a step-tapered shape. The pipe can be reinforced if necessary, or, for uplift loads, dowels can be welded to the top of the pipe for the pile-to-cap connection.

2.3.2.3.4 Monotube Piles.   Monotubes are manufactured by the Union Metal Manufacturing Company in various tapers and diameters, as indicated in Table C-5. Monotubes are produced in 3, 5, 7, 9, and 11 gauge. The pile wall

Driving Monotube piles. (*Courtesy of Union Metal Manufacturing Company.*)

is fluted, and the pile tip is closed with a steel point welded on by the manufacturer. The pile can be reinforced as necessary, and for uplift loads, dowels can be welded to the top of the pile to make the pile-to-cap connection.

2.3.2.3.5 Wood Composite Piles.   This type of pile combines an untreated timber pile lower section with a steel-encased, cast-in-place concrete upper section. Generally a constant-section corrugated steel shell is used and is connected to the top of the timber section with a wedge ring driven into the wood. The shell is filled with conventional concrete to the cutoff grade. The untreated timber pile section is driven with its top below the permanent groundwater level.

2.3.2.3.6 Enlarged-Tip Piles.   An enlarged precast concrete tip, either round or square, is attached at the bottom of some type of pile shaft (see Figure 2-15). The precast tip is usually tapered. The shaft can be a mandrel-driven corrugated shell which is socketed into the top of the concrete tip and filled with concrete after the pile has been driven. The enlarged tip has also been used at the bottom of a pipe or timber pile shaft socketed into the tip. Alternatively, the tip has been made with a 2-ft (0.6-m)-high pedestal at the top, over which a pipe is driven with an internal mandrel engaging the top of the pipe and bearing on the pedestal. The pedestal has a slight taper and wedges into

Attaching a Corwel shell to the top of an untreated timber pile for a wood composite pile. (*Courtesy of Republic Steel Corporation, Drainage Products Division.*)

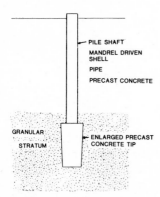

PILE SHAFT
MANDREL DRIVEN SHELL
PIPE
PRECAST CONCRETE

GRANULAR
STRATUM

ENLARGED PRECAST CONCRETE TIP

Figure 2-15 Enlarged-tip pile.

32

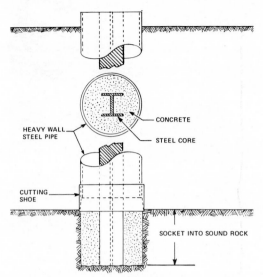

Figure 2-16 Construction of drilled-in caisson.

the pipe. The pipe is filled with concrete after driving. The enlarged concrete tip could also be cast at the end of a precast concrete pile during manufacturing.[75] After the pile has been driven, the annulus created by the enlarged tip is filled by washing in sand or pumping grout.

Dimensions of the enlarged tip can vary, but generally bottom diameters range from 12 to 36 in (300 to 900 mm), and top diameters range from 16 to 40 in (400 to 1020 mm). The height of the tip is generally from 2.5 to 5 ft (0.8 to 1.5 m). The taper will depend on the actual dimensions, which may be dictated by job conditions.

2.3.2.3.7 Drilled-In Caisson. This is a special type of high-capacity pipe pile constructed as shown in Figure 2-16. A heavy-wall pipe or casing fitted with a special drive shoe at its tip is driven to bedrock and sealed off on the rock surface. After the casing is cleaned out, a socket is drilled into the rock with percussion- or rotary-type drilling equipment. The socket is cleaned out, and a steel H-shaped core is placed in the socket. It extends either partway up in the casing or to the cutoff grade. The socket and casing are then filled with concrete. With an alternative method of construction, the steel core is omitted.

3

Pile Material

The inspection of pile material involves various items to ensure that all material meets the requirements of the specifications and conforms with material on which the design was based. The basic pile materials are timber, concrete, and steel, and each has its unique inspection requirements.

The actual procedures for material handling and storage may not be items of inspection. However, the inspector should be aware of improper procedures that may affect the drivability, structural quality, or long-term performance of the piles. If warranted, special checklist-type reports can be prepared for recording inspection data, or such data can be included in the inspector's diary. Improper material-handling procedures can be noted under the remarks section on conventional pile installation inspection forms (see Appendix D).

3.1 TIMBER PILES

3.1.1 Material Specifications The material specification frequently referred to for timber piles is ASTM standard D 25.[39] In 1970 and again in 1973, the 1958 version of D 25 was revised with several major changes, such as (1) the elimination of pile classes A, B, and C, (2) the change in specified butt and tip dimensions from diameter to circumference, (3) the elimination of minimum required tip dimensions, and (4) the reduction in knot restrictions. Another change made was the limitation of a specified dimension to only one end of the pile. The dimension of the other end would result from the ordered length and the natural taper of the tree. The result was that more trees out of a given stand could be harvested for piles. Also, the quality of all piles as measured by permissible knots can now be equal to or less than the quality of the former class C piles as specified in the 1958 version of D 25.

3.1.2 Species. The species may not be specified except under circumstances in which only certain ones are suitable for the loads or environmental condi-

AB Co	– – – SUPPLIER'S BRAND
D	– – – PLANT DESIGNATION
10–81	– – – YEAR (AND MONTH) OF TREATMENT
SPC	– – – SPECIES AND PRESERVATIVE (SEE SYMBOLS BELOW)
12	– – – RETENTION – PCF
45	– – – LENGTH – FT.

Species Symbols		Preservative Symbols			
DF	Douglas fir	C	Creosote	XA	80/20 creosote/petroleum solution
JP	Jack pine	CM	Creosote for marine use	XB	70/30 creosote/petroleum solution
LP	Lodgepole pine	LS	Pentachlorophenol in standard solvent	XC	60/40 creosote/petroleum solution
NP	Red pine	TA	80/20 creosote/coal tar solution	XD	50/50 creosote/petroleum solution
OA	Oak	TB	70/30 creosote/coal tar solution	SB*	Ammoniacal copper arsenate (ACA)
SP	Southern pine	TC	60/40 creosote/coal tar solution	SC*	Chromated copper arsenate (CCA), type A
WL	Western larch	TD	50/50 creosote/coal tar solution	SJ*	Chromated copper arsenate (CCA), type B
WP	Ponderosa pine	TM	Creosote/coal tar solution for marine use	SK*	Chromated copper arsenate (CCA), type C

*For dual treatment C precedes the symbol.

Figure 3-1 Standard timber pile brand.

tions involved. Generally, strength varies with species and also with sub-species. Certain species are not suitable for preservative treatment, whereas other species—for example, greenheart—may be selected for greater durability. The species will be noted on inspection reports received from the point of origin of each pile shipment. Also, for treated piles the species will be shown on the brand (see Figure 3-1) if branding is required, such as for marine piles.[51]

3.1.3 Conditioning and Preservative Treatment.   The treatment of timber piles is governed by either standard C 3 of the American Wood-Preserver's Association (AWPA) or ASTM standard D 1760. Other applicable AWPA standards are C 1, C 18, M 1, M 2, M 4, and P 5. These standards are listed in Appendix A. The inspector should be familiar with these standards, especially AWPA C 3 and ASTM D 1760, as to conditioning methods permitted or required, types of preservatives used, and the specified retention and penetration depth of the preservative. AWPA standard C 3 and ASTM standard D 1760 are not in total agreement.

Piles treated with a preservative should be inspected at the treatment plant. Adequate inspection certificates should accompany each shipment, and the inspector should be furnished with a copy of all certificates. Certificates should show the type of conditioning used, the heating temperature and duration of heating, and the type and retention of the preservative. The types of conditioning include air drying, kiln drying, steaming, the Boulton process, and heating in the preservative.

The type and retention of the preservative will be shown on the brand (Figure 3-1) if the piles are branded. Generally, the amount of preservative to be retained in the wood will be specified in pounds per cubic foot (kilograms per cubic meter). The required retention will vary with the type of preservative, species, and use. For example, for land and freshwater piles, the standard retention for creosote is 12 lb/ft^3 (190 kg/m^3) for southern pine, 17 lb/ft^3 (270 kg/m^3) for Douglas fir, and 6 lb/ft^3 (95 kg/m^3) for oak. For marine use, these become 20 lb/ft^3 (320 kg/m^3) for both southern pine and Douglas fir and 10 lb/ft^3 (160 kg/m^3) for oak. For preservative salts such as ACA and CCA (see Figure 3-1), the standard retention ranges from 0.8 to 1.0 lb/ft^3 (13 to 16 kg/m^3). This type of preservative is not recommended for oak and should not be used when metal fittings are to be attached to the piles.[124]

The penetration depth of the preservative is an important factor, and it is governed by the AWPA and ASTM standards. Minimum required penetrations vary with species and use. For example, for land and freshwater piles, the minimum penetration is 3 in (75 mm) or 90 percent of the sapwood for southern pine, 0.75 in (20 mm) or 85 percent for Douglas fir, and 100 percent of the sapwood for oak. For marine piles, the minimum penetration increases to 4 in (100 mm) for southern pine and 1 in (25 mm) for Douglas fir. The penetration is determined by removing small-diameter cores from the piles, and penetrations will be reported by the inspector at the treatment plant. Core holes must be properly plugged.

For marine piles to be used in waters heavily infested with marine borers, the specifications may require that such piles be given dual treatment. The piles are first treated with a salt preservative such as ACA or CCA. This is followed by a creosote treatment.

3.1.4 Bark Removal.
Sometimes the specifications will permit unpeeled piles, but in general, and especially in the case of all treated piles, piles will be clean-peeled, which means that all the outer bark and at least 80 percent of the inner bark must be removed. Unpeeled piles require no bark removal, and for rough-peeled piles complete removal of the outer bark only is required.

If piles are peeled by a process known as "shaving," some wood below the bark is removed, and the surface of the piles will be relatively smooth. Shaving may weaken the pile in the areas of knots, and therefore the effect of knots may be more pronounced.

3.1.5 Lengths.   Timber piles will be shipped to the jobsite according to approved ordered lengths. If pile material is to be paid for on the basis of furnished lengths, the ordered lengths must be approved by the engineer. A standard brand on each pile should indicate the pile length, but lengths can be readily checked with a measuring tape. Piles shorter than those ordered are not acceptable, but for piles specified according to ASTM standard D 25,[39] the ordered lengths may be exceeded by 1 ft (0.3 m) for piles 40 ft (12 m) or shorter and by 2 ft (0.6 m) for piles over 40 ft in length. If payment for timber piles is based upon the full furnished lengths, the delivered lengths must agree with the ordered lengths within the plus tolerances permitted.

Ordered lengths may be somewhat longer than the lengths expected to be driven. This is to allow for extra lengths which may be required if subsoil conditions vary from those indicated by test borings.

3.1.6 Dimensions.   Frequently, a minimum dimension at the pile tip or butt or both may be specified or may be anticipated if a pile class is specified, such as A or B. However, if piles are ordered according to ASTM D 25, not all dimensions of the delivered piles may be as specified or anticipated. The producer may furnish piles in accordance with the latest version of ASTM D 25. Because of the 1970 revision, timber piles are no longer classified as A, B, or C in ASTM D 25, and the specific requirements such as minimum butt or tip dimensions relating to each of these classes of piles are no longer in effect. Because of the 1973 revision, timber piles are to be specified by either a minimum tip circumference or a minimum butt circumference, but not both. Diameters are no longer used in specifying timber pile dimensions. The minimum circumference furnished at the other end of the pile (tip or butt as the case may be) results from the pile length and taper. The butt circumference is measured 3 ft from the large end of the pile.

The pile inspector should understand that regardless of current ASTM specifications, the engineer responsible for the design is at liberty to specify whatever dimensions or other properties he wants for timber piles. Also, the owner is entitled to receive piles as specified, regardless of industry standards. It is advisable to specify timber piles according to a minimum tip dimension. During driving, stresses at the tip may be critical. Furthermore, piles may not be driven to the full ordered length, and thus the dimension of the pile butt after cutoff will be less than a specified butt dimension.

3.1.7 Pile Taper and Straightness.   Timber piles should have a continuous taper from tip to butt, and the piles should be sufficiently straight that a line from the center of the butt to the center of the tip lies entirely within the body of the pile. Short crooks or reverse bends could cause problems during driving, and piles with these defects should be carefully checked to see that they comply with the specifications on straightness.

3.1.8 Knots. If pile quality is governed by ASTM D 25, the pile inspector should be aware of the differences in allowable knots between the 1958 version of ASTM D 25 and the current D 25. In 1970, ASTM D 25 was revised to remove and reduce some of the restrictions on the sizes of allowable knots. For example, as shown in Table 3-1, the permitted size of knots was increased so that all piles have only to conform with the knot limitations for the former class C piles. Also, the maximum size for permissible knots, regardless of diameter, is no longer specified in D 25, and cluster knots, which were prohibited by the 1958 version of D 25, are now permitted. Knots generally are more numerous along the upper portions of the tree and thus toward the pile tip. Knots at the pile tip could be quite critical and result in pile damage during driving.

If there is any doubt about the quality of the delivered piles satisfying the design requirements, the engineer should be advised. As with dimensions, the engineer responsible for the design may specify the quality of timber piles regardless of industry standards.

3.1.9 Checks, Shakes, and Splits. A "check" is a longitudinal separation of the wood across the growth rings extending from the pile surface inward but not entirely through the pile. A "shake" is a circumferential separation of the growth rings. A "split" is a check that extends through the pile.

The extent of allowable checks, shakes, and splits is limited by ASTM D 25. However, they are permitted by ASTM D 25 to some degree, and for timber

Table 3-1 COMPARISON OF KNOT LIMITATIONS

| Knot Property | ASTM D 25 (1958) | | | ASTM D 25 (1979), All Piles |
	Classes A and B Less Than 50 ft	Classes A and B Longer Than 50 ft	Class C	
Maximum size, single knot	One-third pile diameter; maximum, 4 in	Same as for class C for lower 25%	One-half pile diameter; maximum, 5 in	One-sixth pile circumference (one-half pile diameter); no maximum
Maximum sum of knot diameters in 12 in	Two-thirds pile diameter; maximum 8 in	Same as for class C for lower 25%	The pile diameter; maximum, 10 in	One-third pile circumference (pile diameter); no maximum
Cluster of knots	Not permitted	Not permitted	Not permitted	Permitted; maximum same as for single knot

piles that are not required to conform to ASTM D 25, severe limitations on these types of defects should be imposed, or the defects should be prohibited. Such initial defects in a pile may be made more severe during driving, and in the case of treated timber piles, they could expose the inner untreated pile material to decay or insect attack.

3.1.10 Spiral Grain. Spiral grain should not exceed 180° of twist in any 20-ft (6-m) length of pile. The grain twist may be difficult to determine, especially with treated piles, but it should be spot-checked. The inspection report from the point of origin should cover this.

3.1.11 Butt and Surface Condition. The ends of piles should not be out of square with the pile axis by more than 0.1 in per inch (100 mm per meter) of diameter. All knots and limbs should be cut flush with the surface of the pile.

3.1.12 Soundness of Piles. There should be no evidence of decay or insect attack. The inspection certificate obtained from the point of origin or the treatment plant should cover this, but the pile inspector should spot-check.

3.1.13 Timber Pile Fittings. The specifications may require that the pile tip be protected with a steel drive shoe or that tightly fitted steel bands be put on the pile at designated intervals along its length and at the butt to prevent the pile from splitting or brooming during driving. Special fittings may also include anchorages from the pile to the pile cap. All special fittings should comply with the specifications.

Special fittings attached to the tips of timber piles. (*Courtesy of Associated Pile & Fitting Corp.*)

3.1.14 Handling.   All timber piles should be handled with sufficient care so as to avoid damaging the piles. As a general rule, treated timber piles should not be handled with pointed tools such as timber tongs, cant hooks, or peaveys or with pile chains. Treated piles should be handled so as to avoid puncturing or breaking through the outer treated portion of the piles, which may be as little as 1 in (25 mm). AWPA standard M4[50] permits the use of pointed tools provided that side surfaces of the pile are not penetrated more than $\frac{1}{2}$ in (13 mm). This may be difficult to control. To prevent gouging or other abrasive damage to the treated portion of the piles, it is necessary to prevent treated timber piles from being dragged along the ground.

3.1.15 Unloading.   Timber piles may be unloaded by controlled roll-off. Dumping should not be permitted.

3.1.16 Storage.   Timber piles placed in storage for longer than about a week should be on adequate blocking. They should be supported for protection and to avoid permanent bends. Piles should be stacked on treated or non-decaying material, and there should be an air space beneath the piles. Storage areas should be free of debris, decayed wood, and dry vegetation (fire hazard), and there should be sufficient drainage to prevent the piles from lying in water.

3.1.17 Records.   A simple checklist can be prepared for recording the results of the inspection of timber pile material.

3.2 PRECAST CONCRETE PILES

3.2.1 Design Requirements.   Adequate plant inspection reports should accompany each pile shipment. They should identify the piles and certify that they meet the design specifications, including such things as concrete mix, amount and location of reinforcing steel, 28-day concrete strengths, and effective prestress. The inspector should be furnished with copies of such reports. Inspection reports should be from an independent testing or inspection firm and not from the manufacturer. Piles should be marked or stamped with the date of manufacture.

The concrete mix design may call for special cements such as ASTM C 150[34] types II or V (sulfate-resistant) or for special admixtures[3,4] such as air entrainers. Refer to Section 3.3.3 for more detailed requirements for concrete material.

3.2.2 Lengths.   Precast piles will be shipped to the jobsite according to specified or approved ordered lengths. If pile material is to be paid for on the basis of furnished lengths, the ordered lengths must be approved by the engineer. Each pile should be of the full ordered length except in the case where sectional piles are permitted. Sometimes piles will be ordered with sufficient extra length to permit stripping back the concrete and exposing the reinforcing steel for the pile-to-cap connection (see Section 5.50). Ordered lengths may be somewhat longer than anticipated driven lengths to allow for variations in subsoil conditions.

3.2.3 Dimensions.   Piles should be of the shape and size specified.

3.2.4 Tolerances.   Unless otherwise specified, precast concrete piles should be manufactured to the following dimensional tolerances:

1. **Length:** ± 0.375 in (± 10 mm) per 10 ft (3 m) of length
2. **Width (Diameter):** -0.25 in (-6 mm) to $+0.50$ in ($+13$ mm)
3. **Head:**   Deviation from plane perpendicular to pile axis, ± 0.25 in per foot (± 20 mm per meter) of width (diameter)
4. **Head Surface:**   Irregularities, ± 0.125 in (± 3 mm)
5. **Straightness:**   Deviation from straight line of not more than 0.125 in per 10 ft (1 mm per meter) of length
6. **Wall Thickness (Hollow Core):** -0.25 in (-6 mm) to $+0.375$ in ($+10$ mm)
7. **Internal Core or Void:**   Within ± 0.375 in (± 10 mm) of plan location
8. **Reinforcing Steel:**   Main reinforcement cover, -0.125 in (-3 mm) to $+0.25$ in ($+6$ mm); spiral spacing, ± 0.50 in (± 13 mm)

The inspector can readily check items 1 through 6 above. Field checking of item 7 will not be possible if the piles have solid ends. A cursory check on the cover of the main reinforcement (item 8) can be made where the steel is exposed at the ends of the piles.

3.2.5 Chamfers.   All corners or edges of square piles should be chamfered. The width of the chamfer face should be limited to about 1.5 in (40 mm) so that the reduction in any side dimension due to chamfering is not more than about 2 in (50 mm).

3.2.6 Precast Concrete Pile Fittings.   If the use of sectional piles is permitted, the plans and specifications will detail the type of splice or joint to be used. This may require that special end fittings be cast in the pile sections and that appropriate sleeves, locking devices, or connectors be furnished (see Section 2.3.1.1). If dowel splices are to be used, the specifications may require that the ends of the pile sections be formed with sleeves or holes to accommodate the dowels. All joint or splicing material should conform to the plans and specifications.

The specifications may require special pile tips or tip protection such as steel H or pipe projections or steel shoes. These should be cast into the pile tips and should conform to the specifications.

3.2.7 Exposed Steel. The specifications may require that piles be furnished with reinforcing or prestressing steel extending beyond the butt concrete surface in order to make the pile-to-cap connection. The extension should be of the specified length, and a suitable drive head or follower must be furnished. If exposed steel is not required, all longitudinal reinforcing steel or strands must be cut off flush with or just below the concrete surface.

3.2.8 Pile Coatings. The project specifications may require that piles be coated with bitumen or other materials for protection or to reduce negative friction loads.[65] If coatings are applied by the manufacturer or by a third party at an off-site location, certificates of inspection and/or compliance should be furnished, and the inspector should check on the quality and thickness of the coatings. If the coating is to be applied at the jobsite, the inspector should ensure that all material furnished meets the specifications and that suitable application equipment is available. The actual application of pile coatings is covered in Section 5.11.4.

3.2.9 Pile Damage. Piles should be checked for detrimental cracks, spalling, slabbing, or other damage. Such inspection should take place when the piles are delivered and also just before driving, especially if the piles are going into and out of storage. Damage can occur during transportation and handling. Hairline cracks [not wider than 0.01 in (0.2 mm)] are not considered detrimental, especially for prestressed piles.

3.2.10 Handling. Precast concrete piles should be handled with proper slings attached to predesignated pickup points or inserts. Impact loads should be avoided.

3.2.11 Unloading. Precast concrete piles should be unloaded by lifting them in a horizontal position with a lifting beam (strongback) or sufficiently long spreader slings. If piles are coated, a lifting beam must be used. Dumping or rolling off of precast concrete piles should not be permitted.

3.2.12 Storage. Precast concrete piles should be stored on blocking placed at predesignated pickup points to avoid overstressing and cracking of the piles. Piles placed near the driving rig as driving progresses may be placed on the ground, which should be fairly even. Long unsupported lengths, including overhangs, should be avoided. Blocking used to facilitate the attachment of slings should be placed near designated pickup points so as to avoid overstressing the pile.

Handling a precast, prestressed concrete pile with a three-point pickup. (*Courtesy of J. H. Pomeroy & Co., Inc.*)

3.2.13 Records.   The results of an inspection of precast concrete piles can be recorded on a checklist prepared for this purpose in accordance with the job requirements.

3.3 CONCRETE FOR CAST-IN-PLACE PILES

3.3.1 Design Mix.   An approved design mix[1,6,31,113] with results of tests on standard cylinders should be furnished by the contractor. Copies of these data should be made available to the inspector at the start of pile installation.

Generally, conventional structural-grade concrete with 28-day strengths ranging from 4000 to 7000 lb/in^2 (27.6 to 48.3 MPa) is used for cast-in-place concrete piles. Some special types of piles require special concrete or grout mixes as covered in Chapter 6. Special mixes may be required for pumped concrete.[8] For filling normal-size pile shells, especially under difficult placement conditions, a reduced-coarse-aggregate concrete is often specified. Difficult placement conditions include piles longer than about 50 ft (15 m), piles driven on a batter steeper than 1:4, and pile shells containing heavy reinforcing cages. A typical reduced-coarse-aggregate mix includes 800 lb of coarse aggregate per cubic yard (475 kg/m^3) with a corresponding increase in the sand and cement content.[113]

3.3.2 Concrete Production Facilities.

Concrete may be mixed in portable mixers brought to the pile locations, but generally it will be ready-mixed. Ready-mix concrete may be (1) batched and mixed at a central plant and delivered to the pile locations in agitating or nonagitating trucks (central-mixed), or (2) batched at a central plant and mixed in a truck mixer in transit to or after reaching the jobsite (truck-mixed), or (3) partially centrally mixed, with mixing completed in a truck mixer en route to the job or at the jobsite (shrink-mixed). The central plant may be located at the jobsite.

The plant where concrete is batched and mixed should be inspected for the adequacy of storage facilities for materials, the accuracy and reliability of batching equipment, the condition of mixing equipment, and the appropriateness of operational procedures.[7]

3.3.2.1 Storage Facilities.

Cement must be kept dry whether stored in bulk containers or kept in bags. To avoid contamination, stockpiles of aggregates that have been cleaned, graded, and prepared for batching should be on a hard, clean base, and the area around the stockpiles should be spread with a bedding material of sand, gravel, or rock. Side slopes of stockpiles should have a slope of 7 in or less per foot (0.5 m/m) to prevent segregation. Coarse aggregate should be separated according to type and size gradation. Overlapping of stockpiles should be prevented, and suitable drainage should be provided. All reasonable precautions should be taken to keep the moisture content of aggregates as uniform as possible.

3.3.2.2 Batching Equipment.

Concrete is usually batched by weight. The batching scales should have a recent calibration and certificate of inspection and must be clean and free of interference by other objects. Separate weighing-batching facilities should be provided for cement. The batching–weight recording and cutoff devices must operate accurately. The bottoms of batch bins must be fully sloped in all directions. Water-metering devices, whether at a central mixing plant or mounted on a truck mixer, must be accurate and equipped with indicating dials and totalizers.

3.3.2.3 Mixing Equipment.

All mixing equipment, whether stationary or truck-mounted, must be in good operating condition. The interiors of drums should be clean, and mixing blades should not show signs of wear in excess of 1 in (25 mm). Truck mixers must be equipped with a reliable revolution counter.

3.3.2.4 Operations.

All materials must be accurately batched, and batching should be by weight. Admixtures, if required, must be accurately measured. Mixing drums must be cleaned after each use to prevent an accumulation of hardened concrete on the blades. All wash water must be removed from the mixing drums prior to batching. Cement should be used on the basis of first in, first out. The free-water content of the aggregates should be included as part of the total mix water. Aggregates should be allowed a sufficient time to drain, and it may be necessary to have a moisture meter in the sand batcher to monitor the moisture content. Proper equipment and methods must be used for handling aggregates to avoid segregation and breakage. Segregation of coarse aggregate can be reduced by separating the aggregate into several sizes and batching them separately. Finished screening of aggregates at the batcher is recommended to avoid problems of segregation and contamination.

3.3.3 Concrete Materials. Materials, including cement, sand, coarse aggregate, water, and admixtures, should be inspected for conformity with the specifications and accepted practice.

3.3.3.1 Cement. Cement must be of the type specified or permitted with the approval of the engineer. Mill certificates should be furnished to show that the cement conforms to the requirements of the specifications and ASTM C 150.[34] Type IV cement should not be used for pile concrete. Type III or high-early cement may be permitted for cast-in-place concrete test piles to get a fast strength gain. Types II or V may be specified for sulfate exposure.

Cement remaining in bulk storage for more than 6 months or cement stored in bags for a period longer than 3 months should be retested before it is used to ensure that it meets the requirements of ASTM C 150. If cement is used directly from the mill, it may still be hot and could contribute to a false concrete set.

Cement should be inspected for contamination by lumps caused by moisture. Cement bags should be inspected for rips, punctures, or other defects. If cement is to be batched by bag, the weights of the bags should be spot-checked and should not vary by more than 3 percent.

3.3.3.2 Sand. Sand should be clean, sharp, and well graded—free of silt, clay, or organic material. The specific gravity and/or fineness modulus may be specified for special mixes such as reduced-coarse-aggregate concrete.[113]

3.3.3.3 Coarse Aggregate. The specifications may permit gravel or crushed stone. The use of crushed-rock aggregate requires more cement and sand for comparable workability. Lightweight aggregates are not recommended, and slag aggregates generally are not used. Alkali-reactive aggregates or aggregates from shales, friable sandstone, clayey or micaceous rock, or cherts should not be permitted.[6,28] Aggregates should be uncoated and free of silt, clay, organic material, and chemical salts. The specific gravity of the coarse aggregate may be specified. Aggregates should be well graded, with a maximum size of $\frac{3}{4}$ in (20 m), and the amount of undersize aggregates [less than $\frac{3}{16}$ in (5 mm)] should be held uniform and within 3 percent.

3.3.3.4 Mix Water.   As a general rule, mix water should be potable and should contain no impurities which would affect the quality of the concrete. It should not have a sweet, saline, or brackish taste or contain silt or suspended solids. Very hard water may contain high concentrations of sulfate. Well water from arid regions may contain harmful dissolved mineral salts. If questionable, the water can be chemically analyzed. The quality of the water can be checked by comparing the strength of concrete reached at various ages for a mix using the water of unknown quality with the results of similar age tests on a mix made with water which is known to be acceptable. Impurities in mix water may affect both the compressive strength of the concrete and its setting time.

3.3.4 Admixtures.   The authorized or mandatory use of admixtures will be noted on the design mix report. Special admixtures such as retarders and plasticizers may be required for pumped concrete or special types of piles (see Section 6.3). Admixtures should comply with the specifications or recommended practice.[3,4]

3.3.5 Cold-Weather Operations.   When concrete is placed during cold weather, certain precautions are necessary.[10] Frozen aggregate or aggregates containing lumps of ice should be thawed before being used. It may be necessary to preheat the mix water and/or the aggregate. For air temperatures between 30 and 40°F (−1 and 4°C), it is usually only necessary to heat the water to a maximum of about 140°F (60°C). For air temperatures below 30°F (−1°C), the water can be heated to from 140 to 212°F (60 to 100°C) and the aggregate to about 45 to 55°F (7 to 13°C). Overheating should be avoided. If both the mix water and the aggregates are preheated, it is recommended that the water be mixed with the aggregates before the cement is added so as to avoid a flash set. The temperature of the water-aggregate mixture should not be higher than 80°F (27°C); a temperature of about 60°F (16°C) is preferable.

3.3.6 Hot-Weather Operations.   Special precautions should be taken when concrete is placed in hot climates.[9] If the temperature of the concrete during mixing is above 80°F (27°C), the result could be increased water demand (slump loss) or an accelerated set. The easiest way to control and reduce the concrete temperature is by using cold mix water, which can be mechanically refrigerated, or by using crushed ice as a part of or all of the mix water. Spraying of the coarse-aggregate stockpile can help control temperatures. Mixing time should be kept to a minimum, and mixing drums as well as water tanks and pipes should be painted white.

3.3.7 Mixing Time.   Mixing time starts when the water is added to the mix and should be adequate but not excessive. Minimum mixing times vary with the size and type of the mixer and range from 1 to 3 min. Maximum mixing times can range from 3 to 10 min. For stationary mixers, the minimum mixing time can be established by tests on mixer performance. For truck-mixed concrete, complete mixing requires from 50 to 100 revolutions of the drum at mixing speed. Check the manufacturer's plate on the mixer. If after mixing, the drum speed is reduced to agitation speed or the drum is stopped, the drum should be rotated at mixing speed for from 10 to 15 revolutions just before concrete is discharged.

3.3.8 Elapsed Time.   For normal temperatures, the total time from the start of mixing to discharge should not exceed about $1\frac{1}{2}$ h, and as temperatures increase, the total time should be reduced. The mix should be discharged before 300 revolutions of the drum.

3.3.9 Slump.   Slump tests for each batch of concrete should be made in accordance with ASTM C 143[33] to ensure that the concrete has the specified slump for proper placement in pile casings, shells, or holes. Concrete samples should be taken in accordance with ASTM C 172.[35] See Figure 3-2 for recommended procedure. Some slump-test equipment has a special base to which a hinged bail is attached. The height of the bail in a vertical position is the same as the height of the cone. After the cone is removed as illustrated in step 5 in Figure 3-2, the bail is swung up over the concrete, and the slump is measured from the top of the concrete to the bottom of the bail.

The slump for concrete as delivered to the top of the pile casing or hole should be 5 in (125 mm) for conventional concrete or 4 in (100 mm) for reduced-coarse-aggregate concrete, both with a tolerance of $+2$ in ($+50$ mm) or -1 in (-25 mm). Special types of piles require concrete or grout having different slumps (see Chapter 6). Sometimes it is advisable to check the slump just before the final water is added at the jobsite to avoid too high a slump or a wet mix. The consistency or slump of the concrete can be checked with a calibrated probe such as the K slump tester.[98]

3.3.10 Slump Loss.   Slump loss can be caused by overmixing, by hot weather, by pumping through long lines, or by delays in the delivery and placement of concrete. Overmixing can and should be avoided. If necessary, all the mix water can be added and all mixing done upon delivery at the jobsite. This could prevent overmixing and may help in eliminating slump loss due to hot weather. If concrete is to be pumped to the pile locations, the slump should be increased without changing the water-cement ratio or concrete strength to compensate for the slump loss during pumping.[8] All preparations should be

CONCRETE SLUMP TEST

Purpose of test: *To determine the consistency of fresh concrete and to check its uniformity from batch to batch. This test is based on ASTM C 143: Standard Method of Test for Slump of Portland Cement Concrete.*

Take two or more representative samples—at regularly spaced intervals —from the middle of the mixer discharge; do not take samples from beginning or end of discharge. Obtain samples within 15 minutes or less. *Important:* Slump test must be made within 5 minutes after taking samples.

Combine samples in a wheelbarrow or appropriate container and remix before making test.

Dampen slump cone with water and place it on a flat, level, smooth, moist, non-absorbent, firm surface.

1. Stand on two foot pieces of cone to hold it firmly in place during Steps 1 through 4. Fill cone mold 1/3 full by volume (2-1/2" high) with the concrete sample and rod it with 25 strokes using a round, bullet-nosed steel rod of 5/8" diameter x 24" long. Distribute rodding strokes evenly over entire cross section of the concrete by using approximately half the strokes near the perimeter (outer edge) and then progressing spirally toward the center.

2. Fill cone 2/3 full by volume (6" or half the height) and again rod 25 times with rod just penetrating into, but not through, the first layer. Distribute strokes evenly as described in Step 1.

3. Fill cone to overflowing and again rod 25 times with rod just penetrating into but not through the second layer. Again distribute strokes evenly.

4. Strike off excess concrete from top of cone with the steel rod, so that the cone is exactly level full. Clean the overflow away from the base of the cone mold.

5. Immediately after completion of Step 4, the operation of raising the mold shall be performed in 5 to 10 sec. by a steady upward lift with no lateral or torsional motion being imparted to the concrete. The entire operation from the start of the filling through removal of the mold shall be carried out without interruption and shall be completed within an elapsed time of 2-1/2 minutes.

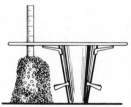

6. Place the steel rod horizontally across the inverted mold, so the rod extends over the slumped concrete. Immediately measure the distance from bottom of the steel rod to the original center of the top of the specimen. This distance, to the nearest 1/4 inch, is the slump of the concrete.

Figure 3-2 Recommended procedure for preforming concrete slump tests.

made for depositing concrete upon delivery, and delivery schedules should be arranged to eliminate delays in placing concrete.

3.3.11 Retempering.   The addition of water to the concrete mix to compensate for slump loss resulting from delays in delivery or placing is permissible provided the design water-cement ratio is not exceeded and the concrete has not attained its initial set. Excess mix water could result in decreased concrete strength. Initial set is not to be confused with a false set, when the concrete appears to stiffen but can be made workable with agitation.

3.3.12 Delivery Tickets.   A delivery ticket must accompany each load or batch of concrete. The delivery ticket is for the purchaser, but the inspector should be furnished with a copy. It should include sufficient data to identify the producer, the project, the contractor (purchaser), the truck mixer used, and the specified concrete mix or strength. Other items of information which should be on the delivery ticket include the date of delivery, the type and brand of cement, the types and amounts of admixtures, the quantity of water, the time batched, the reading of the revolution counter and the time when water was first added, the volume of the batch (cubic yards), and the amount of water added at the jobsite.

3.3.13 Concrete Strength Tests.   Standard 6×12 in (150×300 mm) cylinders for compression tests should be made periodically or as specified in accordance with ASTM C 31[27] to ensure that concrete of the required strength is being furnished. Concrete samples should be taken in accordance with ASTM C 172.[35] See Figure 3-3 for recommended procedure for making test cylinders. The frequency of making test cylinders will vary with the job size and other factors, but generally a test set (a minimum of two cylinders) should be made for each daily pour or for every 50 yd^3 (40 m^3) placed. Also, a test set should be made for each age at which compression tests are to be run (for example, 3 days, 7 days, or 28 days).

Test specimens must be cast in nonabsorbent molds. If cardboard molds are used, they must conform with ASTM C 470.[36] Improper jobsite curing or the use of cardboard molds not conforming to ASTM C 470 may contribute to low-strength test results. Substandard cardboard molds may cause excessive or rapid loss of moisture necessary for proper concrete curing or may produce distorted test specimens. Concrete strengths should be determined by standard cylinder tests in accordance with ASTM C 39.[29] Cube tests result in higher strengths. If cube tests have been performed, the cylinder strength can be considered 80 percent of the cube strength. Grout strengths for special types of piles, as covered in Chapter 6, will be determined by standard cube tests in accordance with ASTM C 91[30] and ASTM C 109[32] (see Sections 6.2 and 6.3). The inspector should ensure that test specimens are properly cast,

CONCRETE TEST CYLINDERS

NOTE: For complete procedure, see A.S.T.M. Designations: C31, C94 and C172.

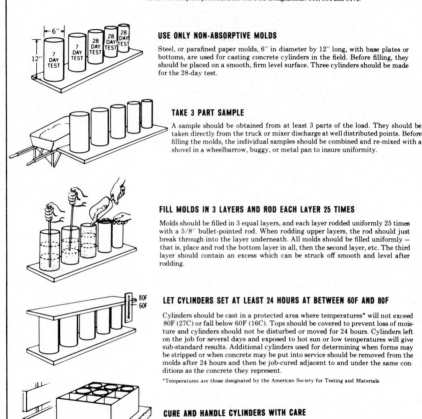

USE ONLY NON-ABSORPTIVE MOLDS

Steel, or parafined paper molds, 6″ in diameter by 12″ long, with base plates or bottoms, are used for casting concrete cylinders in the field. Before filling, they should be placed on a smooth, firm level surface. Three cylinders should be made for the 28-day test.

TAKE 3 PART SAMPLE

A sample should be obtained from at least 3 parts of the load. They should be taken directly from the truck or mixer discharge at well distributed points. Before filling the molds, the individual samples should be combined and re-mixed with a shovel in a wheelbarrow, buggy, or metal pan to insure uniformity.

FILL MOLDS IN 3 LAYERS AND ROD EACH LAYER 25 TIMES

Molds should be filled in 3 equal layers, and each layer rodded uniformly 25 times with a 5/8″ bullet-pointed rod. When rodding upper layers, the rod should just break through into the layer underneath. All molds should be filled uniformly — that is, place and rod the bottom layer in all, then the second layer, etc. The third layer should contain an excess which can be struck off smooth and level after rodding.

LET CYLINDERS SET AT LEAST 24 HOURS AT BETWEEN 60F AND 80F

Cylinders should be cast in a protected area where temperatures* will not exceed 80F (27C) or fall below 60F (16C). Tops should be covered to prevent loss of moisture and cylinders should not be disturbed or moved for 24 hours. Cylinders left on the job for several days and exposed to hot sun or low temperatures will give sub-standard results. Additional cylinders used for determining when forms may be stripped or when concrete may be put into service should be removed from the molds after 24 hours and then be job-cured adjacent to and under the same conditions as the concrete they represent.

*Temperatures are those designated by the American Society for Testing and Materials.

CURE AND HANDLE CYLINDERS WITH CARE

After 24 hours, cylinders for acceptance tests should be placed in moist curing at 73.4 ± 3F (23 ± 1.7C) or sent to a laboratory for similar standard curing. Careful handling during moving is necessary since cylinders which are allowed to rattle around in a box, or the back of a car, or pick-up, can suffer considerable damage.

IMPORTANT: Strengths indicative of the quality of concrete can be obtained only if this procedure is closely followed.

Figure 3-3 Recommended procedure for making standard concrete cylinder test specimens.

handled, stored, sealed, packaged for shipment, and shipped so as not to invalidate test results.

3.3.14 Results of Tests.   The pile inspector should be furnished with copies of the results of all concrete compression tests required by the specifications. The concrete supplier should also receive copies. It is advisable to obtain 3- and 7-day break results at the beginning of the job in order to detect trends in concrete strengths. The results of 7-day tests are also valuable in monitoring concrete strength trends as the job progresses so that, if necessary, remedial measures can be taken before too much concrete is placed. The results of concrete strength tests should be distributed promptly.

3.3.15 Strength Variations.   Some variation in concrete strength as determined by standard cylinder tests is normal, and a few low breaks are not sufficient justification to reject piles. Various criteria have been suggested to determine the acceptability of strength variations (see References 5, 11, 31, 64, and 66). For example, the concrete is considered satisfactory if the average of three consecutive tests is equal to or greater than the required 28-day strength and no test result falls below the required 28-day strength by more than 500 lb/in^2 (3.5 MPa). Another acceptance criterion is that 80 percent of the tests should show strengths greater than the design strength, and not more than 1 test in 10 should show less than the required 28-day strength. A third is that the average strength from consecutive tests should be greater than the required 28-day strength.

If the test results show that the concrete strength is below that specified, the cause of low strength should be investigated. Low strength could be caused by unsatisfactory concrete materials, by improper batching and mixing, or by the use of excess water in the mix. Low cylinder breaks could also result from using improper molds or improperly preparing, curing, handling, capping, or testing the cylinder specimens.

3.3.16 Verification of Concrete Strengths.   If the results of standard cylinder tests are low, cores can be removed from piles for testing. Tests on concrete cores are considered satisfactory if the average of three cores is equal to or greater than 85 percent of the required 28-day strength and if no core strength is less than 75 percent of the specified 28-day strength. The results of tests on cores are normally lower than the test results for standard cylinders, and there are various reasons for this (see References 56, 57, 61, 93, 94, 95, and 101).

It should be noted that the curing rates and strength gains for cast-in-place pile concrete vary according to environmental conditions. For example, curing conditions for concrete cast in a steel shell are ideal, but the rate of strength gain may be lower than that for test cylinders. Also, for uncased piles, concrete cast in saturated soils will cure under constant moisture conditions. Such conditions are desirable for proper curing but may result in slower curing. On the other hand, concrete cast in dry, highly permeable soils may experience a rapid loss of water into the surrounding soil, and this could result in improper curing and loss of strength. Concrete strength in completed piles can also be checked by nondestructive methods such as probe penetration resistance tests, hammer rebound tests, and ultrasonic pulse tests (see References 37, 54, 91, 92, 110, and 112). For some such tests to be meaningful, the surface tested should be free of any laitance or sand and should be representative of the actual concrete in the pile.

Before piles are rejected because the concrete is below the specified 28-day strength, consideration should be given to the natural strength gain with age, to using a higher percentage of the 28-day strength for the design stress, to proof-testing piles, or to using piles at a reduced design capacity. Generally, low-strength concrete is not the fault of the contractor, especially under proper inspection.

3.3.17 Records.   Simple checklist forms can be prepared for recording the results of inspection of the concrete production facilities, including materials, equipment, and procedures. Similar checklist forms, including items on the delivery ticket, can be prepared for recording pertinent data relative to delivered concrete. Other data to be recorded may include the time of delivery, the time concrete was placed, the slump, when test cylinders were made, and the concrete and air temperatures. Some of this information may be shown on inspection forms used to monitor the placing of concrete for cast-in-place piles. See Appendix D for sample forms.

3.4 DRILLING MUD

If a drilling mud or slurry is to be used in installing drilled-hole piles, the type to be used may be specified.

3.5 STEEL PIPE AND MONOTUBE PILES

3.5.1 Material Specifications.   Mill certificates or laboratory test reports should be furnished to show that the pipe or Monotubes conform to the required material specifications, including yield strength. Pipe may be specified by grade with reference to ASTM A 252.[17] The specifications may require new pipe, but sometimes the contractor will propose using used pipe that was not produced under ASTM A 252. This may be for reasons of economy or availability. There is nothing wrong with using used pipe, provided it is in good condition, is drivable, and is weldable by standard methods. Some steels could be rather brittle and very difficult to weld. Test coupons should be taken from each batch of such pipe and the results of laboratory tests submitted to the engineer. The steel should satisfy the minimum yield-strength requirements. The use of used pipe or pipe other than ASTM A 252 must be subject to the engineer's approval.

3.5.2 Lengths. Pipe-pile material may be delivered in single random, double random, or uniform lengths. Single random lengths range from 16 to 25 ft (4.9 to 7.6 m) inclusive, and double random lengths are over 25 ft (7.6 m), with a minimum average of 35 ft (10.7 m). Uniform lengths will be as specified with a tolerance of ± 1 in (± 25 mm). The ordered length may be limited by the mill or the transportation facilities.

The lengths of tapered portions of Monotubes will be determined by the type and size specified. See Table C-5 for data on Monotubes. The lengths of extension pieces for Monotubes will be as ordered: 10- to 40-ft (3- to 12-m) lengths in 5-ft (1.5-m) increments. Generally, payment for material for pipe and Monotube piles is made for the quantity incorporated in the finished foundation. However, if pile material is to be paid for on the basis of furnished lengths, the ordered lengths must be approved by the engineer, and the total delivered lengths of pipe or Monotube piles must be checked. Extra pieces of pipe and extra lengths or pieces of Monotubes may be ordered to provide for piles that may be driven longer than anticipated.

3.5.3 Dimensions. The diameter and wall thickness or gauge should meet the minimums specified. Although a minimum wall thickness or gauge may be specified, the contractor may not be relieved from the responsibility of furnishing thicker walls or heavier gauges if necessary to properly install the piles without damage or to achieve the required pile penetration. Check the contract documents. For tapered Monotubes, the type of lower pile section (designating the degree of taper) should be specified. Table C-2 shows dimensions for standard pipe sizes, and Table C-5 shows data on Monotube piles.

3.5.4 End Finish. Pipe may be ordered with plain ends either flame- or machine-cut, or the specifications may require that ends be beveled for welding. A special end finish may be specified. A milled finish is not necessary.

3.5.5 Fittings for Pipe and Monotube Piles. Pipe may be ordered with closure plates attached, or the plates may be welded on in the field. Monotubes will be furnished with closure points welded on by the manufacturer. Special closure plates or points may be required by the specifications. The diameter and thickness of closure plates or points will be specified. When pipe piles are closed with a flat steel plate, the diameter of the closure plate should be not more than $\frac{3}{4}$ in (20 mm) larger than the outside diameter of the pipe. The specifications may permit splicing pipe piles with steel sleeves with or without

Conical points attached to pipe piles. (*Courtesy of Associated Pile & Fitting Corp.*)

welding. Splicing sleeves may be either outside or inside sleeves and should conform to the specifications.

3.5.6 Welding. The welding on of boot plates or points at the tips of pipe piles will be done on a horizontal rack in advance of pile driving, unless pipe is shipped to the job with closure plates attached. Splice welding of pipe or Monotube piles may be done on a horizontal rack or in the leaders (see Section 5.34). Alternatively, splice fittings may be welded to one end of the pipe on the ground in preparation for splicing in the leaders. The qualifications of welders and all welding should conform with the AWS Structural Welding Code—Steel D 1.1.*

3.5.7 Handling. Sufficient pickup points should be used to avoid bends in pipe or Monotube piles. Generally a one-point pickup is sufficient. Closed-end piles should not be dragged along the ground open end first; if they are, dirt or other debris will be picked up and will collect at the bottoms of the piles when they are lofted.

3.5.8 Unloading. Controlled dumping or roll-off unloading of pipe or Monotube piles may be permitted.

3.5.9 Storage. Pipe and Monotube piles should be stored on adequate blocking off the ground and above any standing water. Sufficient chocks should be used to prevent pile stacks from spreading.

---

*American Welding Society, Inc., Miami, Fla., 1982.

3.5.10 Records. A simple checklist form can be prepared for recording the inspection data.

3.6 STEEL H PILES

3.6.1 Material Specifications. Steel H piles will generally be specified under ASTM A 36[15] or ASTM A 572.[21] Mill certificates or laboratory test reports should be furnished showing that the material meets the specifications as to type of steel and properties, including yield strength. The average yield strength across the full cross section could be less than the specified yield strength without invalidating conformance to the specifications.[70] Coupons for mill tests are customarily taken from the web near a flange where the strength is usually the highest. Also, the rules of purchase[14,18] permit a retest when a test is failed, which means that the specimen has a 75 percent chance of passing. If the specified yield strength is higher than 36,000 lb/in^2 (248 MPa), the identity of all steel must be continuously maintained from the point of manufacture to the pile location, or coupons must be taken from each piece and tested to see that it meets the specifications.

3.6.2 Lengths. If pile material is to be paid for on the basis of furnished lengths, the ordered lengths must be approved by the engineer, and the total delivered lengths of H piles must be checked. Piles will generally be shipped in standard mill lengths of 40 to 60 ft (12 to 18 m). Longer lengths can be obtaind from the mill by special order. Extra lengths of H piles may be ordered to provide for driving piles longer than anticipated.

3.6.3 Dimensions. The pile size and weight per foot should meet the minimum requirements of the specifications. Piles should generally conform to American Institute of Steel Construction (AISC) HP shapes. See Table C-1 for data on HP shapes.

3.6.4 Types. The specifications may permit either rolled or built-up shapes. If built up, the piles should be of the H-section type, with the web and flanges of equal thickness. The web and flanges must be continuously welded together.

3.6.5 H-Pile Fittings. The specifications may require pile tip reinforcement, which could be special steel castings or fabricated points or pile tips built up with steel plates. Splicing material or fittings may also be specified. Steel pile cap plates (see Section 5.42) may be required. All pile fittings should conform to the specifications.

3.6.6 Special Coatings. The materials and method of application of special coatings should conform to the specifications. If coatings are applied off-site,

Special fitting welded to an H pile to protect the tip.
(*Courtesy of Associated Pile & Fitting Corp.*)

certificates of inspection and/or compliance should be furnished, and the inspector should check on the quality and thickness of the coatings. If welding of coated piles is necessary, the special coating must be properly applied to all welded areas and those portions of the pile where the coating has been damaged by welding (see Section 5.11.4).

3.6.7 Welding.   The welding on of pile tip reinforcement will be done on a horizontal rack before piles are driven. Splicing may be completed on the rack, or fittings may be welded to the bottoms of pile sections which are to be added as driving progresses and the splice welding completed in the leaders (see Section 5.34). Pile cap plates, if required, will be welded on after piles have been cut off to grade. The qualifications of welders and all welding should conform with the AWS Structural Welding Code—Steel D 1.1.* Note that special welding procedures may be required for high-yield-strength steel or special steels.

3.6.8 Handling.   Long steel H piles should be lifted in a horizontal position with the webs vertical and with a sufficient number of pickup points to avoid bending. Coated H piles must be carefully handled so as to prevent damage to the coating.

3.6.9 Unloading.   Steel H piles should be unloaded by lifting. Dumping of piles should be prohibited.

3.6.10 Storage.   Steel H piles should be stored on adequate timber blocking to avoid bending. Nesting of piles with flanges vertical is recommended.

---

*American Welding Society, Inc., Miami, Fla., 1982.

Splice fittings for steel H piles. (*Courtesy of Associated Pile & Fitting Corp.*)

Blocking should be placed so as to prevent low spots along the pile in which water could accumulate. If piles are stored in tiers with webs vertical, blocking should be used between each tier at each support point.

3.6.11 Records.   On the basis of the specifications and the items required to be inspected, appropriate forms can be prepared for recording the necessary data.

3.7 PILE SHELLS

Pile shells covered by this section are made of relatively light-gauge corrugated steel and are driven with the aid of an internal steel mandrel. They are considered non-load-bearing and serve primarily as a form to protect the concrete filling as it sets and cures.

3.7.1 Dimensions.   Nominal outside diameters of pile shells should be in accordance with the specifications. For Step-Taper pile shells, the minimum nominal tip diameter may be specified, with the butt diameter resulting from the rate of taper and pile length. If the minimum butt diameter is specified, the required tip diameter will be governed by the taper and pile length. For

Unloading steel H piles. (*Courtesy of Bethlehem Steel Corporation.*)

Step-Taper shells, the rate of taper will be governed by the lengths of the shell sections used. In some cases both minimum tip and butt diameters may be specified. Table C-3 contains dimensional data on the various Step-Taper shell sections. Dimensional data for constant-section shells are shown in Table C-4.

3.7.2 Lengths.   Payment is usually made for pile lengths actually installed. If payment is to be made for furnished lengths, the inspector should verify that the delivered lengths agree with the ordered lengths as approved by the engineer.

3.7.2.1 Constant-Section Shells.   Shells of uniform diameter (constant section) will usually be shipped to the job in mill lengths up to about 80 ft (24 m). However, within limitations shells may be made up by the manufacturer to the required pile lengths. Lengths of shell can be spliced together by butt welding on a horizontal rack to make up the required pile lengths.

3.7.2.2 Step-Taper Shells.   Step-Taper shells will generally be shipped to the job in section lengths of 4, 8, 12, or 16 ft (1.2, 2.4, 3.7, or 4.9 m) as

Steel H piles in storage. (*Courtesy of Bethlehem Steel Corporation.*)

specified. Longer section lengths are also used. Shell sections are usually assembled on a horizontal rack by means of threaded joints to make up the required pile lengths.

3.7.3 Shell Gauges.   The minimum shell gauges may be specified, especially for the lower portion of the pile, to resist high collapsing pressures. For a given thickness, the strength against collapse will vary inversely with the diameter. The contractor may be responsible for furnishing gauges heavier than specified if they are necessary for satisfactory pile installation.

3.7.4 Shell Seams.   Pile shells are generally spirally formed, and the resulting seam should be welded. If the specifications do not address the type of seam, the use of nonwelded (locked) seams should be subject to the approval of the engineer.

3.7.5 Closure Plates.   Step-Taper pile shells will be furnished with boot plates attached. For constant-section shells, the closures may be welded on before shipment to the job, or they may be welded on in the field. The diameter, thickness, and attachment of closure plates should conform to the specifications.

3.7.6 Handling.   Pile shells should be handled carefully at all times so as to avoid permanent detrimental deformations. Closed-end shells should not be dragged along the ground open end first. If this is unavoidable, the pile shells

Step-Taper pile shells delivered to the jobsite nested and bundled. (*Courtesy of Raymond International Builders, Inc.*)

should be lofted (raised to a vertical position) with the closed end up in order to remove any accumulated dirt or other debris.

3.7.7 Unloading.   Dumping of pile shells should not be permitted, but a roll-off method may be used for unloading. Step-Taper pile shells will generally be shipped to the jobsite nested and bundled with steel strapping. Such bundles may be unloaded with a small crane.

3.7.8 Storage.   Pile shells should be stored out of mud or standing water. If in storage for a long period of time, shells should be protected from the elements, and the condition of the shells should be checked before they are used.

3.7.9 Records.   On the basis of the specifications, appropriate forms can be prepared for recording data resulting from the required inspections.

3.8 PILE CASINGS

The casing material used for drilled-hole piles may be specified as to diameter and minimum wall thickness. The casing diameter should be greater than the specified diameter for the drilled-hole piles.

3.9 REINFORCING STEEL

3.9.1 Material Specifications.   Reinforcing steel material is usually governed by ASTM standards A 82, A 615, A 616, A 617, and A 706. Prestressing steel is governed by ASTM A 416, A 421, and A 722. These standards are listed in Appendix A. High-yield-strength steel bars conforming to ASTM A 722, such as Dywidag,* are often used for reinforcement to resist uplift loads. Mill certificates or laboratory test reports should be given to the inspector showing that the material meets the specifications as to type of steel and properties, including yield strength. Reinforcing steel bundles should have identification tags attached.

3.9.2 Dimensions. Longitudinal reinforcement should be bundled according to size and length, which should be in accordance with the specifications. The sizes and diameters of spirals or hoops should be as specified. Longitudinal steel may be spliced to the required lengths by welding, by approved splicers, or by adequate lapping and wiring.

3.9.3 Bends. Hook or L-shaped bends should conform to the plans and specifications. The diameter of all bends should not be less than 6 times the minimum bar thickness or diameter. All bending should be done with the bars cold. Bars that have been bent should not be restraightened.

3.9.4 Reinforcing Steel Fittings. The plans or specifications may require special fittings such as spacers for centering reinforcement in the pile casing or hole.

3.9.5 Surface Conditions. All reinforcing material must be new and free from rust. Before actual use, reinforcing must be free from rust scale, loose mill scale, oil, grease, paint, dirt, and all other coatings which could destroy or reduce the bond between the steel and concrete.

3.9.6 Handling Reinforcing steel should be handled in bundles with appropriate lifting slings located at sufficient pickup points to avoid permanent bending.

3.9.7 Storage. Bundles should not be broken until used. All necessary precautions must be taken to maintain the identification of the steel after the bundles are broken. This can be done by keeping the steel separated according to type, size, and length with a tagged piece in each stack. Reinforcing steel should be stored off the ground on suitable racks or blocking so as to avoid permanent bends. The steel should be stored in a manner to prevent excessive rusting and contamination by dirt, grease, or other coatings that could affect the steel-to-concrete bond.

3.9.8 Records. Data on the inspection of reinforcing steel material can be recorded on simple checklist forms.

* Dywidag Systems International, Lincoln Park, N.J.

Chapter **4**

Pile Installation Equipment

A fundamental knowledge of pile installation equipment is essential for meaningful pile inspection. The inspector should be familiar with the principal components of a pile-driving rig, their functions, and their operating characteristics. Figure 4-1 illustrates the major parts of a typical complete pile-driving rig. Some of these parts are critical to the proper installation of piles. Pile driving is a unique type of construction in that the basic tool used for installation, the pile-driving hammer, is also used to measure the adequacy of the construction as a function of driving resistance.

4.1 EQUIPMENT DATA

The inspector should be furnished with copies of the contractor's submittals covering the equipment and methods to be used. Since the pile-driving hammer is the heart of the driving system, the inspector should also have on hand data from the hammer manufacturer covering the specifications, operation, and maintenance of the hammer to be used.

4.2 RECORDS

Much of the equipment data to be recorded can be reported on conventional inspection forms covering such operations as pile installation and pile load tests. See Appendix D for sample forms. If necessary, special forms can be prepared for recording equipment data, or such information can be included in the inspector's diary or general daily reports.

62

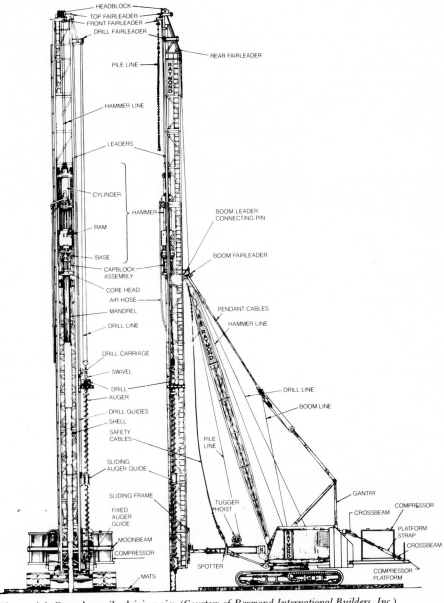

Figure 4-1 Complete pile-driving rig. (*Courtesy of Raymond International Builders, Inc.*)

4.3 LEADERS

The leaders hold the pile and hammer in proper alignment so that eccentric hammer blows can be avoided. Such blows could damage the pile or cause it to be driven off location, or they could invalidate a dynamic driving formula. The leaders also serve to hold the pile in the specified position and alignment, and they provide a means for supporting the pile during driving. Leaders should be of sturdy construction, and they should be fixed at two points, normally at the boom tip and to the spotter at the bottom of the leaders. The use of swinging leaders or spud-type leaders is generally not recommended, except possibly for small jobs or for driving piles on very steep batters. In that case, the leaders should be supported and held in the required position with some type of special frame. Leaders should be equipped with extensions which would permit the hammer to travel below the bottom of the leaders during driving. Thus the use of a follower can be avoided. Leaders also serve as a mounting for ancillary equipment such as a jet or drill.

4.4 SPOTTER AND MOONBEAM

The spotter (see Figure 4-1) fixes the bottom of the leaders to the crane or to the base of the rig. Adjustable or telescopic spotters greatly facilitate pile spotting (see Section 5.15), especially when hydraulically controlled. The leaders can be attached directly to the spotter or to a transverse member called a

Hydraulically controlled telescopic spotter. Rig equipped with a moonbeam for driving side-batter piles. (*Courtesy of Raymond International Builders, Inc.*)

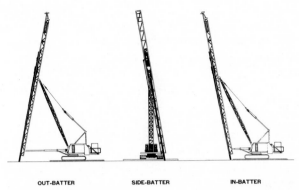

OUT-BATTER   SIDE-BATTER   IN-BATTER

Figure 4-2 Basic rig configurations for driving batter piles.

"moonbeam." The attachment to the moonbeam permits the bottom of the leaders to move laterally for driving side-batter piles. Unless the moonbeam is curved to match the swing radius of the leaders pinned at the boom tip, a sliding frame is required at the bottom of the leaders to accommodate the increase in length as the leaders are pivoted sideways. The combination of a universal joint between the leaders and the boom tip, a live boom, an adjustable spotter, and a moonbeam permits, within limitations, driving piles on any required degree or direction of batter. Figure 4-2 illustrates the basic rig configurations for driving batter piles.

4.5 PREEXCAVATION EQUIPMENT

Preexcavation equipment (see Section 5.12) such as a jet or drill is generally mounted on the leaders on the same driving radius as for the hammer and pile. This facilitates pile installation. If necessary to avoid whipping, the jet pipe or drill stem is supported by a traveling guide. Drill bits or augers should not be larger than the specified size. Drill stems must be of adequate size to handle the necessary water pressures and volumes for effective predrilling and removal of soil cuttings for the size of the hole drilled. Drill stems (including kellys) and jet pipes must be long enough to reach the required preexcavation depths. Jet pumps should be of sufficient size and capacity to provide the required volume of water at the necessary rates and pressures.

4.6 POWER SOURCE

The power source used to operate the pile-driving hammer, such as a boiler or compressor, must be of adequate capacity. Boilers should be sized according to the pounds of steam delivered per hour at the required operating

Auger for predrilling mounted
on box leaders. Note that the
hammer is mounted outboard.
(*Courtesy of Raymond International
Builders, Inc.*)

pressure. However, boilers are generally sized by horsepower, which can be based on the pounds of steam consumed per hour or on the square footage of the heating area. The so-called ASME rating is a misnomer in that the American Society of Mechanical Engineers does not rate boilers. The term "ASME rating" is based on an ASME performance test code which equates a steam consumption of 34.5 lb/h at 212°F with 1 hp (16.4 kg/h at 100°C with 10 kW). Compressors should be rated by the volume of compressed air delivered per minute corrected to standard conditions when operating at the required pressure (standard cubic feet per minute, or scfm). Reference to pounds of steam per hour or standard cubic feet per minute alone without specifying pressure is inadequate, since no amount of steam or air will operate a hammer if it cannot be delivered at the required minimum pressure. The required steam or air pressure varies directly with the weight of the hammer ram.

The hammer manufacturer's data can be used as a guide for determining the required boiler or compressor capacity. See Table B-1 for specified boiler and compressor capacities for hammers of different sizes. The actual required capacities will depend upon such things as the lengths and sizes of piping and hose connecting the hammer to the power source and the number and sizes of elbows, valves, and other fittings, as well as the condition of the hammer (wear of piston rings, etc.) and leaks in the system. The condition of

Various types of bits can be
used on predrilling augers.
(*Courtesy of Raymond International
Builders, Inc.*)

the boiler and the quality of water used could affect the volume of steam
produced and therefore the effective capacity of the boiler.

For air-operated hammers, the consumption figures frequently reported
are based upon adiabatic compression and the required pressure at the hammer. This can be misleading, since no compressor operates fully adiabatically.
For practical reasons, the air is cooled as it is compressed, and its volume
decreases. Therefore, unless the air is reheated after normal compression, the
output of the compressor should be from 30 to 50 percent greater than the
adiabatic consumption figure normally reported.

The hammer manufacturer's data will generally specify the minimum pressure required at the hammer for operation at normal efficiency. Adequate
pressure at the hammer is essential for double-acting, differential, or compound hammers. It is impractical to measure the pressure at the hammer, but
the pressure should be measured as close to the hammer as feasible and in any
case downstream from whatever throating and control valves are used. The
pressure as measured on the downstream side of control valves should be
higher than the required hammer-operating pressure to provide for line
losses between the hammer and the pressure gauge. Experience may determine what pressure must be maintained at the gauge to make the required
pressure available at the hammer. Line losses can be more critical for smaller-

diameter pipe. For example, for a 100-ft (30-m) length of 2-in (50-mm)-diameter pipe carrying 1500 scfm (0.71 m^3/s) of air at 125 lb/in^2 (860 kPa), the pressure drop would be about 10 lb/in^2 (69 kPa). For a 3-in (75-mm) pipe carrying the same volume of compressed air at the same pressure, the drop would be only 1.4 lb/in^2 (10 kPa). Valves and fittings will increase the pressure loss. For example, a 2-in (50-mm) 90° elbow is equivalent to an additional 5 ft (1.5 m) of straight pipe. A 2-in (50-mm) globe valve fully opened is equivalent to adding about 60 ft (18 m) more of pipe.

4.7 TYPES OF PILE-DRIVING HAMMERS

Table 4-1 lists various types of hammers. Typical pile-driving hammers include drop hammers, single-acting hammers, double-acting hammers, differential hammers, compound hammers, diesel hammers, and vibratory drivers. In addition there are special types of hammers, such as air-gun, vibratory-impact, and electrohydraulic hammers.

Powered pile-driving hammers can be classified as air or steam hammers, diesel hammers, and vibratory drivers. They are manufactured in many models and sizes, some having unique characteristics. Table B-1 lists the various makes and models of air or steam hammers, Table B-2 lists the same for diesel

Table 4-1 TYPES OF PILE-DRIVING HAMMERS

Drop hammers
Single-acting hammers
  Steam
  Air
Double-acting hammers
Differential hammers
  Steam
  Air
  Hydraulic
Diesel hammers
  Open-top
  Closed-top
Vibratory drivers
  Low-frequency (to 40 Hz)
  High-frequency (to 140 Hz)
Linear oscillators
  Hydraulic
  Electrohydraulic
Vibratory-impact hammers
Air-gun hammers
  Underwater
  Bouncer
Compound hammers

hammers, and Table B-3 covers vibratory drivers. These tables give the basic specifications for the various models of hammers or drivers.

4.7.1 Drop Hammer.   The drop hammer is the oldest type of pile hammer in use and is simply a heavy weight that is allowed to drop freely on the head of the pile. The drop weight is usually operated between guide rails.

Until around 1900, piles were driven almost exclusively with drop hammers. Today, because of their slow rate of operation and inconsistent delivered energy, drop hammers are seldom used to drive foundation piles. They are sometimes used to drive piles for small projects and in remote areas, and a special type of drop hammer is used for base-driven pipe piles and to install pressure injected footings as described in Chapter 2.

If a drop hammer is used, the inspector should ascertain that the specified weight has been furnished along with special equipment that may be required, such as an automatic trip.

4.7.2 Single-Acting Hammer.   Single-acting hammers are powered by compressed air or steam pressure, which is used to raise the hammer ram for each stroke. The steam or air exhausts on the downstroke. The delivered energy results from the kinetic energy developed by the gravity fall of the ram.

Figure 4-3 shows schematically the operation of a single-acting hammer. At the start of the cycle, the ram has impacted, and air or steam pressure is being admitted into the cylinder below the piston. The upward force resulting from this pressure is about twice the weight of the ram. This pressure raises and accelerates the ram until the lower wedge on the slide bar trips the valves to shut off the air or steam supply and open the exhaust. Because of upward acceleration, the ram continues to move up until its kinetic energy is zero, at which time it starts its gravity fall. Just prior to impact, the upper wedge on the slide bar trips the valves to close off the exhaust and admit air or steam. The complete valve action is not immediate, and the ram continues its downward movement to impact on the pile. By this time the intake valve is completely open. The air or steam pressure builds up rapidly to raise the ram, and the cycle is repeated. The upward acceleration of the ram is assisted by the ram's rebound, which varies with the drive system, the type of pile, and the pile penetration resistance.

4.7.3 Double-Acting Hammer.   Double-acting hammers can be powered by steam, but they are usually powered by compressed air, which is used both to raise the ram and to accelerate its fall. This type of hammer exhausts at both the upstroke and the downstroke, and the operating pressure on the downstroke is applied to the full top area of the piston. Double-acting hammers have light rams and operate at a relatively high speed. They are not as effective in driving foundation piles as single-acting or differential hammers, and they are used principally for driving sheet piles or underpinning piles.

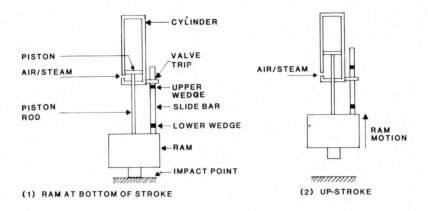

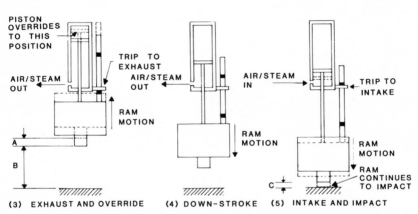

Figure 4-3 Operating cycle for a single-acting air or steam hammer. *Note:* Distances *A*, *B*, and *C* vary with hammer design. An average value for *A* would be about $0.33(A + B)$, where $A + B$ equals the full stroke. The distance *C* ranges from about 1.5 to 3.5 in (38 to 89 mm).

4.7.4 Differential Hammer.   A differential hammer is usually powered by either steam or compressed air. However, this type of hammer has also been designed and built to operate by means of high-pressure hydraulic fluid. The steam, air, or hydraulic fluid is used both to raise the ram and to accelerate its fall. The differential hammer exhausts only during the upstroke.

Figure 4-4 illustrates the operation of a differential air or steam hammer. The upper portion of the cylinder has a larger diameter than the lower portion. On the upstroke, air or steam is admitted into the cylinder between the upper and lower pistons. The air or steam pressure acting on the difference between piston areas causes an upward acceleration of the ram. At the top of the stroke the air or steam pressure is admitted into the cylinder above the large (upper) piston, and the cylinder spaces both above and below the

Vulcan single-acting steam hammer. (*Courtesy of Armco, Inc., Construction Products Division.*)

upper piston are under equal pressure. The accelerating downward force results from the differential-operating fluid pressure acting on both pistons (the effective area equals the total area of the lower piston).

As shown in Figure 4-5, the construction of the differential hydraulic hammer is different in that there is no lower piston. The operation is basically the same as for the air or steam hammer in that during the downstroke, the cylinder spaces both above and below the piston are open to the operating pressure and thus under equal pressure. The accelerating downward force in this case results from the difference in areas between the top and bottom of the piston (the difference equals the area of the piston rod). The hydraulic hammer can be designed with a single piston because the very high operating pressure, such as 5000 lb/in^2 (35 MPa), produces an effective force on the small piston-rod area.

Differential hammers have shorter strokes than comparable single-acting hammers and combine the advantages of the heavy ram of the single-acting hammer with the higher operating speed of the double-acting hammer.

4.7.5 Compound Hammer. The compound hammer is a variation of the differential hammer. Again compressed air or steam is used both to raise the ram and to accelerate its fall. The construction is similar to that of the differ-

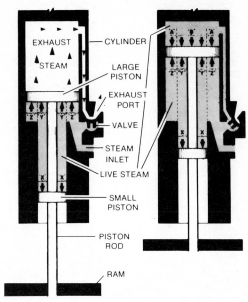

Figure 4-4 Operating principles of a differential air or steam hammer. *Upstroke:* Steam or air force XX on the small piston is balanced by equal steam or air force YY on the large piston. The remaining area of the large piston is acted on by force ZZ, which lifts the ram. (The steam or air above the large piston, which was used on the downstroke, is exhausted.) *Downstroke:* Steam or air force XX on the small piston is balanced by equal force YY on the large piston. The force ZZ on the large piston is balanced by equal force AA. Force B on the remaining area is the net force which pushes the ram down. The area on which B acts is equal to the area of the small piston, including the piston rod. (*Courtesy of Raymond International Builders, Inc.*)

ential hydraulic hammer. The hammer exhausts during the upstroke, at the top of which both the exhaust and inlet valves close, and no additional motive fluid is introduced into the cylinder. The cylinder spaces both above and below the piston are interconnected, permitting the motive fluid to raise the ram and also enter the top of the cylinder as it expands. After the ram reaches the top of its stroke, the continued expansion of the motive fluid, acting on the differential area between the top and bottom of the piston, accelerates the ram on the downstroke.

4.7.6 Diesel Hammer.   Diesel hammers are self-contained power units. The explosion of diesel fuel under the ram or piston raises the ram for the next

Raymond hydraulically powered differential hammer.
(*Courtesy of Raymond International Builders, Inc.*)

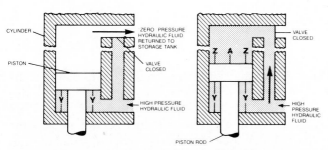

Figure 4-5 Operating principles of a differential hydraulic hammer. *Upstroke:* Hydraulic force YY pushing against the piston and reacting against the bottom of the cylinder lifts the ram. *Downstroke:* Hydraulic force YY is balanced by equal force ZZ. Hydraulic force A on the remaining area is the net force which pushes the ram down. The area on which A acts is equal to the area of the piston rod (*Courtesy of Raymond International Builders, Inc.*)

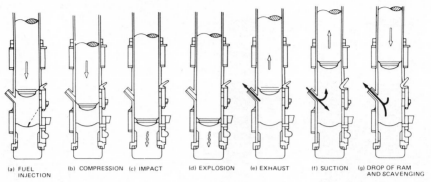

Figure 4-6 Operating cycle for a diesel hammer. (*Courtesy of Mitsubishi Heavy Industries, Ltd., and International Construction Equipment, Inc.*)

stroke. The ram or piston then falls by gravity to impact and drive the pile. Figure 4-6 illustrates the operation of a diesel hammer. The hammer is started by raising the ram or piston with a line (or a separate air or hydraulic pressure system) to the top of its stroke and releasing it, permitting it to fall inside the cylinder. As the ram descends, it closes off the air intake port, activates a fuel pump to inject diesel fuel into the combustion chamber, and compresses the air in the combustion chamber. Some hammers are of the impact-atomization type, whereas others have a spray-atomization fuel-injection system. The ram continues to compress and heat up the air in the cylinder, and at impact, the air-fuel mixture ignites under pressure and heat. The resulting explosion raises the ram for its next stroke. At the start of the upstroke, the exhaust-intake port is opened, and the products of combustion are exhausted. As the ram moves upward, fresh air is drawn into the cylinder. The ram continues its ascent to the top of its stroke, and the cycle repeats.

As long as sufficient pile penetration resistance is encountered, the hammer will continue to operate. If there is little or no resistance to pile penetration, the hammer may stop, although some hammers are designed to operate under soft driving. The hammer can be stopped at any time by cutting off the fuel flow.

There are two basic types of diesel hammers: single-acting (open-top) and double-acting (closed-top). For the single-acting type, the cylinder in which the ram operates is open at the top, and the ram will rise to whatever height results from the explosive force and rebound. For the double-acting type, the cylinder is closed at the top, and entrapped air above the ram is compressed in the bounce chamber as the ram rises (see Figure 4-7). The expansion of this compressed air provides an accelerating force for the ram on the downstroke in addition to that of gravity. Closed-top hammers have shorter strokes and operate at higher speeds than open-top hammers of equivalent energy under the same driving conditions.

Delmag single-acting diesel hammer driving precast concrete piles. *Hammer:* Delmag D62-12 diesel hammer. *Pile:* 24-in-square concrete, 70 to 90 ft long. *Soil:* dense clay. *Job:* Texas Turnpike Bridge, Deerpark, Texas. (*Courtesy of Pileco, Inc.*)

4.7.7 Vibratory Driver. Vibratory drivers apply a dynamic force to the pile from paired rotating weights set eccentric from their centers of rotation and positioned so that when they are rotated, the horizontal forces are canceled and the vertical forces are added. Figure 4-8 illustrates schematically the construction of a vibratory driver.

The oscillator containing the rotating weights must be rigidly connected to the pile for effective transmission of the longitudinal vibrations. Vibratory drivers are more effective for installing non-displacement-type piles (or steel sheeting) in granular or cohesionless soils. The driving effectiveness of the vibratory hammer can be increased by applying a bias weight or force to the nonvibrating portion of the driver (sprung weight).

Most vibratory drivers are of the low-frequency type, with operating frequencies ranging from 0 to about 2000 vibrations per minute, and the oscillator is powered by electric or hydraulic motors. The high-frequency type operates at frequencies ranging from 4800 to about 7200 cycles per minute,

ICE double-acting diesel hammer driving Raymond
Step-Taper piles. (*Courtesy of Raymond International Build-*
ers, Inc.)

which is within the resonant frequency range of most piles. Oscillators for
these drivers are powered by internal-combustion engines.

4.8 PILE HAMMER ENERGY

4.8.1 General. As previously stated, the hammer is the heart of the pile-
driving system, and the determination of pile capacity is often based on the
energy being delivered by the hammer during driving. It is essential, in such
cases, that the actual delivered energy be about the same as the energy used in
any dynamic analysis or driving formula and that the hammer performance
be consistent as production piles are driven. The inspector should know how
hammer energies are developed, how they are affected, the possible energy
losses in the total driving system, and the possible alterations in hammer
energy. The inspector should also be familiar with the basic operation and
maintenance of hammers as they may affect hammer energy.

Pile-driving hammers are available in various sizes with rated energies rang-

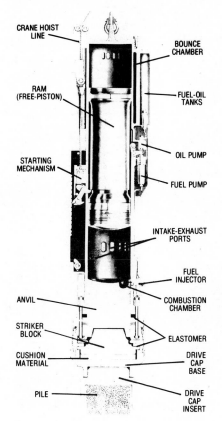

CRANE HOIST
LINE

BOUNCE
CHAMBER

RAM
(FREE-PISTON)

FUEL-OIL
TANKS

OIL PUMP

STARTING
MECHANISM

FUEL PUMP

INTAKE-EXHAUST
PORTS

FUEL
INJECTOR

ANVIL

COMBUSTION
CHAMBER

STRIKER
BLOCK

ELASTOMER

CUSHION
MATERIAL

DRIVE
CAP
BASE

PILE

DRIVE
CAP
INSERT

Figure 4-7 Construction of a closed-top diesel hammer. (*Courtesy of International Construction Equipment, Inc.*)

ing from a few hundred foot-pounds per blow to over 1 million foot-pounds. Normally, foundation piles are installed with hammers with energy ratings ranging from about 10,000 to 100,000 ft·lbf (13.5 to 135.6 kJ). Hammers smaller than about 10,000 ft·lbf are used principally for underpinning work or for installing sheeting. Hammers larger than about 100,000 ft·lbf have been developed to drive long, heavy piles for offshore and other marine structures.

The required type of pile-driving hammer and the required size (rated energy) will generally be specified. For vibratory drivers the required size may be stated in terms of eccentric moment or the dynamic force available at a specified frequency. Generally, hammers somewhat larger than specified could be used, except that the hammer energy used to drive normal-size timber piles should be limited to about 15,000 ft·lbf (20.3 kJ) per blow.

For dynamic pile installation, the required or permissible hammer size can best be determined by a wave equation analysis (see Section 5.19). Such an analysis reflects the characteristics and properties of the various components of the drive system (see Figure 4-9), the pile, and the subsoils. The analysis will

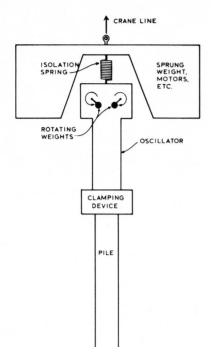

CRANE LINE

ISOLATION SPRING

SPRUNG WEIGHT, MOTORS, ETC.

ROTATING WEIGHTS

OSCILLATOR

CLAMPING DEVICE

PILE

Figure 4-8 Principal parts of a vibratory driver.

Foster vibratory driver. (*Courtesy of L. B. Foster Company.*)

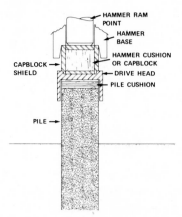

HAMMER RAM
POINT
HAMMER
BASE
HAMMER CUSHION
OR CAPBLOCK
CAPBLOCK
SHIELD
DRIVE HEAD
PILE CUSHION
PILE

Figure 4-9 Principal components of the pile-driving system.

indicate the potential for developing the required pile capacity with the selected drive system, including the hammer, and the possibility of overstressing
the pile during driving. It will also indicate the feasibility of achieving the
required pile lengths.

For impact hammers, the energy delivered depends upon the mass of the
ram and its velocity at impact. The hammer energy is not a function of the
rate at which blows are delivered. Under field conditions, it is very difficult to
measure the terminal velocity of the ram, and in general, the energy is considered to be a function of ram weight and stroke. Hammer speed, or the rate at
which blows are delivered, can be affected by soil resistance, the elastic properties of the soil, pile stiffness, and pile length in addition to faulty hammer
performance. These causes should be considered before condemning a hammer for lack of normal operating speed.

The total energy delivered by a hammer is not the sole criterion for effective pile driving. The shape of the force-time curve should be considered. A
curve with a high peak force and a short time may show the same total energy
as a curve with a lower force over a longer time, but the prolonged force-time
curve is more effective. For this reason, hammers with heavy rams and short
strokes are generally more effective in driving piles than hammers with light
rams and long strokes.

4.8.2 Energy Losses. The delivered energy is generally less than the theoretical rated energy of the hammer, and the actual delivered energy determines
the hammer efficiency. Energy losses associated with air or steam hammers
include mechanical friction, valving timing, and actual stroke length. In addition, for double-acting and differential hammers, the actual air or steam
pressure delivered at the hammer as well as hammer temperature and air or
steam leakage at the hammer could affect the hammer energy. Mechanical-
friction losses also occur in diesel hammers but probably to a lesser degree
than for air or steam hammers. For diesel hammers, energy losses could also

be due to abnormal preignition, which could be caused by an overheated hammer or the use of the wrong type of fuel.

For all types of hammers, driving piles on a batter could influence the hammer energy not only because of a reduction in the gravity fall but also because of increased mechanical-friction losses. For double-acting and differential hammers, the energy reduction is less than that for single-acting hammers, because the energy resulting from the air or steam pressure is independent of the batter. Friction losses could also be aggravated by the use of improper or insufficient hammer lubricants or by the piston rod packing being too tight.

There should be a suitable lubricator mounted in the supply line for air or steam hammers to ensure proper hammer lubrication. When hammers are operated by air, it is necessary to saturate the air supply with oil, especially during hot weather. The cool compressed air cannot carry the oil as effectively as the hot steam, which tends to vaporize the lubricating oil and form a steam-oil mixture. When air is used, the oil tends to flow along the hose lining, and when cold weather is combined with the cold compressed air, the oil tends to drop out and fill fittings such as elbows and valves.

For well-maintained hammers, the efficiency can range from 70 to 80 percent for air or steam hammers and from 80 to 90 percent for diesel hammers depending on hammer design and driving conditions. For poorly maintained hammers, the efficiency can drop to below 50 percent depending on the condition of the hammer.

The energy delivered by the hammer is reduced to effective energy by losses within the balance of the drive system and within the pile and soil. The effective energy develops pile capacity or achieves permanent pile penetration. Losses within the balance of the drive system can be determined or accounted for by a wave equation analysis using known elastic properties of the various components. See Section 5.20 for details on monitoring the performance of the pile-driving system. Energy losses within the pile depend on the pile material, size, and length, and within the soil, on the elastic properties of the soil.

4.8.3 Drop Hammer.   The theoretical energy delivered by the drop hammer can be determined from the weight of the hammer and its fall. However, friction losses will occur between the hammer and its guide rails or leaders. Other energy reductions could result from such things as the force necessary to overhaul the hammer line or the snubbing of the hammer line just prior to impact.

Unless the tripping device is lowered as the pile penetrates, the stroke and thus the delivered energy will vary. Although the variation in stroke may not be significant during the measurement of final penetration if the set is small, the length of the stroke at the final penetration should be known.

When base-driven piles, such as pressure injected footings as described in

Chapter 2, are installed, the drop hammer operates freely inside the pipe or drive tube. The stroke and thus the energy can be monitored by observing a mark on the hammer line as the mark appears above the top of the pipe or drive tube when the hammer is raised.

The inspector should record the weight of the drop hammer and the stroke when logging the pile or measuring final penetration resistance.

4.8.4 Single-Acting Hammer. A single-acting hammer develops its energy from the gravitational free-fall of the hammer ram. The rated energy can be checked by determining the weight of the ram from its material and volume and measuring its stroke. In addition to normal energy reduction due to mechanical losses in the hammer, the delivered energy could be affected by improper positioning of the valve-trip wedges on the slide bar and, within limits, by a change in the operating pressure. If the lower wedge is mounted too high, it will trip the exhaust too soon and short-stroke the hammer. Sufficient steam or air pressure must be furnished to accelerate the ram to the full height of its stroke, but the opening of the inlet valve on the downstroke must be timed so as to avoid letting the full air or steam pressure build up too soon (back pressure) and cushion the blow. A slight rising of the hammer base at the end of the upstroke indicates that the hammer is getting the proper air or steam supply and pressure for a full stroke.

Theoretically, the length of the stroke and therefore the delivered energy will change if the point of impact for the ram is higher or lower than the "design" point of impact. This could occur if the cap block is too high, resulting in a shorter stroke, or if the cap block is highly compressed, resulting in a longer stroke. The added energy due to the longer stroke may be offset by the additional cushioning effect of the steam or air pressure. Energy losses or gains associated with variations in the height of the impact point are not critical.

The cap-block height can be controlled and should be consistent with the hammer design and manufacturing process. For many years wood cap blocks have been used successfully with height changes as much as 4 in (100 m) as the cap blocks became compressed during driving. With modern cap blocks, as discussed in Section 4.9, relatively constant heights are maintained during driving.

The energy of the single-acting hammer can be varied by changing the ram weight or by modifying the stroke. The ram weight can be changed by replacing the ram or by adding or removing pieces. The stroke can be modified by relocating the wedges on the slide bar, by changing slide bars, or by using a movable trip combined with a multiple-wedge slide bar. Movable trip devices can be remotely controlled by the operator. When the stroke is shortened by raising the bottom wedge, a higher operating pressure will be required. It is better to change the slide bar to short-stroke the hammer so that the hammer can be operated without having to increase the air or steam pressure and a higher operating speed will be maintained.

Using available information from the hammer manufacturer, the inspector should check to see that the hammer is equipped and adjusted for the specified rated energy. See Table B-1 for hammers for which the energy can be adjusted. Single-acting hammers are open-type hammers. Thus the stroke can be readily measured and monitored.

4.8.5 Double-Acting Hammer.   For double-acting hammers, the delivered energy depends upon the ram weight and stroke plus the force developed by the operating pressure acting on the piston. The correct pressure must be at the hammer. Ideally, because of pressure losses in the supply lines, valves, and fittings, such pressure should be measured directly at the hammer, but this is impractical. However, pressure measurements should be taken as close to the hammer as practical and certainly somewhere between the control valve and the hammer. Frequently, a pressure gauge is mounted at the compressor or boiler, in which case sufficient excess pressure to compensate for line losses should be observed on the gauge, and the control valve should not be adjusted during the measurement of final pile penetration resistance.

The maximum kinetic energy developed by any double-acting hammer cannot exceed the total weight of the hammer multiplied by the length of the ram stroke. However, double-acting hammers are usually closed-type hammers, and thus the stroke cannot be measured or observed during operation.

4.8.6 Differential Hammer.   Like the delivered energy of the double-acting hammer, the delivered energy of the differential hammer results from the ram weight and stroke plus the force from the operating pressure of the air, steam, or hydraulic fluid. It is important that the proper operating pressure be maintained, especially during measurements of final pile penetration resistance. The statements on the measurement of operating pressure in the preceding section on double-acting hammers apply equally to differential hammers. However, the similarity ends there, and double-acting hammers should not be considered in the same class as and equal to differential hammers.

The hammer energy could be affected by improper positioning of the valve-trip wedges on the slide bar. If the lower wedge is too high, it will close the exhaust too soon and admit fluid pressure above the piston, causing the hammer to short-stroke. If the upper wedge is too low, it will prematurely open the exhaust and close the upper portion of the cylinder to the fluid pressure before the ram can make a full stroke, and it is possible that the blow will be cushioned.

As with single-acting hammers, the energy delivered by differential hammers can also be varied by changing rams, by relocating wedges, by changing slide bars, or, for some hammers, by remotely adjusting the position of the valve trips. Differential hammers are generally open-type hammers, and the ram stroke can be observed. The inspector should check on the ram weight, the slide bar used, the positioning of the wedges, and any stroke adjustments made during driving. See Table B-1 for hammers for which the energy can be adjusted.

For differential hammers, a slight rising of the hammer base at the start of the downstroke indicates that the hammer is delivering full energy. The maximum energy that this type of hammer can deliver is equal to the total weight of the hammer times the ram stroke.

4.8.7 Diesel Hammer. As with steam or air hammers, the actual delivered energy depends on the mass of the ram or piston and its terminal velocity at impact. The actual kinetic energy is somewhat less than the potential energy because of friction losses and the slowing down of the ram during compression of the air at the bottom of the cylinder. The methods used to determine the rated energy of diesel hammers vary within the industry. Many rated energies for single-acting diesel hammers are based on the weight of the ram or piston and its stroke, but there is no uniformity on the lengths of strokes used in rating these hammers. Some manufacturers use the maximum stroke attainable. Others use a more conservative and realistic normal stroke or a "standard" stroke. The actual stroke depends upon the quantity and type of fuel burned, the type of pile being driven, and the driving resistance (the harder the driving, the longer the stroke).

The rated energy for a double-acting (closed top) diesel hammer is based on an equivalent stroke which includes a factor for the downward accelerating force resulting from the expansion of the air compressed in the bounce chamber (top of the cylinder) during the piston upstroke. The equivalent stroke is related to the pressure built up in the bounce chamber as indicated in the manufacturer's data. It should be noted that some diesel hammers can be converted from the single-acting to the double-acting mode of operation or vice versa (see Table B-2).

Some manufacturers may include in the total rated energy a combustion force. However, only the impact energy should be considered effective in driving the pile. The explosive force is primarily for raising the ram for its next stroke, and its influence on the pile penetration is negligible at final resistance.

Some diesel hammers are equipped with interchangeable pistons or rams of different weights (see Table B-2). The ram that is used will determine the impact energy. The impact energy is also affected by the timing of fuel ignition. Abnormal preignition (ignition prior to impact) could decrease impact velocity or, in extreme cases, prevent impact. Abnormal preignition could be caused by improper fuel (highly volatile fuel with a low flash point), by overheating of the hammer, or by improper timing of the spray atomization of the fuel. Some hammers may be designed to preignite; the manufacturer's specifications should be checked.

The energy resulting from the explosion of the diesel fuel influences the stroke and depends upon the type and amount of fuel injected and the efficiency of combustion. Evidence of poor combustion is a black exhaust, whereas a light blue exhaust indicates good combustion. The type and quantity of fuel used should be in accordance with the manufacturer's data. Some models have a constant-volume metering fuel pump for providing a constant volume of fuel per ram stroke. Other models have a variable-volume metering device with an adjustable fuel setting that is accessible to the operator, thus permitting fuel adjustments while the hammer is operating. For constant-volume metering, the fuel pump can be checked to see if it is delivering the correct amount of fuel. This is done by disconnecting the pump and activating it for several strokes while measuring the quantity of fuel dispensed.

The explosive energy available to raise the ram to the top of its full stroke depends on the driving resistance. If the driving resistance is low, much of the explosive energy is absorbed by the pile-soil system, and little may be left to raise the ram. Under such conditions, the ram stroke will be shortened, and in extreme cases, the hammer may stop.

The inspector should check the piston weight being used, the mode of hammer operation (single- or double-acting), and the fuel setting. See Table B-2 for hammers that can be modified. All single-acting diesel hammers should be equipped with a stroke indicator, and all double-acting hammers should have a bounce-chamber pressure gauge so that the hammer energy can be monitored.

It is important that the stroke or equivalent stroke be determined and recorded during the measurement of final pile penetration resistance. Unlike the stroke of a steam or air hammer, the stroke of a diesel hammer varies with pile penetration resistance and must be monitored.

Pile capacity curves could be developed through the use of a reliable diesel wave-equation program which correctly models the total hammer operation, including the thermodynamics, and reflects the internal energy losses.[108,109] Such capacity curves could be made available for the specific project in the form of either pile capacity versus blows per inch for a range of strokes or blows per inch versus stroke for a given pile capacity.

4.8.8 Vibratory Driver. Vibratory drivers can be rated according to the eccentric moment developed or the amount of dynamic force delivered at a specified steady-state frequency. The eccentric moment depends on the mass of the rotating weights (or rollers) and their eccentricity. Some vibratory drivers have adjustable or interchangeable weights, as indicated in Table B-3, which lists basic specification data for different vibratory drivers.

The available dynamic force varies with the square of the frequency and is also a function of the eccentric moment. The frequency at which the driver operates depends on the type of pile and its weight, the type of soil into which the pile is being driven, and the available horsepower. A limiting factor may be the design of the oscillator. For some vibratory drivers (see Table B-3), the operating frequency can be varied by changing the sprocket ratios of the drive. For the resonant driver, the available dynamic force depends on the type of rollers (eccentric weights) being used and their size.

Some vibratory drivers can be operated in tandem or twin-tandem modes, in which case the dynamic force is either doubled or quadrupled. The inspector should check on such things as the adjustment of eccentric weights, the type of rollers being used and their size, the sprocket ratio used, and the mode of operation (tandem or twin-tandem).

The force acting on the pile consists of the dynamic force and the weight of the driver plus any bias weight or downcrowd applied. The dynamic (oscillatory) force acts in both compression and tension to break down the pile-soil friction, allowing the total weight on the pile to push it into the ground. With time, the dynamic force averages zero, and the net effective force producing pile penetration is the total applied weight. However, to achieve pile penetration, the soil resistance must be overcome. This requires continuous vibration of the pile. The energy demands may increase with pile penetration, and continued vibration of the pile may be limited by the available horsepower.

For vibratory driving, the inspector should observe and record the horsepower being applied, the operating frequency, and the rate of pile penetration.

4.9 HAMMER CUSHION, OR CAP BLOCK

The hammer cushion, or cap block, is inserted between the striking part of the hammer (ram) and the pile or drive cap to condition the blow by reducing peak forces. Thus both the pile and the hammer are protected from damage. However, the cap block must effectively transmit the hammer energy to the pile, and the ability to transmit such energy depends upon the elastic properties of the cap-block material. In the past, most cap blocks consisted of a hardwood block (see Figure 4-10). This type of cap block becomes crushed and burned during pile driving, and the result is variations in elastic properties and the need for frequent changing. Now most cap blocks are of laminated construction, with alternating layers of aluminum and Micarta disks or similar material as illustrated in Figure 4-11. Others are made of material such as asbestos or woven steel wire. These cap blocks are generally stiffer than the wood cap blocks and more efficiently transmit hammer energy to the pile. Also, some of these hammer cushions retain constant elastic properties and have a relatively long life. The elastic properties and energy-transmitting characteristic of these cap blocks can be determined quite accurately. Not all permanent-type cap blocks are equally effective.

Mechanical cap blocks have been developed. They consist of a cylinder, a

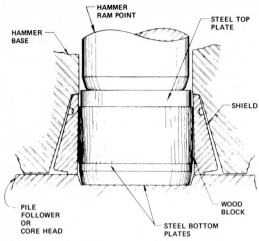

Figure 4-10 Wood cap block. (*Courtesy of Raymond International Builders, Inc.*)

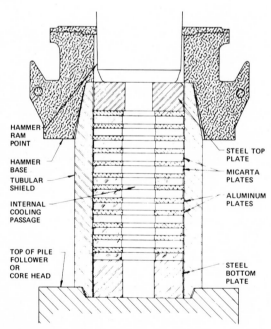

Figure 4-11 Aluminum-Micarta cap block. (*Courtesy of Raymond International Builders, Inc.*)

piston, and disk springs or other types of springs. The hammer ram strikes the piston and compresses the springs. This reduces peak forces and prolongs the duration of the hammer blow. Cap blocks having consistent elastic properties must be used if piles are being driven to a penetration resistance determined by a wave equation analysis using those elastic properties (see Section 5.19).

The minimum type of cap block should be as specified. The contractor may be required to submit details on the type of cap block he intends to use. The inspector should be furnished with copies of such submittals. The indiscriminate or unauthorized use of highly compressible cap blocks such as wood chips, pieces of wire rope, etc., should be prohibited. The replacement of a wood cap block just prior to final driving should not be permitted especially if piles are being driven to a specified penetration resistance (see Sections 5.17.2, 5.18, and 5.19). The inspector should record the type of hammer cushion used and a description, including height, diameter, and thickness of disks, and he should note on the driving record (see Section 5.32) when the hammer cushion is changed.

4.10 DRIVE CAP, DRIVE HEAD, OR BONNET

Generally, some type of cast- or forged-steel drive cap or head is used to fit the hammer base to the top of the pile and to uniformly distribute the hammer blows to the pile top. The hammer energy must be transmitted through the drive cap, and energy losses within the drive cap are usually quite small.

Drive caps should be of the correct size and provide full bearing over the entire cross section of the pile. Drive caps for precast concrete piles should be sufficiently loose so as not to restrain the piles from their tendency to rotate during driving. When sectional precast concrete piles are driven, a special drive cap may be required to accommodate any protrusions above the surface of the joint fitting, such as rods, bolts, pins, or raised portions. The joint manufacturer should be consulted for any special equipment or procedures necessary.

Drive caps for H piles are often of the H shape to fit the size and configuration of the piles. Pipe-pile drive caps can be of the inside or outside type and constructed to accommodate a variety of pile sizes as illustrated in Figure 4-12. The pipe-pile drive cap must fit the pile diameter accurately and have a machined surface to fully engage the end of the pipe. Similar requirements are necessary for caps to drive Monotubes.

The inspector should check that a drive cap of the proper size and shape is being used and that there is a proper fit between the drive cap and the pile. An improper or poorly fitted drive cap will cause damage to the top of the pile, which will invalidate the measurement of pile penetration resistance, or it will cause structural damage to the pile.

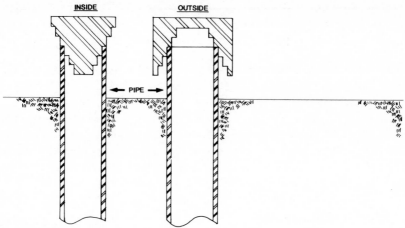

Figure 4-12 Types of drive caps for pipe piles. Drive caps are made to fit pipes of various sizes.

4.11 PILE CUSHION

A pile cushion is necessary between the drive head (or follower) and the top of a precast concrete pile. The primary purpose of the pile cushion is to protect the pile from damaging compression and tension stresses. The cushion also serves to distribute the hammer blows uniformly over the pile head and to compensate for any irregularities on the top surface of the pile.

The pile cushion generally consists of layers of hardwood or softwood boards or plywood. Other suitable materials can be used. The pile cushion must protect the pile while at the same time transmitting sufficient hammer energy to the top of the pile. The required height or thickness of the pile cushion varies with job conditions and affects the energy losses within the cushion. If pile cushions are made of wood or some other material that disintegrates during driving, a new cushion should be used to drive each pile.

The type of wood or other material and the thickness of the cushion should be as specified, or the properties should be like those used in a wave equation analysis or in the establishment of the driving criteria. The inspector should record the type of pile cushion used, the thickness, and a description.

4.12 FOLLOWER

The follower is a structural member used as an extension of the pile in order to drive the head of the pile below the ground or water surface or below the level which the hammer can reach while still engaged in the leaders. In that case, the use of suitable hammer extensions in the leaders may eliminate the need for a follower. The follower may also be required to accommodate reinforcing steel or prestressing strand which may project beyond the head of a precast concrete pile for the pile-to-cap connection (see Section 5.50). A special follower may be required for driving sectional precast concrete piles (see Section 4.10).

Followers should be of steel and sufficiently rigid or stiff to assure adequate transmission of hammer energy. The bottom of the follower should be formed like or fitted with a drive cap suitable for the type of pile being driven. For precast concrete piles, a pile cushion will be required between the pile head and the bottom end of the follower.

The use of a follower may be subject to the approval of the engineer, and the contractor may be required to submit details on the follower to be used. In this case the inspector should be furnished with copies of such submittals. If a follower is used, the inspector should record on the driving log the type (material) of follower and its size, length, and weight.

Chapter 5

Pile Installation

Piles are installed by dynamic, drilling, or vibratory methods or by a combination of such methods. The use of proper equipment, methods, and techniques is critical to achieving a pile foundation that will perform as designed for the expected life of the structure. The primary responsibility of the inspector is to see that the piles are installed according to the plans and specifications, and with due concern for unforeseen conditions. This includes the application of equipment, methods, and techniques that will assure a satisfactory foundation for the owner. This chapter will cover the general details involved in pile installation.

5.1 SUBSOIL INFORMATION

Pile foundations should not be designed or installed without adequate subsoil information.[13,88] This is obtained by means of conventional test borings to recover soil and rock samples for analyses and tests. If the analyses and tests are to be meaningful, the depth to which test borings are taken must be below the depth to which piles may be installed. Various types of in situ soil tests can also be made in the bore hole to determine soil properties. The inspector should have access to the subsoil information and should be familiar with the existing subsurface conditions which may affect pile installation. It should be noted that test-boring data only show conditions existing at the location of the boring and that conditions could vary widely between bore holes. A general knowledge of the geologic history of the area is helpful for anticipating possible variations in subsoil conditions.

5.2 UNDERGROUND STRUCTURES

It is not the responsibility of the inspector to determine the existence, location, and condition of underground structures, including pipelines. However, the inspector should be advised of such structures and should be alert to potential damage during pile installation.

5.3 PILE INSTALLATION SEQUENCE

The installation of piles generally proceeds according to a planned sequence established at the start of the job. This sequence may be dictated by the owner's requirements but is usually prepared by the contractor with the aim of accomplishing the work in a logical and expeditious manner. The installation sequence is important for proper planning by other contractors responsible for such operations as site preparation, dewatering, the construction of access roads and ramps, and pile layout. The inspector should be furnished with a copy of the proposed construction schedule and sequence.

5.4 SITE PREPARATION

The specifications will usually require that excavation be carried out to at least the pile cutoff grade before piles are driven. However, there may be conditions such as extreme variations in pile cutoff grades or unusual subsoil conditions or closely spaced pile groups or a very high water table which would make excavation to below pile cutoff impractical before piles are driven. In such cases, piles may be driven through overburden (soils which will subsequently be removed). An alternative would be to cut the site down to a uniform grade equal to the lowest or average pile cutoff elevation and backfill as necessary after the piles have been driven.

If possible, pile contractors should be provided with a dry, clear, level working site, one that is unencumbered with pile cap excavations, braces, shores, or overhead structures such as piping or wires. This will expedite their work. They also require access to pile locations for equipment and material and adequate storage space for pile material. The responsibilities for all or some of these requirements may be covered in the contract documents.

Except for shallow pile cap excavations, excavation banks should be properly sloped or adequately sheeted and braced or tied back to take all possible surcharge loads during and after pile installation and to protect the piles from detrimental ground movements. Groundwater and surface water should be controlled to provide reasonably dry work areas. How site preparation is handled can affect pile installation. The site preparation or lack thereof should be noted in the inspector's diary.

5.5 IDENTIFICATION OF PILES

Each pile in the project should have a unique designation (pile number), and this should be noted on the pile plans and used on all pile-driving logs, pile reports, and other job records. Piles may be numbered consecutively or within each group, with the group being given a unique designation. This could be by coordinates tied into the grid system established for the job or according to intersecting numbered or lettered column lines or simply by a letter.

5.6 STAKING OUT PILE LOCATIONS

The contract documents will indicate who is responsible for staking out the pile locations. It may be the pile contractor, but for practical reasons, it is usually the general contractor who has basic survey and layout responsibilities.

The inspector should be familiar with the pile layout, including the positions and sizes of pile groups, the number and arrangement of piles within each group, and the locations of isolated piles. In general, piles will have a uniform spacing or a standard group arrangement. The positions of pile location stakes should be checked. This can generally be done visually by comparing the group layout with the pile location plans, by counting the number of stakes, and by checking on any nonuniform spacing in the field stakeout. Frequently pile groups are also in line and have some uniform spacing. The inspector should request that obvious discrepancies in the alignment or spacing of pile location stakes be checked. Distances between pile groups can be checked to detect any major survey errors.

The inspector should also check on the layout of pile groups containing both vertical and batter piles. Depending on the direction and degree of batter and on the estimated or actual pile lengths, it may be necessary to relocate piles to avoid pile interference.

The inspector should be aware of possible construction activities which may dislodge or move pile location stakes before piles are installed, including the movement of personnel around the site. It is advisable to check the locations and number of pile stakes within each group immediately before piles are driven.

5.7 PILE SPACING

Although pile spacing will be indicated on the plans, the inspector should be familiar with circumstances that may dictate an increase in pile spacing or a change in the pile installation sequence. Normal center-to-center pile spacing is about twice the average diameter or diagonal dimension of the pile, but not less than 24 in (0.6 m) for point-bearing piles or 30 in (0.8 m) for friction piles. The required spacing for friction piles is generally greater than that for point-bearing piles. Special types of piles may require increased spacing as indicated in Chapter 6. If there is any evidence of pile interference during driving, such as driving a pile into a pile already driven, it may be necessary to increase the pile spacing or relocate batter piles or change the degree of batter. The possibility of pile interference increases with increasing pile length and flexibility. Using a stiffer pile or increasing the pile spacing beforehand is recommended for very long, flexible piles.

5.8 MARKING OFF PILES

When the specifications require that complete driving logs be recorded, it will be necessary to have the piles marked off, usually in 1-ft (or 0.25-m) intervals over their entire length or over a portion of their length. If piles are marked off, the length from the pile tip should be indicated on the pile at 5-ft (or 1-m) intervals.

Even when piles are not marked off for logging, the total furnished length as ready for driving should be measured and marked at the pile butt. This is to facilitate the determination of pile pay lengths after driving. Such marks should not rub off and should withstand the weather long enough so that final pile measurements can be obtained. It is not necessary to mark Step-Taper shells for length only. The top shell diameter, with a known tip diameter and

The upper portion of the pile is marked off for determining the driving record. (*Courtesy of Raymond International Builders, Inc.*)

known shell section lengths, indicates the total length of the pile before cutoff. The lengths of pipe used in composite-type piles should be marked.

Pile marking, including the measurement of lengths, should be done with a steel measuring tape. Cloth tapes can stretch. It is generally the pile contractor's responsibility to mark off piles.

5.9 INDICATOR PILES

The specifications may require that indicator piles be installed at designated locations to determine the pile lengths to be ordered or to help establish the installation criteria. Pile load tests may be conducted on selected indicator piles. Indicator piles should be installed with the same equipment, methods, and techniques that will be used to install the production piles. The inspector must keep a complete record of indicator pile installation, including full details on the equipment used and the piles installed. It is recommended that complete driving logs be recorded.

5.10 OVERBURDEN

Overburden is soil through which piles are installed but which will be removed after pile installation. The overburden extends from the ground surface at the time of pile installation to the pile cutoff elevation.

Sometimes it is necessary or advisable to install piles through overburden. Chapter 6 covers some special types of piles for which this procedure is recommended. Driving piles through overburden may be subject to the approval of the engineer. The inspector should be alert as to the possible effects of overburden on the driving criteria, the need for a follower, the pile butt location, the cutting off of piles to grade, and pile payment. Also, the subsequent excavation of the overburden could expose the piles to damage, and special precautions may be required. There should be an understanding and agreement between the owner, the engineer, and the contractor as to how these matters will be handled.

5.11 PILE PREPARATION

Pile preparation includes splicing to the required lengths; the attachment of special fittings such as closure plates, pile shoes, or bands; and the application of special coatings.

5.11.1 Timber Piles. The preparation of timber piles for driving may require the attachment of steel drive shoes at the pile tip or steel bands at the pile butt

A protective steel point is attached to the tip of a timber pile. (*Courtesy of Associated Pile & Fitting Corp.*)

or, in addition, steel bands at specified intervals along the pile. The pile tip may have to be shaped to fit the drive shoe, which should be fastened as specified. Sometimes the tips of timber piles are sharpened to a point even though drive shoes are not used. It is doubtful that this facilitates pile penetration. Since timber piles should not be used as point-bearing piles, the practice of pointing piles is not considered detrimental.

The top of the pile must be sawed square with the pile's axis and chamfered as necessary to fit the drive cap. Sometimes a steel ring is fitted to the top of the pile to prevent splitting. If treated piles are used, all cuts to fit the pile to the drive cap or to install the ring should be treated after driving in accordance with Section 5.41 unless the top portion of the pile is subsequently cut off.

5.11.2 Steel Piles and Shells

5.11.2.1 Splicing. Steel piles, including HP shapes, pipe piles, Monotubes, and constant-section shells, may require splicing by welding on the ground to make up the necessary pile lengths. Assembling Step-Taper shell sections into full pile lengths is not considered splicing. Joints between such shell sections are screw-connected. The welding rack must be constructed to hold the pile sections in accurate alignment and should provide for rotating the piles to ensure good welding throughout. All welding must be done by competent welders who are certified, if possible, in accordance with the AWS Structural Welding Code—Steel D 1.1.*

*American Welding Society, Inc., Miami, Fla., 1982.

Splicing may be subject to the approval of the engineer, or the splicing requirements, including the preparation of the ends to be spliced, may be shown on the plans or covered in the specifications. The specifications may indicate the required size and extent of welding, such as tack, continuous, or a minimum length. For H piles that are to be spliced by butt welding, the ends should be properly scarfed with a cutting torch and a suitable guide. Milled ends are not necessary. It is advisable that the splice develop the full strength of the section. Special splice fittings are available for HP shapes and pipe. Pipe piles are generally spliced by butt welding, and the specifications may require backup rings. When straight-sided Monotube sections are added to tapered sections, the straight-sided portion is telescoped into the end of the tapered portion, and a full fillet weld is made. The splicing of straight-sided Monotube sections will require a butt weld. The manufacturer's recommendations for splicing Monotubes should be followed. Constant-section pile shells will be spliced by butt welding.

Pile preparation may include attaching splice fittings or plates to the bottom ends of pile sections for later splicing in the leaders (see Section 5.34). The number of splices in a pile and the splice locations may be limited by the specifications. The inspector should determine that all splicing is done according to approved or specified procedures.

5.11.2.2 Pile Tips.   For the preparation of HP shapes for driving, the specifications may require the attachment of special drive shoes or some other type of tip reinforcement. Special drive shoes may also be required for pipe piles, or the tips may be closed with flat steel plates. All welding should conform to AWS specifications.

Tip closures for Monotubes and Step-Taper shells will be attached by the manufacturer. If constant-section shells are furnished without closures, the plates will have to be welded on in the field.

5.11.2.3 Special Attachments.   The specifications may call for special attachments such as cathodic protection cables for steel piles. Such installations must conform to the manufacturer's or owner's specifications.

5.11.3 Precast Concrete Piles.   Splice or joint fittings for sectional precast concrete piles will be attached to the piles during the casting process. If special drive shoes or points are required for precast concrete piles, they will be attached to the piles during manufacture.

5.11.4 Pile Coatings.   The specifications may require special coatings for pile material protection or to reduce negative friction loads. Various types of coating materials are available, but the type used should conform to the specifications. Such coatings may have to be applied at the jobsite, and the manufacturer's recommendations must be followed, especially for epoxy coatings.

Applying bitumen prime coating to precast concrete piles with a roller. (*Courtesy of Parsons, Brinckerhoff, Quade & Douglas, Inc.*)

Natural bitumen (asphaltic) coatings are commonly used to reduce negative friction loads and may be applied to steel H piles, pipe piles, or precast concrete piles.[65] The type of bitumen may be specified according to penetration, with reference to ASTM D 946.[40] The penetration designation, such as 85–100, indicates the minimum and maximum penetration in tenths of a millimeter when testing is done according to ASTM D 5.[38] A higher penetration number indicates a softer material. Pile coatings must be applied according to the manufacturer's recommendations for such things as temperature, surface preparation, and priming. The surface to be coated must be clean and dry. A primer must be used on concrete to make the surface impervious to the bitumen, and it must be allowed to dry thoroughly (6 to 24 h) before the bitumen is applied. Application of the hot [300 to 350°F (150 to 175°C)] bitumen can be by mopping, brushing, or spraying. When applied at a plant, the bitumen is often poured on the piles when they are in special forms. The thickness of the coating will be specified and may vary from 1 to 10 mm (0.04 to 0.4 in). The inspector should check the thickness.

The application of bitumen coatings in the field is a difficult and messy operation, especially in hot weather, when the bitumen tends to soften and run off. In such cases, a stiffer (lower-penetration) bitumen may be required, at least for an outer coat. Protection from direct sunlight and spraying with water may help.

The coated piles should be protected from possible damage to the coating and should not be handled for at least 4 h or until the coating is relatively dry.

The final bitumen coat for a precast concrete pile is poured on and troweled. (*Courtesy of Parsons, Brinckerhoff, Quade & Douglas, Inc.*)

Except when piles are lofted, coated piles should be handled in a horizontal position with a lifting beam to prevent the slings from slipping. Damaged areas such as those caused by lifting slings should be repaired.

For negative friction loads, the portion or length of the pile to be coated will be specified. It is important that the coating be limited to the specified portion of the pile, which will generally be the upper part of the pile.

5.12 PREEXCAVATION

The specifications may require or permit pile preexcavation, or its use may be subject to the approval of the engineer. The principal methods of preexcavation are prejetting and predrilling, which includes the wet-rotary process. Other methods, such as the dry-tube method, have been used. Piles may also be jetted during driving.

Predrilling can be done by either the dry process or the wet process. For the dry method, either a short-flight or continuous-flight auger can be used. For the wet method, a continuous-flight, hollow-stem auger or a hollow drill stem is used, and water or drilling mud is circulated through it. The type of bit required at the auger tip or the end of the drill stem depends on the soil (or rock) formation to be drilled. Either direct or reverse circulation can be used with the drill-stem method, depending on which is more effective. Figure 5-1 illustrates the wet-rotary process using direct circulation. For reverse circulation (see Figure 5-2), the hole is kept filled with water or drilling mud, and the

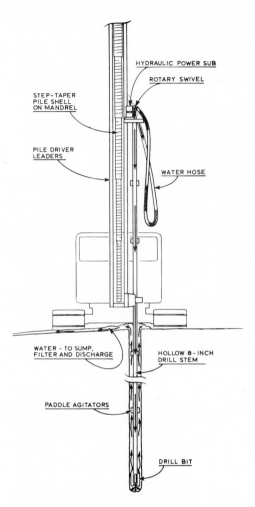

HYDRAULIC POWER SUB

ROTARY SWIVEL

STEP-TAPER
PILE SHELL
ON MANDREL

PILE DRIVER
LEADERS

WATER HOSE

WATER - TO SUMP,
FILTER AND DISCHARGE

HOLLOW 8-INCH
DRILL STEM

PADDLE AGITATORS

DRILL BIT

Figure 5-1 Arrangement for
wet-rotary preexcavation. (*Courtesy of Raymond International Builders, Inc.*)

soil or rock cuttings are removed through the drill stem, usually with the assistance of an air lift. For the wet-drill process, a hollow-stem auger would replace the drill stem.

The type of preexcavation to be used will depend on the soil conditions. Jetting is more effective in granular soils than in cohesive soils. Dry predrilling can be used in cohesive soils, and wet predrilling is effective in both types of soil. Predrilling is more controllable than jetting.

Preexcavation may be required to assist in pile penetration of dense or hard upper strata or to facilitate pile installation or to reduce or eliminate pile heave. If jetting during driving is permitted, there will generally be certain restrictions on the size of the jet, the volume and pressure of the water used, and the depth of jetting. Driving the pile below the jetted depth will also be required.

The dry process is used for predrilling out-batter piles with a continuous-flight auger. (*Courtesy of Raymond International Builders, Inc.*)

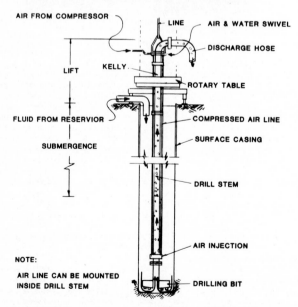

AIR FROM COMPRESSOR

LINE AIR & WATER SWIVEL

DISCHARGE HOSE

LIFT KELLY

ROTARY TABLE

FLUID FROM RESERVIOR

COMPRESSED AIR LINE

SUBMERGENCE

SURFACE CASING

DRILL STEM

AIR INJECTION

NOTE:

AIR LINE CAN BE MOUNTED
INSIDE DRILL STEM

DRILLING BIT

Figure 5-2 Setup for reverse-circulation drilling. (*Courtesy of Raymond International Builders, Inc.*)

100

Prolonged jetting or drilling without advancing the jet or drill should be prohibited. Jetting should not be permitted in soils containing large gravel or cobbles. These could collect at the bottom of the jetted hole, making subsequent pile driving impossible. If piles are jetted during driving, the proper procedures must be followed. At least two jets should be used, and they should be operated on opposite sides of the pile. The use of three or four jets provides more equal jetting around the pile. Each jet should have its own water supply and be operated at the same pressure and depth. Jets and drills must be stiff enough or be guided to ensure a straight hole.

5.13 PILE HANDLING AND LOFTING

Piles should be handled and lofted carefully so as to avoid damage that could hamper the proper installation of a pile or affect its structural capacity or long-term performance. Hollow piles such as pipe, Monotube, or shell piles should not be dragged along the ground open end first. This could result in picking up soil or other debris. Treated timber piles should not be handled with pointed tools that could puncture the treated portions.

Precast concrete piles must be handled and lofted at the designated pickup points. Sometimes holes are cut in the web or flange of H piles for attaching a lifting shackle. This is permissible if the portion of the pile with the holes will

A precast concrete pile being lofted with a two-point pickup. (*Courtesy of Parsons, Brinckerhoff, Quade & Douglas, Inc.*)

A Raymond Step-Taper shell is lofted with a one-point pickup. (*Courtesy of Raymond International Builders, Inc.*)

subsequently be cut off. An alternative would be to weld a lug on the pile to prevent the lifting sling or chain from sliding off as the pile is raised to a vertical position. The same could be done for pipe or Monotube piles.

When coated precast concrete piles are lofted with a multiple-point pickup, the top sling should be tied to the bottom sling to prevent the top sling from slipping. Usually, for negative friction loads, the bottom portion of the pile is not coated, and the bottom sling will hold. If piles are coated along their full length, or if a one-point pickup is used, provisions must be made to prevent the sling or pile chain from slipping. In addition to being unsafe, such slipping could seriously damage the coating. In some cases, lugs can be welded or attached to the pile.

5.14 PILE LENGTH IN THE LEADERS

If the total payment or part of the payment for piles is based on the length of pile raised in the leaders, the inspector should record such length for each pile. It should be noted that additional lengths of pile may have to be added during installation. If the added length of pile was included in the pay length of a prior pile (and subsequently cut off), the pay length of the pile being lengthened should be adjusted so that double payment for pile material is not made.

5.15 PILE SPOTTING

The tip of the pile (or auger or drill) should be accurately spotted over the pile location stake. To avoid errors due to parallax, the positioning of the pile can be checked by measuring to two reference stakes 90° apart. The use of fixed leaders attached to a live crane boom and an adjustable spotter facilitates the accurate positioning of the pile. Sometimes a template can be used to assure accurate positioning. H piles should have their flanges oriented as shown on the plans.

5.16 PILE ALIGNMENT

Piles are installed either vertically (plumb) or on a batter. The degree or rate of batter and the direction of batter will be indicated on the plans. Both the

The pile tip should be accurately spotted on the pile location stake. (*Courtesy of Raymond International Builders, Inc.*)

The alignment of the pile should be checked before driving. (*Courtesy of Raymond International Builders, Inc.*)

leaders and the pile should be positioned as accurately as possible to the alignment required by the plans. For drilled piles or when piles are preexcavated, the drill stem or jet pipe must also be properly aligned. If batter piles are installed, the piles or holes must be oriented in the direction shown on the plans.

Before driving starts and after the pile point has been properly spotted, the alignment of the pile and equipment should be checked with a carpenter's level. For batter piles, the level can be held on a simple wood template cut to the correct batter angle and held against the leaders, pile, or drill stem. The pile or drill rig should be on a stable and level hardstanding (preferably timber mats) to prevent the rig from tilting when there is ground subsidence. Pile hammers should be operated in leaders, and the use of fixed leaders is recommended to help maintain the required alignment. The alignment of piles should be checked periodically during driving, and such checks should be made on exposed lengths of not less than about 5 ft (2 m).

If piles are to be driven through overburden or water and the final cutoff grade is below the ground or water surface, the initial alignment of the pile is critical. Any misalignment could result in the pile butt being off design location at cutoff. The amount of mislocation would increase with increasing depths of overburden or water.

If pile alignment below the ground surface is considered critical enough to require an axial alignment tolerance for the full length of the pile, only those types of piles should be used for which the axial alignment after installation can be determined throughout the pile length. These include pipe, Monotube, and shell-type piles plus those precast concrete and steel H piles which are fitted with a full-length inspection duct in which an inclinometer can be lowered to measure the axial deviations.

Any type of pile could be deflected off the required axial alignment during driving. This could be caused by subsurface obstructions, sloping rock surfaces, densification of the soil during driving, and certain subsoil conditions such as fissured rock or cavernous limestone. Under soft-soil conditions, the forces of gravity could cause flexible piles driven on a batter to be deflected downward as they are driven. Also, flexible drill stems or jet pipes used for preexcavation could be deflected off line by gravity forces. The chances of such bending increase with increasing pile (or drill or jet) lengths or flexibility.

Excessive deviations from the specified axial alignment can sometimes be controlled by using a stiffer pile (or drill or jet), by predrilling, or by removing obstructions. Under some conditions, such as driving piles in fissured or cavernous rock, there is no practical method for eliminating pile bending.

5.17 INSTALLATION CRITERIA

Piles can be installed by a deadweight method, by dynamic impact, by drilling, by jacking, by vibratory driving, or by a combination of these methods. The specifications may require that each pile be installed without interruption. The specifications may also establish the installation criteria or state the method for establishing the criteria. Piles may be installed to a predetermined length, to a specified tip elevation, to a specified minimum penetration resistance (usually stated in hammer blows per inch), or according to a combination of these criteria. The installation criteria may also be stated in terms of a required pile bearing capacity based upon a specified driving formula, a dynamic analysis, or the results of a load test. The required bearing capacity may be stated in terms of the ultimate load or design load with a specified factor of safety.

Installation criteria involving predetermined pile lengths are usually determined by the application of an established static analysis considering the size and shape of the pile and based upon known soil properties. Installation criteria involving predetermined tip elevations may be based upon a similar static analysis combined with a knowledge of the profile of the bearing strata. Installation criteria based upon a specified penetration resistance can be determined by either a conventional dynamic driving formula or a wave equation analysis (see Section 5.19). A minimum-size hammer will be specified as part of the penetration resistance criteria.

If the required hammer size is not determined by a wave equation analysis, it may be selected through the use of an arbitrary rule of thumb. Some of the general rules are reasonable and are based upon empirical data and experience. However, requirements such as the hammer energy in foot-pounds being numerically at least 3 times the pile weight in pounds are totally unreasonable and unnecessary. A more realistic ratio would be 1:1 or, at the most, 2:1. Such rules governing the required ram weight range from 25 to 200 percent of the pile weight, which indicates their arbitrary bases.

5.17.1 Deadweight.
For the deadweight method, the ultimate capacity of the pile as installed is generally limited to the amount of weight applied. This is not a practical method for installing piles. If it is used, the amount of weight applied should be recorded. Jetting during installation can assist in pile penetration.

5.17.2 Dynamic Impact.
For piles to be installed by dynamic impact, the required pile length and/or penetration resistance may be established by load-test results. The use of load tests is recommended. The final driving resistance may also be established from indicator piles installed immediately adjacent to

Step-Taper piles are driven with a heavy, rigid mandrel. (*Courtesy of Raymond International Builders, Inc.*)

test-boring locations. As stated, the required penetration resistance may be specified on the basis of a wave equation analysis, or it may be determined by a conventional driving formula. The applicability of a specified penetration resistance or the use of a dynamic formula will depend upon the drivability or stiffness of the pile. The stiffer the pile, the more effective the hammer blows in obtaining pile penetration and overcoming soil resistance. Therefore, light-weight, springy piles may appear to have a high capacity by a dynamic for-mula, whereas in reality much of the hammer energy is being absorbed elas-tically. On the other hand, a heavy, stiff pile may appear to have a low capacity by a dynamic formula, whereas in reality the hammer blows are fully effective in achieving pile penetration and mobilizing capacity. A wave equation analy-sis reflects pile stiffness or drivability. If a required penetration resistance under a given hammer is specified, consideration should be given to the effects of pile stiffness. A heavy, stiff pile will generally penetrate deeper than a lightweight, springy pile for the same penetration resistance. Also, the light-weight, springy pile may not be achieving the required capacity at the specified driving resistance.

For piles that are installed dynamically, the source of energy necessary to achieve the required pile penetration is the pile-driving hammer. For piles that are installed to a predetermined length or a predetermined tip elevation (or driven to sound bedrock), the actual energy used to dynamically install the piles is not critical to the pile bearing capacity. The energy, of course, must be sufficient to achieve the necessary pile penetration, and the amount of energy applied may be an important consideration from the contractor's viewpoint in achieving a reasonable pile production rate.

For piles that are driven to a specified minimum penetration resistance, determined by a conventional dynamic pile-driving formula or by a wave equation analysis or by the results of pile load tests, the actual energy deliv-ered by the hammer to the top of the pile is critical at the time the resistance to penetration is measured. The energy delivered to the pile during the entire driving of the pile is not so critical except as it may affect the ability to achieve pile penetration and a good production rate.

The energy delivered to the pile depends on the hammer energy lost in the drive system; therefore, the introduction of fresh cap-block material just prior to the measurement of final penetration resistance should not be allowed. If a follower is to be used, the required driving resistance may have to be adjusted to compensate for energy losses within the follower. The use of a follower should be subject to the engineer's approval. The use of hammer extensions may eliminate the need for a follower. The required penetration resistance may also have to be adjusted when batter piles are driven, especially when piles on steep batters are driven with a single-acting hammer.

The adherence to an established driving resistance permits each pile to seek its own required capacity regardless of normal variations in the depth, density, and quality of the bearing strata or variations in pile length. This characteristic is not found in several of the special types of piles described in Chapter 6.

5.17.3 Drilling. Drilled piles will generally be installed to a required depth. The drilling operation and soil cuttings should be observed, as this will be helpful in evaluating the subsoil conditions at each pile location and correlating them with the conditions at test-pile locations. Under the right conditions, such as an adequate-size hole, the absence of groundwater, and the insertion of a temporary steel liner, the hole may be entered and the bottom inspected or tested to ensure that an adequate bearing stratum has been reached. Chapter 6 covers drilled piles in greater detail.

5.17.4 Jacking. For piles installed by jacking, the ultimate capacity is generally limited by the reaction available to resist the jacking force. The jacking force may be resisted by an existing structure such as for underpinning, by a superimposed deadweight, or by soil anchors. If this method is used, the jacking force should be recorded.

5.17.5 Vibratory Driving. If piles are to be installed with a vibratory driver, the specifications may require that the piles be driven to a required length or tip elevation. Additional subsoil information based upon closely spaced borings may be necessary to establish required pile lengths. The driving criteria may involve a minimum rate of penetration for a specified dynamic force and operating frequency or the power to be applied. The specifications may require that the installation criteria be verified by means of a conventional impact hammer and/or load test. The specifications may also require that the final penetration resistance of all piles be checked with an impact hammer, in which case the minimum acceptable penetration resistance and the hammer size will be specified. Vibratory driving is more effective for installing friction piles. It is not recommended for point-bearing piles unless the final seating is done with an impact hammer.

5.18 DRIVING FORMULAS

Since the middle 1800s, dynamic pile-driving formulas have been used to determine the static bearing capacity of the pile as a function of the resistance of the pile to penetration. More than 400 such pile-driving formulas have been suggested, and for the most part, they tend to equate the energy delivered to a pile (the weight of the pile hammer times its fall, WH) to the distance the pile moves (S) against a soil resistance (R): $WH = RS$. Some of these formulas are used to solve for the ultimate bearing capacity of the pile, and others include a factor of safety resulting in a safe, allowable bearing capacity. Many of these formulas contain various factors to account for the different energy losses in the drive system and in the pile-soil system. Some formulas use the rated energy of the pile-driving hammer, whereas others contain an efficiency factor because it is recognized that hammers are not 100 percent efficient. When the results of such conventional dynamic driving formulas are compared with the results of actual pile load tests, a relatively wide scatter is noted (see References 73, 82, 99, 103, 114 to 116, and 123). However, such formulas have been successfully used for many years when combined with experience and sound judgment. Driving formulas range from the relatively simple Engineering News formula:

$$R = \frac{2WH}{S + 0.1}$$

to the rather complicated types such as the Hiley formula:

$$R_u = \left(\frac{e_f W_r h}{S + \frac{1}{2}(C_1 + C_2 + C_3)}\right)\left(\frac{W_r + e^2 W_p}{W_r + W_p}\right)$$

There is no indication that the more complicated of these empirical formulas are any more accurate than the simple ones. All can show a wide scatter when compared with load-test results. These formulas can be used for relatively light loads and where they have been calibrated for the pile and soil conditions. Pile-driving formulas are discussed in detail in various publications.[62,67,97]

5.19 WAVE EQUATION ANALYSIS

A more accurate and rational dynamic analysis requiring the use of a computer is the one-dimensional wave equation analysis (see References 80, 84, 85, 96, 102, and 111). The wave equation analysis can take into accurate account the various factors which could affect the pile's static capacity as determined by dynamic methods. In the absence of soil freeze or relaxation, it could give an accurate measure of the static capacity of the pile based on dynamic measurements. The accuracy and reliability of a wave equation analysis depends on how the hammer-cushion-pile-soil system is modeled (especially for diesel hammers and mandrel-driven piles), how the computer program was written, and the accuracy of the input data. Not all wave equation computer programs are equally valid, and the proper selection of input data is often a matter of sound engineering judgment based upon experience.

It should be noted that the wave equation analysis also indicates the maximum compression and tension stresses in the pile material during driving. This information is useful in selecting a pile with a cross-sectional area that is adequate for withstanding driving stresses or in limiting the hammer energy that can safely be delivered to the pile. The wave equation analysis is also an excellent method for selecting the optimum hammer and drive system for the pile-soil system involved and the desired pile capacity. In the absence of soil freeze (see Section 5.28), it also shows any limitations in developing pile capacity for any pile-hammer combination.

5.20 MONITORING THE PERFORMANCE OF A PILE-DRIVING SYSTEM

When the pile-soil capacity is mobilized dynamically and the way to satisfy a required bearing capacity is determined by measuring the resistance to pile penetration, it is essential that the driving energy delivered to the pile be known. The energy developed by the pile-driving hammer is transmitted through various components of the pile-driving system and is subject to certain losses in each of these components. If the hammer efficiency is known, the energy transmitted to the top of the pile can be readily determined by a wave equation analysis inasmuch as the elastic properties and energy-transmitting characteristics of the components can be determined by routine tests or are known for the materials involved.

The actual energy delivered by the hammer depends on the ram mass and the terminal velocity of the ram at impact. If the terminal velocity can be measured, and assuming that the ram mass is known, the true hammer efficiency can be determined. Methods and devices have been proposed and used to measure the terminal velocity, including high-speed photography, radar, and instrumentation mounted on the ram, such as a velocity transducer or an accelerometer. None of these have been developed into a practical field tool or method.

A special piece of equipment known as a "pile-driving analyzer" has been used to monitor hammer performance.[63,78,105] Accelerometers and force or strain transducers are attached to the pile near its top or to a "follower" inserted between the pile and the drive system. A properly designed and calibrated load cell can be used as the force-measuring device. From the data obtained, the force or energy delivered to the top of the pile can be computed.

The inspector can monitor hammer performance by observation. In Chapter 4, the various factors affecting hammer energy and performance are discussed. The inspector should check the makeup of the hammer, including the ram weight and slide bar used and the positions of the trip wedges. During driving, the inspector can check the operating pressures and operating speed and look for evidence of poor hammer maintenance such as excessive air or steam leaks. When hammers are operated by air, the detection of leaks is much more difficult than when steam is used. The inspector should also check the various drive-system components for conformance with the specifications or approved contractor's submittals.

The hammer speed will vary with the type of pile and driving resistance,

Pile-driving analyzer used to monitor hammer performance on a test stand. (*Courtesy of Pile Dynamics, Inc.*)

and although speed is not critical to delivered energy, the hammer should run at approximately the rated speed during final driving. If the hammer runs too slowly, this may be a symptom of faulty performance. Slow speeds could be caused by the condition of the hammer being poor, by insufficient lubrication (see Section 4.8.2), by piston rod packing that is too tight, or by inadequate operating pressure, which in turn could be due to an undersize boiler or compressor or to undersize supply lines or to obstructions in the supply lines such as partially closed valves or a deteriorated hose lining.

5.21 BATTER PILES

If piles are to be installed on a batter, the possible interference with adjacent vertical piles or between piles battered toward each other should be investigated. The possibility of pile interference increases with pile length and flexibility and the degree of batter. It may be necessary to relocate the piles or change the degree or direction of batter. The specified penetration resistance to which piles are to be driven may require modification because of reductions in hammer efficiency, especially when single-acting hammers are used to drive piles on steep batters.

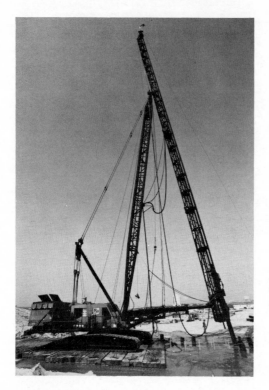

Driving out-batter piles. (*Courtesy of Raymond International Builders, Inc.*)

5.22 NEGATIVE FRICTION

The specifications may require special installation procedures to offset potential negative friction loads such as predrilling an oversized hole and filling the annulus between the pile and the soil with a heavy bentonite slurry, gravel, or some other suitable type of material. Other alternatives are driving the pile through a permanent sleeve or coating the pile with bitumen (see Section 5.11.4). If piles are coated, special precautions such as predrilling with or without a temporary casing may be specified to protect the coating from damage during driving.

5.23 INTERRUPTION OF PILE DRIVING

Generally the specifications will require that the piles be driven their full lengths without interruption. If the driving of a pile is interrupted, the time, cause, and duration should be noted on the driving record. Interruptions may be caused by splicing in the leaders, by equipment breakdown or servicing, by cap-block changes, or by weather. Where soil-freeze conditions exist, any prolonged interruption in pile driving will result in an increase in pile penetration resistance when driving is resumed. In extreme cases, it may not be possible to achieve further pile penetration without damaging the pile. In such cases, if the pile is not long enough or has not reached the required bearing strata, it may be necessary to abandon and replace the pile. A wave equation analysis may indicate how hard the pile can be safely driven to break the freeze.

5.24 ABRUPT CHANGES IN DRIVING RESISTANCE

Sudden increases in driving resistance, either real or apparent, could be caused by the pile hitting underground obstructions or hard soil strata, by the introduction of fresh cap-block material, by the brooming of the butts of timber piles, by the cracking or spalling of the butts of concrete piles, or by the elastic yielding of steel piles. Sudden decreases in pile-driving resistance could be caused by the brooming of timber pile tips, by the breaking below ground surface of timber or precast piles, by the plastic yielding of a steel pile, or by any pile encountering soft soil strata.

Abrupt changes in the penetration resistance should be investigated to determine the cause. If such changes are not investigated, or if pile breakage is found to be the cause, the pile should be rejected. The investigation may indicate that some remedial measures must be taken, such as changing pile installation equipment or methods or using a different type of pile.

5.25 DRIVING PRECAST CONCRETE PILES

When, during the driving of precast concrete piles, the resistance to penetration at the pile tip is very low, the pile hammer energy should be reduced to avoid building up excessively high tensile stresses in the pile. Low tip resistance could occur during the initial driving of piles in prejetted or predrilled holes or if jetting is done during driving. Low tip resistance could also occur when the pile tip encounters a void or a very soft soil stratum. Under such conditions, the compression stress induced by the pile hammer is reflected at the pile tip as a tensile stress. This could crack the pile or, in the case of sectional piles, tend to project the bottom section ahead of the rest of the pile. In this case, the joint between sections must be capable of resisting the tensile forces. If unwelded sleeve-type joints are used, the sleeve must be long enough to keep the pile sections engaged. Hammer energy can be reduced by short-stroking the hammer (see Sections 4.8.4 and 4.8.6) or, for diesel hammers, by adjusting the fuel setting (see Section 4.8.7). After the tip resistance has built up, the full hammer energy can be applied.

If the tip resistance is sufficient, the compression stress induced by the hammer is reflected at the tip as a compression stress. When this stress wave reaches the top of the pile, it could be re-reflected as a tensile stress if the drive system does not have enough weight and stiffness to offer sufficient resistance.

5.26 OBSTRUCTIONS

Obstructions may be buried timber, logs, or tree stumps, boulders, old concrete foundations, slag or rock fill, miscellaneous rubbish fill, or other objects which could prevent the pile from reaching the necessary penetration or cause the pile to bend or drift off location or which may damage the pile. Obstructions near the ground surface will be evident if the pile tends to drift off location at the start of driving or if the pile refuses to penetrate. The presence of deep obstructions may be difficult to detect, and such obstructions could seriously damage the pile or prevent the pile from obtaining the necessary bearing capacity. Deep obstructions may be indicated by an unexpected refusal of the pile to penetrate or by substantial differences in tip elevations for adjacent piles. Such conditions should be investigated by test borings. The inspector should observe the pile driving or installation carefully to detect any unusual occurrence which may indicate pile damage or misalignment.

It may be necessary to remove or dislodge obstructions to install piles properly. Sometimes they can be pushed aside, broken up, or pierced with a spud. Shallow obstructions can often be removed, but special methods may be required to break up or bypass deep obstructions, or the pile may have to be relocated.

The tips of steel H piles are very susceptible to overstressing and deformation when encountering obstructions such as boulders or an uneven rock surface. The use of some type of reinforced tip for steel H piles is recommended if obstructions exist. The tips of timber and precast concrete piles also can be damaged by obstructions, especially the tips of timber piles. The use of steel drive shoes may help prevent tip damage, but if too much reliance is placed on the reinforced tip and the pile is driven too hard, it may be damaged elsewhere. If obstructions such as boulder formations are known to exist, timber piles should not be used.

Although pipe, Monotube, and shell piles can be damaged by obstructions, any damage can be determined by visual internal inspection after the piles are driven. If noninspectable-type piles are driven in ground that is known to be obstructed, or if there is evidence of obstructions during driving, some of the piles should be pulled for inspection as the work progresses. This can be done with a vibratory extractor. Such sampling may not reveal all damaged piles, and so if some serious damage is found, consideration should be given to changing the type of pile or method of installation to help resolve the obstruction problem. A complete record should be kept on all piles pulled.

The responsibility for obstructions and associated pile damage may be provided for in the contract documents. Normally the owner assumes responsibility for his ground and should make an adequate subsurface investigation so that the presence of obstructions is revealed beforehand. The engineer has the responsibility for selecting the proper pile for the existing conditions. The contractor has certain responsibilities such as furnishing suitable equipment and using proper installation methods and techniques. He also may be responsible for furnishing adequate pile material, but in general, problems caused by obstructions are beyond his control.

5.27 OVERDRIVING

Overdriving of piles causes pile damage and should be avoided. Whether or not piles are being overdriven is often a matter of judgment based upon the pile material involved, the subsoil conditions, the driving equipment used, and the installation method. Pile damage could occur when the pile material is exposed to dynamic stresses during driving which are higher than the yield or ultimate strength of the material. A proper wave equation analysis can reveal the driving stresses to which the pile may be subjected. Generally, pile material can withstand driving stresses about 10 percent higher than the yield or ultimate strength. This is because of the very short duration of each peak stress. Pile damage could also occur under prolonged hard driving resulting in a type of fatigue failure. This is especially true for timber piles. Overdriving of timber piles could cause brooming at the pile tip or butt, splitting of the pile, or actual pile breakage. If a sudden high resistance to penetration is encountered when driving timber piles, driving should stop immediately. Banding timber piles with tightly fitted steel bands at regular intervals along the piles may reduce the chances of brooming or splitting, but excessively prolonged hard driving should still be prohibited.

Steel piles could deform by plastic yielding, by rupture, or by both. Damage to precast concrete piles could be in the form of cracks, spalling, or actual breakage. Overdriving is critical only when the structural material of the pile is being driven and the structural integrity of the pile can be impaired.

5.28 SOIL FREEZE   *Thixotropy*

Some cohesive-type soils exhibit a decrease in shear strength when being remolded and disturbed by pile driving, but they regain their strengths with time after pile driving stops. This is known as "soil freeze" or "setup." During driving, the penetration resistance is relatively low, and a specified penetration resistance based upon a dynamic formula or a wave equation analysis is not applicable. Under freeze conditions, the application of dynamic driving formulas including the wave equation should be on the basis of retap data. The occurrence of soil freeze can be checked by retapping piles sometime after final driving. The driving resistance will show a sharp increase. The amount of soil freeze and the rate at which it occurs can vary over a wide range. Some soils show substantial soil freeze in a matter of hours, but others may require days or even weeks to regain full strength.

5.29 RELAXATION

"Relaxation" is a term applied to a decrease with time of the final pile penetration resistance. It could result from driving friction piles into dense, fine, submerged sand, inorganic silt, or stiff, fissured clay or from driving point-bearing piles into a friable shale or a clay stone.[123] Where soil conditions indicate that relaxation could occur, some piles should be retapped after they and adjacent piles have been driven. A reasonable retap program would be to retap the first pile driven in each group after all piles in that group have been driven. As part of this program, to check for long-term relaxation, the last pile driven each day can be retapped at the start of the next workday. If, upon retapping, it is observed that the original final driving resistance has decreased, all piles should be retapped, and further checking should be done until penetration resistance and/or depths of penetration are satisfactory.

Under certain subsoil conditions, relaxation may be compensated for by driving the piles initially to a resistance greater than that normally required. The feasibility of this procedure and the extent of overdriving required could be determined experimentally. When pile tips are being driven to friable shale and relaxation is occurring, the piles should not be overdriven or subjected to prolonged hard driving. This could aggravate and continue the relaxation due to progressive breaking up of the shale. Driving should stop as soon as the tip encounters sound shale.

5.30 PILE HEAVE

When displacement-type piles are driven in soft, saturated, cohesive soils, ground heave may occur, especially when such piles are closely spaced.[90] Under such conditions the possibility of pile heave should be checked. This can be done by taking accurate level readings on the tops of driven piles before and after adjacent piles have been driven. However, for corrugated pile shells, such check-level readings should be taken on a telltale pipe resting on the closure plate at the pile point. Upward movement of the tops of such shells is not harmful when due to shell stretch.

When pile heave is observed, piles should be redriven as specified after pile driving has progressed beyond the pile heave range. Cast-in-place concrete should be placed in pipe, Monotube, or shell piles only after heave has stopped and heaved piles have been redriven. In the case of piles not suitable for redriving (for example, uncased, unreinforced, cast-in-place concrete piles), if heave should occur, the driving sequence and/or methods of installation must be modified to eliminate heave, and all heaved piles should be replaced. Alternatively, the pile type can be changed.

The specifications may limit the amount of pile heave that can occur before redriving is required, or they may provide that all heaved piles be redriven. The specifications may require that piles be redriven to the original penetration resistance or tip elevation or both. Point-bearing piles should be reseated, but for friction piles, heave is not critical. If ground or pile heave occurs, the effects on existing adjacent structures should be observed. Pile heave can be controlled or eliminated by using proper preexcavation methods, by increasing the pile spacing, or by installing nondisplacement-type piles.

The inspector should record the results of heave-level readings and all redrive data. The contract documents may delineate the responsibilities for pile heave and subsequent redriving. If the contractor is to be reimbursed for redriving piles, he may be paid on a per pile or hourly basis, or he may perform such work on force account. The inspector must record the necessary information to determine pay quantities.

5.31 RETAPPING PILES

When it is necessary to redrive or retap piles to a specified penetration resistance, the work should be done with the same drive system that was used for initial driving or an equivalent system except as noted below for concreted shell piles. If the hammer is cold, it may not deliver its full stroke until it has warmed up. In this case, the measured pile penetration under the first few hammer blows may not be indicative of the actual driving resistance.

If soil freeze has occurred, the retap penetration resistance will be higher than the final resistance as measured during initial driving. In some cases, the pile may refuse to penetrate further. In other cases, prolonged redriving may break the soil freeze, and then the pile will drive more easily. If retapping is done only to ensure an adequate penetration resistance or to check on soil freeze, it is not necessary to continue redriving until the soil freeze is broken.

Retapping or redriving of uncased cast-in-place piles should not be permitted. Redriving on concreted shell piles is permissible providing the proper hammer–pile cushion system has been established by prior use or designed by a wave equation analysis. For pipe or Monotube piles not originally driven with an internal mandrel, the concrete filling provides a much stiffer pile and results in a more effective transmission of hammer energy. Therefore, for such piles, the actual retap resistance will be less than the original final resistance for the same formula capacity. This effect may be compounded if the redriven pile is shorter because of being cut off after initial driving. A wave equation analysis will show the comparable final resistances for the loads involved.

5.32 DRIVING RECORD

Probably the most common duty of the pile inspector is to record the pile-driving logs. However, the inspector's responsibilities include more than just counting blows. They involve making a complete driving record for each pile. Appendix D contains several examples of forms that can be used to record the data. The engineer responsible for pile inspection may want to design and print forms that meet the specific job requirements and ensure that the desired information is recorded.

Some basic information should always be recorded, such as the date, the pile designation, the pile type, size, and length, the ground elevation at the pile location, and the drive system data. The drive system data include the hammer model, type, and size, the cap block and pile cushion type and dimensions, the drive cap type and weight, and the follower type, size, and

Logging the pile. (*Courtesy of Raymond International Builders, Inc.*)

length. Data which are constant throughout the job do not have to be recorded for each pile. If piles are spliced in the leaders, the lengths of added pile sections must be recorded. If piles are installed through overburden, the overburden depth should be recorded. General information identifying the project, the location, the owner, and the contractor can be printed on the forms.

The inspector should observe and record occurrences during pile installation which may affect the structural integrity or bearing capacity of the pile or prevent it from meeting the specifications or which may affect existing adjacent piles or structures. This could include evidence of possible pile damage such as a sudden increase or drop in penetration resistance, or evidence of the pile hitting an obstruction or an adjacent pile, or evidence of the pile drifting off location or off alignment.

The inspector should note on the driving record any interruptions in pile installation including the time, causes, and duration and any indications of equipment malfunction.

5.32.1 Impact Driving Record. The specifications may require that the number of hammer blows required for each foot (or meter) of pile penetration be recorded. This is especially true for test piles. However, the general practice is to record the driving log during final penetration of the pile and give the final driving resistance in blows per inch. The basic driving log can be observed by marking the pile off at 1-ft (or 0.25-m) intervals (see Section 5.8) and counting the number of hammer blows delivered as adjacent marks pass a fixed reference point. If the pile is penetrating rapidly, it may be impossible to record blows per foot (or 0.25 m), and under such conditions, the total number of blows for a given length of penetration may be recorded. A convenient

Measuring final penetration resistance. (*Courtesy of Raymond International Builders, Inc.*)

method for observing final driving resistance in blows per inch is to put random marks on the pile and count the number of blows delivered as one of the marks passes adjacent inch marks on a rule held near the side of the pile. The same type of system can be used for metric measurements.

In the case of piles that are inserted in predrilled or jetted holes, or in the case of very heavy piles and soft-soil conditions, a pile will run into the ground under its weight and the weight of the hammer. The depth of run should be recorded if complete driving logs are required.

For double-acting and differential hammers, the compressor or boiler pressure should be monitored and recorded periodically. For a closed-top diesel hammer, the bounce-chamber pressure must be recorded at the time of final driving. If an open-top diesel hammer is used, the stroke must be recorded at the final driving. This may require a second inspector to observe the stroke indicator or the rise of the piston above the top of the cylinder as the final penetration resistance is being measured and recorded. An instrument called the Saximeter* has been developed to acoustically measure the stroke as well as count the hammer blows. Figure D-12 shows a Saximeter blow count–stroke form.

Driving will be stopped by the rig foreman when the inspector is satisfied that the installation criteria have been met. Driving records may be required for piles to be driven to a predetermined length or tip elevation as a check on pile capacity. If piles are to be installed to a specified tip elevation, the pile length and the ground surface elevation must be known. In addition, for batter piles, the extra length required to reach the prescribed tip elevation must be considered.

Generally, with a minimum tip elevation, the piles must also be driven to a minimum penetration resistance below that elevation. In this case and for piles driven solely to a specified penetration resistance, driving can stop when that is achieved. However, the specifications may require that the minimum penetration resistance be maintained over a specified depth. If the specifications do not provide for this, and unless the pile is at absolute refusal, driving should continue until the specified resistance is maintained over at least 3 in (75 mm). The inspector should exercise judgment and not require driving that could damage the pile or reduce its capacity (see Sections 5.26 and 5.27).

After the prescribed tip elevation and/or penetration has been reached, the contractor may want to continue driving the pile butt to the cutoff grade to avoid cutting off the pile. This should not be permitted if there is any danger of damaging the pile. If it is allowed, the driving record should indicate the pile length or tip elevation at the time the installation criteria were satisfied and the extra length driven at the contractor's expense.

*Pileco, Inc., Houston, Tex.

5.32.2 Vibratory Driving Record.   If piles are to be installed with a vibratory driver, the details of the driver, including the make, model, and eccentric moment, must be recorded in addition to the normal pile data. During pile installation, the inspector must record the steady-state frequency at which the driver is operated, the dynamic force developed, and the rate of penetration of the pile. This will require a stopwatch to measure the penetration in feet or inches (meters or millimeters) per second.

The required penetration rate may be specified or result from pile load tests. If the specifications require that the final driving be done with an impact hammer or that the resistance be checked with such a hammer, the inspector must record the information on the equipment used and the results of such driving (see Section 5.32.1).

5.33 MONITORING PILE INSTALLATION

The pile-driving analyzer has been used to monitor pile installation.[78,79,81,104] Sometimes the data obtained from the field instrumentation (an accelerometer and force or strain transducers attached to the top of a pile) are recorded on tape and used as direct input (actual energy delivered to the pile) in a conventional wave equation analysis. This eliminates the basic assumption of hammer efficiency and the computations necessary to determine the energy transmitted through the drive system. The field data can also be used in a special program called CAPWAP,[104] which is based on a conventional wave equation analysis but adjusts some of the soil resistance parameters to get a match between the computed and measured time-force curves.

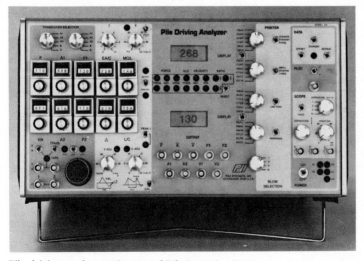

Pile-driving analyzer. (*Courtesy of Pile Dynamics, Inc.*)

The field data can be fed into a microprocessor at the jobsite to determine the predicted capacity of the pile as it is being driven. The procedure is based upon the Case method,[78] and a closed-form wave equation solution is used which considers the pile as a single, long, elastic element and which uses the wave-equation-type soil parameters. This solution is not as accurate or precise as the standard one-dimensional wave equation analysis.[111] Although the pile capacity is displayed for each hammer blow, the depicted capacity is sensitive to operator control and adjustment. Experience and sound judgment are necessary for the reliable use of this equipment. The use of the correct type of accelerometer and the correct mounting are critical. Accelerometers should be of the high-g type so as to pick up the full range.

This method for monitoring pile installation is not suitable for all types of driven piles. For example, for Step-Taper piles, the normal slack in joints between mandrel sections and possibly in the engagement of the mandrel and the shell drive ring during driving can cause very erratic results that can be seriously misinterpreted. The same problem may exist with certain types of sectional precast concrete piles. The method is also not applicable to piles installed with a temporary driven casing.

The compression and tension stresses in the pile during driving can also be displayed and may indicate effects on the structural integrity of the pile (see Section 5.54). If measurements are taken during retapping of the pile, the effects of soil freeze or relaxation may be determined depending on the time interval between initial driving and retapping.

5.34 SPLICING IN THE LEADERS

Splicing in the leaders can be accomplished by using the pile rig to place the pile section to be added. The section is held while the splice is made. A service crane can be used instead of the rig so that the rig is free to continue driving. In the latter case, the installation sequence and splicing procedures, including pile lengths added, must permit the rig to get back on the spliced pile.

If splicing in the leaders is permitted, the type of splice and the maximum number of splices allowed in a pile may be specified. The specifications may prohibit splices from being closer to the pile cutoff than a stated distance. The required strength of the splice or joint may be stated as a percentage (50 to 100 percent) of the strength of the pile section or in terms of being capable of resisting all driving and service-load stresses. The approved splice may be detailed on the plans or may be in a contractor's submittal, in which case the inspector should be furnished with a copy.

The individual pile sections to be spliced must be in accurate axial alignment. Before a section of pile is added, the top of the driven portion may have to be prepared for the splice. For example, any damaged portion must be cut off, and the top of the pile may have to be evened off for full contact with the added piece or the splice fitting. The specifications may require that the top of a steel pile be scarfed for butt welding. For welded splices, the specifications may require a certified welder and indicate the required extent of welding, such as tack, continuous, or a minimum length.

Where soil conditions are such that soil freeze or setup can occur rapidly, the use of pile splicing during driving should be limited. Under extreme conditions, it may be impossible to resume further penetration of the pile after the splice has been made without endangering the pile or the splice. If splicing is necessary under such conditions, the type of splice used should be one which can be completed in the shortest length of time, such as a sleeve-type joint or a mechanical joint. Splicing in the leaders can be expedited by attaching splice fittings and completing half the splice while the pile section is on the ground.

The inspector should carefully record the lengths of pile sections added during driving and the type of splice used. Records must be accurate enough to determine pay quantities.

5.34.1 Timber Piles. The splicing in the leaders of timber piles is rarely permitted. If it is allowed, the splicing method should be clearly detailed on the plans or should be subject to the approval of the engineer. Care must be exercised in getting a uniform and complete contact between abutting pile surfaces and a fairly close match in diameters. For treated piles, the end surfaces to be joined and all holes and cuts must be properly treated with a preservative. All fittings including bolts should be galvanized. If piles are to be spliced with metal fittings, piles treated with a salt preservative should not be used because of potential corrosion.[124]

5.34.2 Precast Concrete Piles. There are several types of precast-pile splices or joints as discussed in Chapter 2. These include various types of mechanical joints, welded joints, sleeve joints, and dowel joints. Many are specifically designed for installing sectional precast concrete piles. Some of these joints cannot take bending or tension. This should be considered when using or approving a splicing method, especially for very long piles, or when driving piles in obstructed ground, or when the tip resistance to penetration can become very low during driving (see Section 5.25).

5.34.3 Pipe Piles. Pipe piles can be spliced by using either inside or outside drive sleeves with or without welding. Splices can also be made by butt welding, and the specifications may require a backup ring.

5.34.4 Monotube Piles. Two different splicing procedures are used for Monotube piles depending on whether a constant-diameter section is being added to a tapered section or to another constant-diameter section. In either case the manufacturer's recommendations should be followed.

5.34.5 H Piles.   Steel H piles are spliced with a simple butt weld or with special splice fittings. Also, steel fishplates can be welded on, or a combination of butt welds and fishplates can be used. If special splice fittings are used, they should at least be tack-welded. It is common practice to attach splice fittings or fishplates to the section to be added while it is still on the ground. This facilitates joining the pile section to the driven pile, holds the pieces together, and shortens the welding time in the leaders.

5.34.6 Constant-Section Shells.   If constant-section shells have to be spliced, butt welds are usually used. Special corrugated sleeves may be available, and these should be welded to the shell body. It is difficult and time-consuming to splice this type of pile shell in the leaders; therefore, the piles should be made up to full length on the ground. One of the problems with splicing in the leaders may be getting the mandrel back into the shell after splicing. Also, the mandrel must be long enough to take the added shell. Another problem is getting the corrugations of the two shell sections to match for proper welding. Where necessary for pile buildup after driving is completed, short lengths of shell can be readily added.

5.34.7 Step-Taper Shells.   The required pile length is generally made up on the ground. If it becomes necessary to add shell sections during driving, the mandrel is withdrawn and the sections to be added are slipped up onto the mandrel and screw-connected to the driven shells. The joints are waterproofed with an O-ring gasket or by other methods.

5.34.8 Composite Piles.   When pipe-shell composite piles are driven, the pipe portion can be driven first and the shell section added. The joint can be a slip-type sleeve or a drive sleeve. For wood composite piles, the shell portion is generally attached to the timber portion with some type of wedge ring, which is driven into the top of the timber pile.

5.35 VARIATIONS IN PILE LENGTHS

If possible, extreme variations in pile lengths in any one group should be avoided. If pile tip elevations for adjacent piles or piles within a group vary by more than about 5 ft (2 m), the cause should be investigated. Length variations could be caused by obstructions or unusual subsoil conditions such as cavernous limestone formations or highly variable glacial deposits. There may be no practical remedy for extreme variations in pile lengths. In some cases additional piles may be required, or piles may have to be relocated. Length variations could also result from the gradual densification of the subsoil and a shortening of the piles as driving progresses. To minimize this, pile driving for large groups should start at the center of the group and continue outward uniformly.

5.36 INTERNAL INSPECTION

Pipe, shell, and Monotube piles can be visually inspected internally after being driven. Inspection can be done with the help of a powerful spotlight or by reflecting sunlight down the pile with a mirror. In some cases a droplight can be lowered inside the pile. This affords an opportunity to detect any damage or misalignment that might have occurred or the presence of water or foreign matter. If water, soil, or other foreign matter is observed in the pile, the depth of the water or the distance from the pile top down to the surface of soil in the pile can be determined by lowering a weighted steel tape. If the bottom of the pile cannot be seen because of water in the pile or because the pile is bent, the pile can be sounded with a steel weight at the end of a line. The impact of the weight on the steel tip or on soil can be detected by feel or sound.

Since all piles are subject to damage and misalignment during driving, the

Inspecting a driven pile shell by reflecting sunlight down the pile with a mirror. (*Courtesy of Raymond International Builders, Inc.*)

revealing of defects puts the inspectable-type piles at a disadvantage with the noninspectable types such as timber piles, precast concrete piles, steel H piles, and certain special types of piles such as auger-grout piles. However, from a quality control viewpoint, inspectability is an advantage. If a problem exists, it is better to know about it and take the necessary corrective action.

5.37 PILE ALIGNMENT AFTER INSTALLATION

The specifications may require that piles be installed within a stated alignment tolerance. This is an impractical requirement if both inspectable and noninspectable piles are permitted unless the specifications require that the noninspectable piles be fitted with inspection ducts in which an inclinometer can be lowered to measure alignment. The alignment tolerance may be specified in degrees or as a rate such as 1 in in 2 or 4 ft (20 or 40 mm/m) or as a percentage of length such as 2 or 4 percent. The alignment tolerance may also be specified in terms of a minimum radius of curvature.

The specifications should be clear as to how the tolerance is to be applied, such as to each incremental length of the pile or to the overall pile length. Alignment tolerances applied to the overall pile length are not considered practical or warranted. In general, for fully embedded foundation piles, alignment tolerances are too restrictive. Before piles are rejected because of failure to meet the alignment tolerance, consideration should be given to the practicality of the specifications and the actual effects of the misalignment.

The approximate axial alignment of pipe, Monotube, or shell piles can be checked by using a mirror and reflected sunlight or a spotlight to see if the full pile length is visible. If any portion of the pile tip can be seen, the pile should be considered satisfactory regardless of the specified tolerance. Alignment can also be checked by lowering a plumb bob or weighted tape inside the pile and noting the offset for a given depth or the depth at which the plumb bob touches the opposite side. The effects of taper must be considered. For pipe piles, the alignment can be checked by lowering a proving "plug," the diameter and length of which are designed to prevent the plug from passing a bend in the pile having a minimum specified radius of curvature. If necessary, deviations from axial alignment can be measured with some type of inclinometer lowered inside the pile or inside a duct fitted to the pile. The use of such instruments on all piles for routine jobs is considered impractical.

In most cases, the alignment check for noninspectable piles can only be made on the portion of the pile extending above the ground surface or exposed by subsequent excavation. The checking can be done with a carpenter's level. If only a very short length of pile is exposed, such measurements are meaningless.

Misalignment of piles below the ground surface can take various shapes, as illustrated in Figure 5-3. In Figure 5-3a the pile is straight, but its axis is

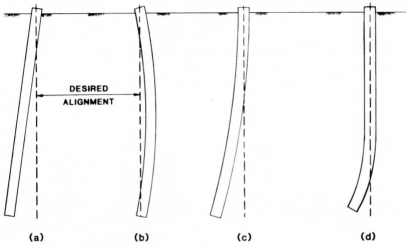

(a)   **(b)**   **(c)**   **(d)**

Figure 5-3 Typical shapes of misaligned piles.

inclined at a slight batter. In this case, a tolerance of 1 on 10 should be considered satisfactory. The pile could be bent somewhere between the butt and the tip, with the tip on location as shown in Figure 5-3*b*, or off location as indicated in Figure 5-3*c*. The bend could be sharp (called a "dogleg") or smooth, having various radii. The misalignment shown in Figure 5-3*d* is quite common for piles overdriven to a hard stratum or a sloping rock surface, and it often goes undetected.

Pile misalignment could be caused by subsoil conditions such as dense or hard sloping strata, obstructions, cavernous limestone, or fissured rock, by flexible pile material, or by the use of inadequate or improper methods and equipment. If misalignment is caused by subsoil conditions, and if the specified pile material has been furnished, the contractor should not be held responsible for the misaligned piles. The contract documents may indicate actual responsibility for misaligned piles and corrective measures, including replacement. If axial alignment of piles is critical, or if misalignment is highly possible because of subsurface conditions, consideration should be given to using a type of pile for which the alignment can be checked.

The most critical portion of a pile for alignment is the upper portion as it enters the pile cap or structure. The length of this portion could be 10 to 12 ft (3 to 4 m) for embedded foundation piles. A reasonable tolerance could be 5 to 10 percent of the length. In general, long, sweeping bends in friction or point-bearing piles are not considered detrimental. The capacity of bent piles, including those having sharp bends or doglegs, can be checked by an analysis involving structural and soil-mechanics principles.[58,89,100] Except possibly for very sharp doglegs in extremely soft soil, the soil resistance is generally more than sufficient to restrain the pile from buckling under its design load. If the capacity of a bent pile is in doubt, it can be checked by a proof load test. Usually there is no need to reject misaligned piles. In many cases they will carry the full design load satisfactorily, and if they do not, they can be downgraded, and additional piles can be installed.

5.38 DAMAGED PILES

Piles can be damaged at the tip, along the shaft, or at the butt. Tip damage for timber piles, precast concrete piles, or steel H piles cannot be detected unless the piles are pulled for visual inspection. Damage along the pile shaft could be in the form of a reduction in the cross-sectional area, a break in the pile, or, in severe cases of overdriving, a folded bend in the pile. The break could be a crack or tear or actual separation. Except for pile shells or casing which can be visually inspected internally after being driven, such deformations cannot be observed unless the pile is pulled or excavated or some type of dynamic or ultrasonic test is conducted on the pile (see Section 5.54).

Pile damage is usually caused by subsurface obstructions, soil pressures, rock fissures or crevices, or some other type of subsoil condition. Damage may also result from using the wrong type of pile for the driving conditions, and rarely is the contractor at fault.

When treated timber piles are driven into rubble fill or soils containing heavy gravel or sharp boulders or other types of obstructions, there is a danger of splintering or gouging the pile surface, and this may render the protective treatment ineffective. In such cases it may be advisable to pre-drill and drive piles through a temporary casing installed through the obstructed zone. It would be prudent not to use treated timber piles under such conditions.

Reductions in the cross-sectional area for pipe, shell, or Monotube piles can be detected during routine internal inspection. For pipe or constant-section shells, the occurrence of a reduction in area can be determined by lowering a proper-size "proving ball" inside the pile. The specifications may limit the allowable decrease in the cross-sectional area. Reductions up to 25 percent are reasonable. In general, the actual reduction would have to be estimated on the basis of measurements or visual inspection. For shell, pipe, or Monotube piles, reductions in the cross-sectional area can sometimes be controlled or eliminated by the use of heavier gauges or wall thicknesses, by preexcavation, by filling a section of driven pipe with concrete before adding and driving additional pipe lengths, by inserting dummy cores in pile shells, or by filling the shells with water until they are ready to be filled with concrete.

Tip damage to steel H piles can often be prevented by suitable tip reinforcement. Some types of pile damage can be prevented by using proper drive heads, by protecting precast concrete piles with a suitable cushion, and by avoiding overdriving. Damaged pile butts can be trimmed off and the pile built up as necessary. The inspector should note on the driving records those piles that are rejected because of damage.

5.39 PILE CUTOFF

It will not be the inspector's responsibility to mark cutoff grades on piles. However, a satisfactory system must be used by the contractor's survey crew to give the inspector the necessary information for determining pile lengths for record and payment purposes. The inspector may not be present when cutoff grades are marked on piles or when piles are actually cut off.

The inspector can generally identify the piles from the pile location plan. For solid-type piles, he will need a legible footage mark on each pile to determine pile length. For hollow-type piles, installed lengths can be determined by lowering a weighted steel tape. For piles that are to be built up (the pile top is driven below grade), the cutoff grade can be indicated as some stated distance above the mark placed on the pile. For piles installed through overburden, the cutoff grade is indicated as some distance below the mark.

It may be necessary to cut off piles immediately after driving to provide rig access to other pile locations or to permit the rig to swing off the driven pile. In such cases, the inspector should record the pile length cut off and ensure that a legible footage mark is on the pile. Such cutoffs may not be to the specified grade, and so a subsequent cutoff will be required.

For a complete record and depending on the pile payment method, the inspector may be required to record the lengths of all cutoffs, properly identified as to pile designation. In such cases, the system used for marking and cutting off piles must provide the inspector with the necessary information. He may have to take measurements before piles are cut off.

The cut should be perpendicular to the longitudinal axis of the pile and within the tolerance specified. It is not unreasonable to require that piles be cut off to within 1 in (25 mm) of the specified elevation. Piles should be cut off below all damaged portions and built up as necessary. By visually checking all piles in a group or adjacent piles against the pile plans, the inspector can often detect major errors in pile cutoff elevations.

5.40 PILE CUTOFF LENGTHS

Pile lengths which are cut off will be the property of the owner if pile material is paid for on the basis of furnished lengths, or they will become the property of the contractor if piles are paid for on the basis of the length from tip to cutoff grade. In either case, the contract may require the contractor to dispose of such waste piling.

Frequently, pile cutoff lengths are used to build up piles to grade or spliced into piles to make up the required length. If in such cases all pile material is paid for on the basis of ordered lengths or the full length in the leaders is paid for, the inspector must keep accurate records to avoid duplicate payments.

5.41 TREATMENT OF TIMBER PILE BUTTS

The butts of treated timber piles should be treated with preservatives in accordance with the specifications. In general, three coats of hot creosote oil must be applied, and then the end surface of the pile must be sealed with a heavy application of coal-tar pitch. The specifications may require the application of as much creosote as the wood will absorb within a specified length of time. It may be necessary to use a band that goes around and projects above the top of the pile to retain the creosote during that period. All framing cuts and holes made in the pile must be adequately treated.

5.42 CAP PLATES

For steel H piles which are installed to carry very high design loads and which are capped with concrete, the specifications may require that steel cap plates be welded to the tops of all piles for adequate load transfer by bearing between the piles and the concrete caps. Cap plates should be fully welded unless there is full bearing contact between the pile top and the plate. In this case, the plates should at least be tack-welded to the piles. Generally, the piles are embedded a sufficient length into the concrete caps to transfer the load through bond and bearing without the need for cap plates.

5.43 PILE BUILDUP

Pile butts that are too low in elevation can be built up to the proper grade. This is readily accomplished for cast-in-place concrete piles by adding a section of shell or pipe before concrete is placed. For other types of piles, especially where the specifications prohibit splices occurring along the upper portion of the pile, it may be necessary to verify with the engineer the acceptability of a pile buildup. In some cases, the bottom of the pile cap can be lowered to accommodate piles with the tops driven below the required cutoff grade.

5.44 PILE BUTT LOCATIONS

The permissible tolerance for the butt location will generally be specified and may vary with the pile size, the number of piles in a group, and possibly the design load. The establishment of a butt location tolerance implies an acceptance of a pile load in excess of the design load. The amount of overload would depend on the tolerance allowed. Butt locations can be critical for single piles carrying high loads. Tolerances can be more liberal as the number of piles in the group increases. Normal tolerances range from 3 to 6 in (75 to 150 mm) but may have to be greater for timber piles because of their natural bends.

Final pile positions should be checked as the work progresses so that, if necessary, additional piles can be installed before the equipment is moved away or before it can no longer reach the required locations of the added piles. If piles are found to be installed beyond the permissible tolerance for the butt location, the resulting loads on the piles should be checked, and remedial measures should be taken as directed by the engineer. Two additional piles may be required to correct the mislocation of a single isolated pile. The number of additional piles required in any one group may be determined by the number necessary to balance the group to maintain the design center of gravity. Added piles must be installed at the proper locations. If a pile or pile group to be corrected is adjacent to a property line, the locations of additional piles should be checked to ensure that those piles do not encroach on other property. If it is impractical to install additional piles, it may be possible to compensate for mislocation by bracing the tops of the piles with grade beams or other types of construction.

The specifications may require that an as-built survey be made and a record plan be prepared showing the actual location of all pile butts, including the butts of added piles. The inspector should be furnished with copies of the survey data and should record all the necessary details for piles added.

Pile butt mislocation could be caused by subsurface obstructions or other soil conditions that tend to move the pile during driving. Mislocation could also result from errors in pile stakeout, careless spotting of the pile (or drill or jet), equipment not capable of holding the piles in position, or the use of improper installation methods. If all piles in a group are off location in the same direction and by about the same amount, a layout error should be suspected.

In general, it is not necessary to reject mislocated piles. They are usually included as pay piles but possibly with a reduced design load. The contract documents should be checked as to responsibility for mislocated piles and remedial work. The inspector must record the data required to satisfy the contract terms.

5.45 CLEANING OUT PILES

5.45.1 Open-End Pipe Piles.
The specifications may require that pipe piles driven open-ended be cleaned out and filled with concrete. The length of pile to be cleaned out may vary from a few feet at the top to the full length.

Open-end pipe piles which pick up an immovable plug during driving will behave as displacement-type piles and may require periodic cleaning out to achieve the necessary penetration. Soil inside such piles can be removed by

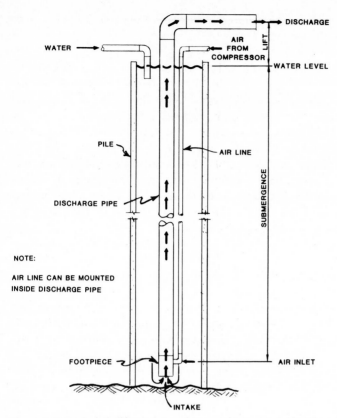

Figure 5-4 Typical air lift. (*Courtesy of Raymond International Builders, Inc.*)

drilling, by washing with a jet with or without an air lift (Figure 5-4), or with various types of grab buckets. It may be necessary to break up large boulders with some type of churn drill chopping bit or cable tool or with a hammer grab. Care must be taken to avoid removing soil from beneath the pile tip.

If a pile tip is driven into a granular stratum and an unbalanced hydrostatic head exists, attempts to completely remove the soil plug may cause a sand boil at the pile tip, and this could affect the pile's capacity or, in severe cases, adjacent structures. A sufficient length of soil plug must be left in place to seal off the pile tip.

5.45.2 Pile Shells and Casings.   Unless pile shells and casings, including pipe and Monotubes, are kept covered until concrete can be placed, various types of debris could fall in. Foreign objects can often be removed with some type of grab or hook. Pieces of wood can sometimes be speared with a pointed length of reinforcing steel or floated to the top by filling the shell or casing with water.

If pile shells are torn by obstructions, groundwater or soil or both can enter. If soil gets into pile shells, it can often be removed by washing with a low-pressure jet, sometimes in combination with steam pressure or with an air lift. If the tear in a shell is small, the soil will enter very slowly. In such cases, the shell can be kept full of water to maintain a positive hydrostatic head inside the pile, and concrete can be placed by tremie (see Section 5.47.3). If the tear is large, the pile will probably have to be rejected.

Water can be removed with a bailing bucket, a steam syphon, or a small, submersible pump. If the lift is not too high, a conventional suction pump can be used. If water is entering the shell slowly, the shell can often be dewatered and immediately filled with concrete. If the flow is rapid, the shell can be filled with water, and concrete can be placed by tremie.

5.46 PLACING REINFORCING STEEL

The number and arrangement of longitudinal bars and the diameter of the reinforcing cage should be as specified or as detailed on the plans. Longitudinal steel to resist bending should be tied with hoops or a spiral with the specified spacing or pitch and should have sufficient spacers to center the cage in the pile casing or hole. The specifications may permit steel to be tied, or they may require welding. Longitudinal steel to resist uplift loads may be bundled and placed in the center of the pile. Frequently, high-yield-strength steel bars are used for tension reinforcement (see Section 3.9.1). Except for short dowels, reinforcing steel for cast-in-place piles should be placed before concrete is poured in that portion of the pile containing reinforcement.

All steel must be free from dirt, rust scale, loose mill scale, oil, grease, and any other coating which would affect the steel-to-concrete bond. The concrete cover should be at least 3 in (75 mm) for uncased cast-in-place concrete piles and $1\frac{1}{2}$ in (40 mm) for cased piles.

5.47 PLACING CONCRETE FOR CAST-IN-PLACE PILES

Chapter 3 contains details on the requirements for concrete for cast-in-place concrete piles. A minimum distance between pile driving and concrete placement may be specified. Tests have indicated that vibrations from pile driving have no detrimental effect on fresh concrete,[55] and a criterion of one open pile between the driving and concreting operations is considered satisfactory. However, for practical reasons a minimum distance of 10 ft is often specified, or concreting is permitted for piles in groups adjacent to that being driven. Concrete should not be placed, however, until pile driving has progressed

Placing concrete in a pile shell.
(*Courtesy of Raymond International Builders, Inc.*)

beyond the heave range and all heaved piles have been properly reseated (see Section 5.30). Also, concrete should not be placed as long as relaxation is occurring (see Section 5.29).

Open piles should be kept covered until concreted to prevent debris from falling in, and the shell or casing should extend above ground level to prevent groundwater from entering. The pile casing or hole should be inspected just before it is filled with concrete, and it should be free of all foreign matter and contain not more than about 4 in (100 mm) of water unless tremie placing of concrete is permitted. Tests have indicated that more than 6 in (150 mm) of water in the bottom of a normal-size pile tends to wash out the cement paste, and uncemented coarse aggregate is left at the pile tip. Water can be drawn down to about 4 in with conventional equipment such as a bailing bucket. It is unnecessary and unreasonable to require that piles be mopped dry.

Concrete should be placed in each pile shell, casing, or hole without interruption. The partial filling of piles should be avoided unless the next truck-load is standing by. This requires knowing the concrete volumes necessary to fill the piles and keeping track of the piles filled out of each truckload or batch.

If it is necessary to interrupt the concreting process long enough so that the concrete could take its initial set or harden, steel dowels should be inserted in the top of the concreted portion of the pile. When concreting is resumed, all laitance should be removed, and the concrete surface should be flushed with neat fluid grout. For normal-size piles, this is virtually impossible to do if the concrete level is more than a few feet below the ground surface.

When concrete is discharged from the mixer, the concrete flow must not be restricted by a partially opened gate. Concrete chutes must be steep enough so that the concrete flows freely and does not have to be pushed or shoveled. If a hopper or concrete bucket is being used, concrete should not be discharged directly from the mixer into the hopper or bucket; it should be discharged into a funnel-type "downpipe" centered over the hopper or bucket. When discharged from the hopper or bucket, the concrete should be drawn off from the center.

The concreting procedure for cast-in-place piles is a critical part of the installation process, and therefore the inspector must be present during concreting operations and record the necessary information. Appendix D contains an example of a form (Figure D-21) that can be used for inspecting the concreting operation.

5.47.1 Concrete Volume.

The volume of concrete placed in each cast-in-place pile should be approximately equal to the theoretical volume of the pile. The inspector should have a record of the theoretical volumes. Tables C-3 to C-8 contain tabulated data on concrete volumes for different types of piles. Each day the volume of concrete delivered and placed should be checked against the theoretical volume for the linear footage of piles filled. Also, the pile footage filled by each truckload is a useful check. The amount of wasted concrete must be considered, and this can be estimated.

If the volume placed is less than the theoretical volume by more than about 10 percent, the cause should be investigated. Unless the volume of concrete is accurately measured as the concrete is discharged from the mixer, a true comparison cannot be made. This requires that the actual yield from the mixer trucks be determined periodically by emptying a truck into a hopper of known volume. It is important that the delivered volumes be accurate. If they are less than what was ordered or what is shown on the delivery ticket, the contractor is paying more than he should, and there is a good chance of piles being partially filled by the last truckload. If the delivered volumes are more than what was ordered or what is shown on the delivery ticket, the yield will not agree with theoretical volumes, and voids in the piles may be unfairly suspected.

5.47.2 Conventional Placement.

The mix design of concrete and the equipment and techniques used to place the concrete must be such as to prevent segregation. Concrete should be of the proper slump (see Section 3.3.9), and it should be deposited in a rapid, continuous pour through a steep-sided funnel centered at the top of the pile. The funnel must be supported off the pile in order to allow the displaced air in the pile to escape. The diameter of the discharge end of the funnel should not be larger than about 10 in (250 mm). When conventional concrete is used, about a pailful of flowable grout should be poured into the pile shell before concrete is placed. Pregrouting is not necessary when reduced-coarse-aggregate concrete is used.[113] The top 6 to 10 ft (2 to 3 m) of the concreted pile should be rodded. Mechanical vibration of concrete is unnecessary and could promote bleeding.

5.47.3 Tremie or Pumping Placement.   The tremie or pumping method[8] should be used for placing concrete through water. Concrete can be poured into the tremie tube or pumped through a pipe stinger. The bottom of the tremie should be closed with an expendable plug or a hinged flap valve before the tremie is lowered through the water. A movable plug can be inserted in the top of the pipe stinger just before concrete is pumped to prevent the concrete from coming in contact with water in the pipe. The tremie or pipe must be resting on the bottom of the shell, casing, or hole before concreting begins. It should then be raised only a few inches to start the flow of concrete and to ensure good contact between the concrete and the bottom of the casing or hole.

As the tremie or pipe is raised during concreting, it must be kept below the surface of the concrete in the pile. Before the tremie or pipe is withdrawn completely, sufficient concrete should be placed to displace all free water and watery concrete.

5.47.4 Bleeding.   Bleeding is evidenced by a collection of water and cement on top of the concrete after placement. Bleeding could also occur within the concrete, forming vertical holes or pipes in the concrete. It could be caused by excess water in the mix or by poorly graded aggregates. The amount of mixing water could be reduced by using a water-reducing admixture. If the quality of aggregates is the problem, corrective measures should be taken to improve the gradation.

5.47.5 Cold-Weather Concreting.   For concrete placed in pile shells, casings, or holes, cold weather is not as critical as it is for concrete placed in above-ground forms. However, suitable precautions should be taken (see Section 3.3.5), including obtaining accurate weather forecasts. The temperature of concrete as placed should not be less than about 45°F (7°C). Concrete should be discharged promptly upon delivery. The exposed portions of freshly poured cast-in-place concrete piles should be adequately protected from freezing. This can be done by covering them with salt hay or soil or, in extreme cases, by using tarps and heaters. After the concrete has set, the piles should be inspected for frost damage. Damaged portions must be repaired.

5.47.6 Hot-Weather Concreting. If the weather is extremely hot, special measures may be required to keep the concrete temperature down to acceptable limits during mixing and placing (see Section 3.3.6). The time between mixing and placing should be reduced to a minimum, and concrete must be placed promptly upon delivery. The temperature of the concrete as placed should be below 80°F (27°C) to avoid flash sets.

5.47.7 Concrete for Special Types of Piles. See Chapter 6 for other concreting requirements for special types of piles.

5.48 PILES OVERLOOKED

Before the pile rig is moved away, the inspector should check that all piles in the immediate area have been installed, including added and replacement piles.

5.49 EXTRA RIG MOVES

Deviations from the established pile installation sequence (see Section 5.3) result in out-of-sequence moves for the pile rig. Extra moves may also be needed to return to an area of work to drive replacement or overlooked piles or to move to any area to drive piles added to the scope of the work.

The contractor may be entitled to payment for extra or out-of-sequence moves or for additional work that is required to install added piles according to the terms of the contract. The inspector should record the times involved for all extra or out-of-sequence moves and identify in the record the rig involved and the reasons for such moves.

5.50 PILE-TO-CAP CONNECTIONS

The plans or specifications may require that the tops of piles be anchored into the pile caps. For steel piles, including pipe and Monotubes, this can be done by welding short dowels to the piles. For cast-in-place concrete without internal reinforcement, dowels can be embedded in the concrete at the pile butt. Internal reinforcement, if used, can be extended into the cap. However, if such pile-to-cap connections are required for uplift loads, reinforcing steel should extend the full length of cast-in-place concrete piles.

For timber piles, special fittings consisting of steel bars or straps can be bolted or otherwise fastened to the tops of the piles. For treated timber piles, all exposed steel, including bolts, must be galvanized, and all holes or other cuts must be treated with several applications of hot creosote oil followed by a seal coat of coal-tar pitch. In such cases, piles treated with a salt preservative should not be used because of potential corrosion of the metal fittings.[124]

For connections involving precast concrete piles, the piles could be made with the longitudinal or prestressing steel projecting the required length beyond the pile butt. For such piles, a special drive cap or follower is required to accommodate the steel extension. In other cases, it may be necessary to strip the concrete back from the top of the pile to expose a sufficient length of reinforcing steel or prestressing strand for the pile-to-cap connection or for attaching additional lengths of steel. The pile top has to be left a sufficient height above the cutoff grade, and stripping must be done carefully to avoid damage to the pile. To make the cap connection, the precast pile may also be cast with dowel holes at the top. Steel dowels are grouted into the holes after the pile has been driven.

5.51 PILES MOVED OFF LOCATION

After being installed, piles could be pushed off location by various types of construction activity or by general ground movements. Ground movements could be caused by heavy adjacent surcharge loads. Under soft-soil conditions, heavy construction equipment should not be permitted to operate immediately adjacent to piles. Excavations should not be made along one side of piles only without bracing the piles or the excavation bank. General ground movements could result from unstable slopes or from inadequately braced or tied sheeting. Heavy rains could cause ground loss or movement.

Pile shells not yet filled with concrete can sometimes be pulled back into position. If concrete has already been placed in pile shells, or if uncased cast-in-place concrete piles are being used, piles that have been pushed off location should be inspected for breaks. If the piles cannot be inspected properly or repaired satisfactorily, they should be rejected and replaced.

If timber piles, precast concrete piles, or steel piles are pushed off location, they should be inspected for breaks or severe bends. It may be necessary to excavate alongside piles. If a pile can be pulled back into position, the force applied to the pile should be limited to avoid breaking the pile. This is especially true where there is a long moment arm, such as in marine construction.

5.52 HIGH-CUTOFF PILES

If after installation and cutoff a portion of an unreinforced shell-type concrete pile extends more than about 5 ft ($1\frac{1}{2}$ m) above the adjacent ground surface, the unsupported length may have to be braced or stay-lathed until backfill operations have been completed or until the pile has been incorporated into the structure. Otherwise, the pile should be protected from accidental impact by barricades. This may be especially critical for batter piles.

Backfilling around high-cutoff piles must be done carefully, and preferably by hand. Construction equipment must not be allowed to hit the piles, and the backfill should be placed in uniform lifts around the piles to avoid lateral loading.

5.53 EXCAVATING OVERBURDEN

If piles have been installed through overburden, the excavation to the pile cutoff grade must be done carefully so that the piles are not damaged. Hand excavation is recommended.

5.54 INTEGRITY TESTING

Various methods for determining the structural integrity of an installed pile have been proposed and discussed.[77,106,118,119] These methods include extraction, excavation, exploratory boring and drilling, dynamic response, and compression testing. Other methods such as the use of closed-circuit television and radiometry require advance preparation during pile installation. Some of these methods, such as pile extraction or deep excavation, may not be totally "nondestructive" or practical or possible.

The sonic[118] and dynamic response[106] methods are based on measuring (or observing on an oscilloscope) the time it takes for a reflected compression stress wave to return to the top of the pile. Some waves will be reflected by a discontinuity in the pile shaft. When the stress wave velocity is known for the pile material involved, the depth to the discontinuity can be determined.

Not all testing methods are applicable to all types of piles, and frequently anomalous results are obtained which are subject to alternative interpretations. For example, an irregular pile shape such as the combination of steps (drive rings) and corrugations in Step-Taper piles may result in misinterpretation of the test results.[118]

Integrity testing is rarely specified in the contract. It is not a routine procedure conducted on many jobs. It may be required by the engineer after the job gets under way if the structural quality of some installed piles is suspect or the contractor's methods are questionable. Such testing is usually conducted by a specialist.

Integrity testing can create problems. For example, there is the cost of the testing, as well as delays caused by the testing and the causes of defects. Also, there is the cost of replacing piles if they are found to be defective. It may be very difficult to determine the responsibilities for the costs involved in and resulting from such testing. Problems also arise in the interpretation of the test results and the seriousness of any "defects" considered to be found. All this may lead to litigation involving further costs. The need for integrity testing can often be avoided by selecting a suitable pile for the soil conditions and loading requirements and by thoroughly inspecting the piles during installation. If integrity testing is contemplated, consideration must be given to the limitations of the various methods and the possible need for further investigations to check the results of such testing.

5.55 REJECTED PILES

Sometimes piles that are initially rejected because of nonconformance with the plans and specifications can be salvaged and accepted if satisfactory remedial measures are taken or if repairs are made subject to the approval of the engineer. Rejected piles are either abandoned and replaced or withdrawn and replaced. The specifications may require that abandoned piles be cut off below the ground surface and that pile shells, casings, or holes be filled with concrete or sand. The contract documents will indicate the financial responsibility for rejected piles. This will depend on the cause for rejection. For example, if obstructions are the cause, the contractor is generally reimbursed for the rejected piles as well as for any replacement piles or associated work.

5.56 REPLACEMENT PILES

The need for and location of replacement piles should be determined without delay so that these piles may be installed while the pile rig is close by and has access to the required pile locations. The designation of each acceptable replacement pile will be the same as for the original pile it replaces except that a letter suffix will be added, such as A, B, or C. The inspector must record all appropriate data for each replacement pile, and such piles must be shown on the original pile location plan and on any as-built plans. Payment for replacement piles will depend on the contract terms. For example, if they replace piles rejected because of obstructions, the contractor may be reimbursed for all such piles. If they replace a pile rejected for reasons under the contractor's control, the contractor may be paid for one equivalent replacement pile.

5.57 PILE LENGTHS

The inspector must be familiar with the contract payment terms for pile lengths. Payment could be for furnished lengths or for installed lengths or for both at different prices. The furnished lengths could be the approved lengths ordered and delivered to the job or the lengths raised in the leaders. Some type of payment may be made for pile lengths installed through overburden from the ground surface to the pile cutoff elevation.

The inspector must record whatever pile lengths are necessary to determine pay quantities, but regardless of contract terms, the pile lengths as installed from pile tip to cutoff must be recorded. If pile tip and butt elevations are recorded, they should be referenced to an established permanent datum which is identified.

For pipe, Monotube, or shell piles the installed lengths can be measured by lowering the weighted end of a steel tape inside the piles after they have been driven and cut off to grade and before concrete is placed. A cloth tape should not be used because of stretch. The thickness of the closure plate should be added to the actual measurement. For timber piles, precast concrete piles, and steel H piles, the installed length of a pile can be determined by measuring the length driven and subtracting the cutoff length. The driven length will include all lengths added in the leaders. For measuring the installed lengths of special types of piles, see Chapter 6.

5.58 PAY QUANTITIES AND METHODS

The inspector may have to record or verify the quantities of pay items. Payment for the piles could be by lump sum, principal sum with adjustment prices, unit price, or a combination of these methods. In addition, separate payment may be made for other items of work. The inspector should be familiar with the contract terms and conditions relating to payments.

Payment for piles could be on the basis of furnished lengths or installed lengths or both. Installed lengths could be from the tip to the cutoff elevation or, in the case of installing piles through overburden, to the adjacent ground surface elevation. The latter case applies only to piles that are temporarily cut off at the ground surface. It does not apply to piles driven below the ground surface with a follower or to types of uncased cast-in-place concrete piles normally installed through overburden, such as auger-grout piles (see Section 6.2.9). For cased cast-in-place concrete piles that are driven through overburden and for which payment is made for the length from the pile tip to the ground surface, the concrete is generally placed to the actual cutoff grade, and a credit is applied for the concrete omitted through the overburden at a stated unit price. Usually no extra payment is made for withdrawn, rejected, or abandoned piles, for pile splicing, or for cutting off piles. The normal exception is for piles rejected because of obstructions. Pile buildups may be included in the total pile footage installed.

If pile materials are paid for on the basis of full ordered and furnished lengths, the waste piling actually becomes the property of the owner. The contract documents may require that the contractor dispose of this material, and if it has any salvage value, the approximate quantities should be recorded and proper credits given to the owner.

5.58.1 Lump-Sum Method.   If the contract specifies a lump-sum payment, it is only necessary to verify that all work has been completed in accordance with the plans and specifications or subsequent revisions. Revisions should be covered by change orders. If additional work is performed under a work order, the satisfactory completion of such work should be verified.

5.58.2 Principal-Sum Method.   With this method, a principal sum is quoted (1) for a specified number of piles having a stated total base aggregate length or (2) for a specified number of piles having a stated base individual length or (3) for a combination of (1) and (2). Unit prices may be quoted for added or omitted (credit) piles or for added or omitted (credit) pile footage resulting from piles being driven longer or shorter than specified or for both piles and footage.

For final payment, the principal sum is adjusted on the basis of added or omitted piles and increases or decreases in pile lengths. The methods of adjustment may involve the base aggregate length, and adjustments may be made on individual pile lengths. Adjustments to the principal sum will be either plus or minus depending upon whether they represent added or omitted work. The method of payment and therefore the method for adjusting the principal sum on the basis of pile quantities installed, as set forth in the contract, should be thoroughly understood so that information that is needed to make the necessary payment computations can be properly recorded and certified. The examples in Appendix E illustrate the application of the principal-sum method.

5.58.3 Unit-Price Method.   All piling may be paid for on the basis of unit prices. Sometimes the furnishing of pile materials and the installation of piles are paid for under separate unit prices. Payment for furnishing piles may be made for the full lengths ordered and delivered to the jobsite or for the length of each pile raised in the leaders. Ordered lengths are generally subjected to the approval of the engineer. The furnished pile lengths as well as the installed lengths must be recorded accurately.

5.58.4 Combination Method.   Sometimes the lump-sum method is combined with either the principal-sum method or the unit-price method. For example, the mobilization and demobilization of the pile installation equipment and the contractor's spread may be paid for on a lump-sum basis, with payment for piles on either a principal-sum or unit-price basis.

5.58.5 Other Pay Items.   Other items of work relating to pile installation are frequently paid for on a unit basis. Included are those items which may or may not be required. For required items, the extent of the work may not be known in advance. Examples are as follows:

Load Testing: Per test (for a stated total load)
Reinforcing Steel: Per pound
Preexcavation (Drill or Jet): Per foot or per pile
Overburden Footage: Per foot
Retapping Piles: Per pile or per rig hour
Use of Casing (Drilled Piles): Per foot
Extra Grout (Auger-Grout Piles): Per cubic yard
Extra Moves: Per rig hour
Cribbing: Per rig hour
Delays Caused by Others: Per rig hour or day

Some of the above items may be included in the lump sum or principal sum as stated in the contract, in which case unit prices would apply to additional such work. Frequently more than one load test is required, and if some load testing is not included in the base price, a separate unit price will be quoted for the initial test to cover general mobilization of testing equipment and materials.

The inspector must keep accurate records of other work that is performed in connection with pile installation and that is to be paid for separately.

5.58.6 Force-Account Work. When the contractor is authorized to perform work on a force-account basis, he is usually reimbursed for all labor, material, and equipment involved in such work, with appropriate factors for small tools, payroll costs, overhead, and profit. For force-account work, the inspector should verify that the work was performed and also the quantity and type of labor furnished (including supervision), the type of equipment used, the quantities and types of materials used, and the time involved in such work.

5.59 PILE CAPS

Pile installation will generally be considered complete when the piles are capped or otherwise incorporated into the structure. Properly designed and constructed pile caps are necessary for the satisfactory performance of the pile foundation.

5.59.1 Cap Excavation. Pile cap excavations must be to the required depth and lateral dimensions to provide for the required embedment of pile butts and specified edge distances. The excavation should be free of groundwater, and the bottom of the excavation should be level and clear of all loose material. If the soil at the bottom is very soft, a working mat should be installed. This base course could consist of about 4 in (100 mm) of lean concrete or about 6 in (150 mm) of compacted cinders or well-graded gravel or crushed rock. The base course is not considered a part of the pile cap, and if it is installed, the excavation level should be lowered accordingly. The size or shape of pile caps may be revised from that shown on the plans if redesigns are required because of added piles or other field conditions.

5.59.2 Pile Butts.   Pile butts must extend the required embedment length above the bottom of the excavation or top of the base course. The top and sides of all pile butts must be clean and free of all dirt and other foreign matter. The plans or specifications may require some type of pile-to-cap connection (see Section 5.50).

5.59.3 Forms.   Forms must be sufficiently tight to prevent the leakage of mortar, and they must be properly constructed and braced so as to retain the wet concrete without distortion. Shapes, positions, dimensions, and edge distances to piles should be checked for conformance with the plans or subsequent revisions. Subject to the approval of the engineer or if permitted by the specifications, side forms may be of soil provided it will stand without caving in and the sides of the bank are cut neat to the minimum required dimensions. Proper provisions must be made for the accurate positioning and support of anchor bolts.

5.59.4 Reinforcing Steel.   Reinforcing steel should be of the specified type and size. It should be positioned and spaced according to the plans or subsequent redesigns and supported on metal or plastic chairs or small concrete blocks. All steel must be clean and free from dirt, rust scale, loose mill scale, oil, grease, and any other coating which could affect the bond. Reinforcing should have a minimum concrete cover of 3 in (75 mm) or as may be specified.

5.59.5 Concrete.   All concrete must be in accordance with the specifications regarding type, strength, ingredients, and slump. See Sections 3.3 and 5.47 for applicable control provisions. For example, the coarse aggregate will be larger and the slump lower than those used for concrete for cast-in-place piles. Forms or excavations should not contain free water, and concrete should be spread and compacted with vibrators unless a superplasticized concrete is permitted.[83] If soil is used for the sides of the form, all precautions must be taken to prevent caving of the soil during concrete placement. Anchor bolts or other embedments as called for on the drawings should be placed in accurate positions as concrete is poured or immediately thereafter.

5.59.6 Curing.   Until it has cured, concrete should be protected from extreme heat or cold. Precautions must be taken to prevent a rapid loss of moisture from the concrete during the curing period. Completed caps should be kept wet for at least 10 days after the placement of concrete. Wind could have a substantial drying effect. The concrete could be protected by windbreaks or covers if necessary.

5.59.7 Payment.   Generally, the construction of pile caps is not done by the pile contractor. However, if such work is included in the pile contract, the inspector should verify that all pile caps were completed according to plans and specifications or subsequent redesigns. Pile caps may be paid for on a unit basis per cubic yard, or separate unit prices may apply to such things as excavation, formwork, reinforcement, and concrete. Depending upon contract payment provisions, the inspector should keep accurate records of the appropriate quantities involved. If pile caps are redesigned, the required additional quantities should be recorded separately.

5.60 RECORDS

Chapters 2 and 3 and the foregoing sections suggest a considerable amount of data that can be recorded for pile installation. Chapters 6 and 7 will suggest additional data. The types and amounts of data to be recorded will depend on the extent of inspection and engineering control deemed necessary to ensure that a pile foundation is constructed that performs as designed for the expected life of the structure and to establish a complete record of the job.

Attention is directed to the several comprehensive pile summary report forms shown in Appendix D. Some type of system should be established for preparing an orderly and complete record of pile installation. With such records, the final disposition or status of all piles is determined, including that of original contract piles, rejected piles, replacement piles, and added or deleted piles. Such records are necessary for determining progress and final payment quantities. In addition to accounting for all piles by means of summary records, it is advisable to keep a current record on the piling plans as to pile installation progress. With appropriate symbols, the status of all piles can be followed, and areas that can be released for subsequent construction can be clearly defined.

Although Appendix D contains examples of various types of inspection forms which can be used as a guide, it is recommended that inspection forms be designed for the specific inspection requirements for the project involved.

6

Special Types of Piles

Chapter 5 dealt with the engineering considerations generally associated with the installation of conventional types of piles. Some types of piles require special considerations primarily because of the methods used to install them. Some of what has been covered in Chapter 5 applies to almost all types of piles, including the special piles discussed in this chapter. The engineer should determine what considerations in Chapter 5 are applicable to these special piles.

Special types of piles include the drilled-hole pile, the auger-grout pile, the cast-in-situ pile, the pressure injected footing, and the enlarged-tip pile. The installation process for each of these was described in Chapter 2. There are many other special types of piles, but they are not commonly used in the United States.[75,120] The inspector should be familiar with the inspection requirements associated with the piles covered in this chapter.

The installation process for some of the following described special types of piles does not provide for a dynamic measurement of penetration resistance. Such measurements reveal variations in subsoil conditions as piles are driven and permit each pile to be installed to the required capacity regardless of such variations. Therefore, for piles not having that capability, more closely spaced test borings may be required to define adequately the vertical position, thickness, and competence of the bearing strata.

6.1 DRILLED-HOLE PILE

6.1.1 Subsurface Investigation. Subsoil information is needed not only for design purposes but also to determine which installation method and equipment can or must be used. Normal-size test borings and samples may not be sufficient. It may be advisable to drill some large-diameter test holes to deter-

146

mine actual conditions. The vertical positions and thicknesses of both unstable and impervious strata must be known. Enlarged bases (underreams) can be formed only in cohesive soils. A knowledge of groundwater conditions, such as the position of the water table, the permeability of water-bearing strata, and artesian conditions, is critical.

6.1.2 Required Dimensions.   The required shaft diameter will be specified. If a casing is to be used, its specified diameter will be greater than the required shaft diameter. If it is necessary to drill through the casing, the controlling diameter will be that of the smallest auger or bit to be used. If the shafts are to be underreamed, the diameter and possibly the height of the enlarged bases will be specified. Generally the bottom diameter of the base is less than about 3 times the shaft diameter. The slope of the roof of the underream may be specified instead of the height.

6.1.3 Required Lengths.   The required elevation of the bottom of the hole may be specified individually or for each area of similar subsoil conditions. For the latter, the area boundaries should be indicated on the plans. As the work progresses, the inspector should log the material removed during excavation and be alert to any changes in the drilling operation which may indicate subsoil conditions other than those anticipated, such as changes in the rate of advance of the drill or changes in the type or consistency of the soil cuttings. Any observed changes should be investigated in case pile lengths may have to be adjusted.

If the drilled hole is large enough and free of water, and providing a temporary steel liner is inserted, the soil at the bottom of the hole can be inspected or tested for adequacy. In other cases, a test boring can be made within the drilled hole and soil or rock samples recovered. Such test borings can reveal if the bearing stratum is of adequate thickness and capacity.

6.1.4 Unstable Soils.   If the hole is to be drilled through unstable soil such as soft clay, soft silt, peat, water-bearing sand, or loose granular soil, it will be necessary to install a steel casing through the zones of unstable soils and/or use a drilling mud slurry to maintain the hole. For water-bearing loose soils, the casing should be advanced ahead of the drill bit or auger to avoid overbreaks and having water-filled pockets behind the casing. In such cases, when the casing is withdrawn, the entrapped water can cause the concrete to slough off and thus expose the reinforcement or reduce the cross section of the pile (necking).[117] If the soil is extremely soft, the steel casing should not be removed.

6.1.5 Excavation.   The method used to construct the drilled-hole pile will depend on the subsoil conditions.[74,107,122] Holes must be drilled to the required diameter and depth. Drilling will usually be done with a short-flight auger or bucket drill. If soil conditions permit using the dry method, the excavation procedure is routine.

If the casing method is used, a slurry may be required during drilling through the unstable soils to maintain the hole until the casing can be set in place. Sometimes any cohesive soil being drilled may form a natural slurry with the groundwater or added water. However, there is very little control over this type of slurry, and in most cases, a bentonite-type drilling mud is used. The casing may be set with a vibratory driver and should extend into an impervious stratum so that the bottom is sealed off. Generally the slurry is removed from within the casing with some type of bailing bucket before drilling is continued with a smaller-diameter drill that will pass through the casing. However, some slurry is usually trapped behind the casing. If there is no impervious stratum, the slurry displacement method should be used. When drilling is done through the slurry, the auger or bit should permit the slurry to flow through as the drill is raised. Otherwise a vacuum may be formed below the drill, and this may permit the soil to slough off into the hole.

6.1.6 Groundwater Control.   If groundwater is permitted to enter the hole, either through the side or from the bottom, the rate of flow may be such as to cause soil erosion, which can result in contamination of the concrete, or the collection of unsatisfactory bearing material in the bottom of the hole, or loss of the bearing capacity of the soil at the bottom of the hole. In extreme cases, such conditions could preclude drilling the hole to the required depth. Temporary or permanent steel liners should be inserted, and if necessary, the hole should be filled with water or slurry to balance the hydrostatic head.

If an artesian aquifer is encountered, the water pressure may be such as to prevent the drilling of the holes or the proper placement of concrete. Under such conditions, the drilling of relief wells may provide a solution.

6.1.7 Use of Slurry.   Drilling mud can be premixed or mixed in the holes as the work progresses. The slurry must be of sufficient density and specific gravity to offset hydrostatic and lateral soil pressures and to maintain the hole. The shear-strength characteristics of the slurry, its viscosity, and its density may be specified and should be controlled to obtain optimum conditions for the displacement of the slurry during the concreting process. Tests to determine the density, viscosity, shear strength, and pH should be carried out initially until a suitable mix has been established. The FPS* specification recommends a density of less than 68.6 lb/ft^3 (1.10 g/ml) according to a mud density balance test, a viscosity of from 30 to 90 s according to the Marsh

*Federation of Piling Specialists, London, England.

Funnel* test, a shear strength of from 0.03 to 0.20 lbf/ft^2 (1.4 to 10 N/m^2) according to a shearometer test, and a pH of from 9.5 to 12.

All reasonable steps should be taken to prevent contamination of the slurry. Discarded slurry which has been pumped or displaced from a drilled hole should be removed from the site. If slurry is to be reused, the quality should be checked periodically to ensure conformance with the specifications.

6.1.8 Cleaning the Hole Bottoms. After drilling has been done to the required depths, the bottoms of the holes should be cleaned of loose material as may be specified. A cleanout bucket should be used. If a hole is to be underreamed, the underreaming tool should not be permitted to ride up while underreaming is being done. A small amount of loose material at the bottom of the hole is not considered detrimental.

6.1.9 Inspection of Bottom. If it is necessary to enter the hole for direct inspection of the bearing material or conditions at the bottom of the hole, the hole must be a minimum of 2 ft (0.75 m) in diameter, and a full-length steel casing must be inserted. All safety precautions must be taken, such as ensuring that the hole is free of noxious gas and has an adequate fresh-air supply, controlling groundwater, maintaining adequate methods of communication, furnishing lifelines and adequate hoisting equipment, and having support personnel in attendance at the top of the hole at all times. A hole can be purged of gas and supplied with fresh air by pumping air through hoses extending to the bottom of the hole.

6.1.10 Reinforcing Steel. Reinforcing steel should be fabricated and placed in accordance with Section 5.46. When the casing method is used, the reinforcing cage will extend to the bottom of the hole. Generally no extra reinforcement is placed in the underream. For the dry and slurry displacement methods, the steel cage may extend only through the upper portion of the hole. For the dry method, the steel cage is placed after the concrete has been placed to about the bottom elevation of the cage. For the slurry displacement method, the cage should not be permitted to rise as the slurry is displaced by the concrete.

When the casing method is used, the inspector should check the elevation of the top of the cage before and after concrete has been placed to determine if the cage has moved up or down. An upward movement would indicate that the concrete (and cage) was raised up during withdrawal of the casing. This could have caused a defect such as a void, soil inclusions, or a necking down of the shaft, and the possibility should be investigated. This could be done by

*Standard RP 13B, American Petroleum Institute, Washington, D.C., April 1980.

coring the shaft or by using nondestructive methods such as ultrasonic pulse testing (see Section 5.54). Reductions in cross-sectional areas are difficult to determine. A downward movement may indicate that the steel has buckled or that splices have slipped because of the weight of the fluid concrete as it moves down around the steel during withdrawal of the casing.

6.1.11 Placing Concrete.   After excavation, the holes should be filled with concrete without delay. A relatively large quantity of concrete may be involved for each hole, and scheduled deliveries must be sufficient to avoid cold joints. The inspector should note the time it takes to make each pour, and when the weather is hot, he should monitor the air and concrete temperatures (see Sections 3.3.6 and 5.47.6). Slump loss could occur with time or high temperatures.

For concrete placed by conventional methods into a dry, unlined hole without reinforcement or with widely spaced reinforcement and with no underream, the slump should be from 4 to 6 in (100 to 150 mm). If the drilled hole contains closely spaced reinforcement, or if there is an underream, or if a temporary liner is used, the concrete slump should be from 5 to 7 in (125 to 175 mm). If concrete is to be placed by tremie or pumping to displace drilling mud, the slump should be from 6 to 8 in (150 to 200 mm).

For the dry or casing method, and providing the hole can be dewatered, concrete may be placed by conventional methods (see Section 5.47.2). Concrete must be deposited vertically in the center of the hole through a funnel hopper or an elephant trunk so that it does not hit the side of the hole or the reinforcement. The chuting of concrete directly into the hole must be prohibited. For holes which are deeper than about 20 ft (6 m) or which extend through soils that could slough off during concrete placement, a temporary steel liner or casing should be inserted before concrete is deposited. A liner may also be required to seal off the flow of water, for that could affect the quality of the concrete.

If the casing method is used, the hole should be completely filled with concrete before the casing is withdrawn. Sufficient concrete must be placed in the casing, and extra casing lengths should be used if necessary, to completely fill the hole to the ground surface, including the space occupied by the casing, or the top of the hole must be protected with a steel liner. The concrete must have sufficient head to displace all the slurry that may be trapped behind the casing.

For the slurry displacement method or when concrete is to be placed through water, the tremie or pumping method must be used (see Section 5.47.3). The pour must be started slowly so that the entire bottom of the hole is filled before the tremie or pipe stinger is raised. The concrete must displace all the slurry, and sufficient concrete should be placed to also displace all watery and poor-quality concrete.

In cold weather, pile tops must be protected from freezing in accordance with Section 5.47.5. See Section 5.47 for other concreting requirements, including checking on concrete volumes. Due to drilling irregularities, the actual concrete volume per pile could be greater than the theoretical volume by about 10 to 15 percent. Table C-7 shows the volumes to be expected.

6.1.12 Withdrawing the Casing.   The steel casing or liner should be withdrawn with a vibratory extractor to reduce the possibility of concrete arching in the casing. After each use, the steel casing should be thoroughly cleaned of all concrete to prevent a buildup of hardened concrete, for this buildup could contribute to arching and cause the fresh concrete to be lifted with the casing.

6.1.13 Casing Left in Place.   Steel casings or liners should be left in place through zones of extremely soft soils or to protect the integrity of the concrete shaft.

6.1.14 Finishing Pile Tops.   Drilled holes will generally be filled with concrete to some distance above the specified cutoff grade, and then the piles will be trimmed back to grade. All laitance must be removed. The top of each pile should be protected from contamination by surface water and loose soils through the use of a steel sleeve placed before the concreting operation.

6.1.15 Drop in Concrete Level.   If the level of concrete in the pile shaft drops after the concreting operation is completed, the cause may be the fresh concrete pushing into very soft surrounding soils under its own weight. This can be prevented by leaving a steel liner in place. Before concrete is added to bring the pile to the required cutoff grade, and if the concrete has started to set, reinforcing steel dowels should be inserted in the top of the pile, and all laitance and contaminated concrete should be removed.

6.1.16 Installation Sequence.   When piles are to be installed through soft soils, and especially if steel liners or casings are not left in place, it may be necessary to install the piles in a staggered sequence to permit the concrete in completed piles to set up before adjacent piles are drilled. Otherwise, the weight of unset concrete may be sufficient to allow the concrete to break through the wall of soft soil between the completed pile and that being drilled.

6.1.17 Records.   The dimensions and installed lengths of all drilled-hole piles should be recorded, and the elevations of the tops of piles should be recorded and referenced to a permanent, fixed datum. For the dry method and possibly for the casing method, pile lengths can be determined by measuring, with a steel tape, the depth of the hole from a fixed reference and deducting the distance down to the cutoff grade. For the slurry displacement method, it may be necessary to determine pile lengths from the depth drilled as measured by marks on the drill stem (see Section 6.2.13). The inspector should record the lengths of the drill stems being used. This system can be used for all installation methods. In addition, the volume of concrete used for each pile should be recorded.

6.2 AUGER-GROUT PILE

6.2.1 Required Lengths.   Required pile lengths may be specified for each area of similar subsoil conditions. However, additional subsoil data may be required to define the bearing strata and establish pile lengths. Subsurface conditions could change radically within very short distances, and the inspector should be alert to any changes in the drilling operation which may indicate different subsoil conditions, such as changes in the torque required to drill, changes in the rate of advance of the auger, or changes in the type or consistency of soil cuttings. During drilling, the auger flights are kept full, and therefore the soil cuttings observed at the ground surface are not indicative of the soils which the lower portion of the auger is penetrating. Therefore, the observation of soil cuttings gives, at best, a rough estimate of subsoil conditions. Any observed changes should be investigated as to cause in case pile lengths may have to be adjusted.

6.2.2 Equipment.   The auger flights should be continuous from top to bottom, with no gaps or other breaks. The discharge hole at the bottom of the

Installing Augercast piles. (*Courtesy of Lee Turzillo Contracting Company.*)

auger should be below the bar containing the cutting teeth. Augers over 40 ft (12 m) long should be laterally supported by intermediate movable guides spaced a maximum of 20 ft (6 m) apart.

The mortar pump should be a positive-displacement piston-type pump capable of developing pressures at the auger tip during grout pumping greater than any hydrostatic pressure or lateral soil pressure at rest. A pressure gauge should be mounted in the grout line as close to the auger head as practical. Some means must be provided for monitoring the discharge volume of the grout pump. This could be a metering device at the pump discharge end, or the volume discharged per pump stroke could be determined and the number of strokes counted. The volume per stroke can be determined if the cross-sectional area of the pump cylinder is known and the stroke is measured. A stroke counter can be mounted on the pump.

The grout pump may be calibrated by determining the number of strokes necessary to fill a box of known volume. For such a calibration to be accurate, the grout pumped into each pile must be of the same consistency, and the pump must be operated at the same speed and stroke as for the calibration. If the theoretical volume of the pile is known, the pump calibration can be converted into the number of pump strokes required to fill each linear foot of pile. Grout volume in the hose lines and auger must be considered.

6.2.3 Grout. The grout mix and consistency may be specified or submitted by the contractor for the engineer's approval. This includes admixtures used to improve the pumpability of the grout and to retard its set. The inspector should be furnished with a copy of such approved submittals.

The grout consistency for each batch or truckload of grout should be checked periodically by the flow cone test according to specification CRD C-79.* Strengths should be determined from cube tests in accordance with ASTM C 91[30] and ASTM C 109.[32]

The grout should be of the proper consistency to be pumped, yet not too fluid. If the water-cement ratio is less than about 4.5, the grout mix is too dry. If the grout splashes when poured into a container of grout, or if, when flowing down a chute, the mix gets a glossy sheen (sand grains disappear below the water and cement surface), the grout is too wet.

6.2.4 Drilling. When drilling is done to the required depth, the auger should be advanced continuously at a rate which will prevent the removal of excess soil. If the auger is advancing too slowly or rotation is continued without advancement, the removal of excess soil could have a detrimental effect on adjacent structures or piles. After the required depth is reached, rotation of

---

*CRD C-79, *Test Method for Flow of Grout Mixtures* (flow cone test), U.S. Corps of Engineers, Waterway Experiment Station, Vicksburg, Miss., December 1977.

the auger should practically stop. Auger flights full of soil assist in maintaining the hole and subsequent pumping pressures and help prevent the removal of excess soil.

6.2.5 Pumping Grout.

At the start of grout pumping, the auger should be raised from 6 to 12 in (150 to 300 mm), and after grout pressure has built up, indicating the discharge of grout, the auger should be redrilled to the original depth before the pile is formed. A positive pressure must be maintained during grout pumping. To ensure a properly filled, full-size hole, the pumping pressure, considering all line losses, should be greater than any hydrostatic or lateral soil pressures in the hole. However, when auger-grout piles are installed in very soft soils, excessively high pumping pressures should be avoided. Such pressures could cause upward or lateral movement of unset adjacent piles. Under such conditions, it is advisable to install piles in a staggered sequence. Pumping pressures are normally reduced during final withdrawal of the auger.

6.2.6 Withdrawing the Auger.

During the pumping of grout to form the pile, the auger should be withdrawn in a smooth, continuous motion and not in jerks or lifts. A three- or four-part lift line is recommended. The auger may turn very slowly in the direction of advance during withdrawal, but in no case should a counterrotation be permitted. The rate of withdrawal should be such that a positive pressure is maintained in the grout line at all times. Unless these precautions are taken, necking down or discontinuities of the grout shaft could occur, or soil inclusions could build up in the grout column unless the soil is sufficiently stiff to maintain the hole.

6.2.7 Interruptions and Pressure Drops.

The formation of each pile should be a continuous, uninterrupted operation once grouting has started. If the grouting process is interrupted or the grouting pressure drops below acceptable levels, the auger should be redrilled to the original tip elevation and the pile re-formed.

6.2.8 Volume of Grout.

The volume of grout placed in each pile could be 10 to 20 percent greater than the theoretical volume of the hole created by the auger. The normal wobble of the auger will create a hole larger that the auger diameter. The determination of the volume of grout placed in the pile should not start until the grout pressure peaks. Table C-7 contains data on grout volumes.

If the grout take (the amount actually pumped into the pile) is less than the theoretical amount, the pile should be rejected and replaced, and the cause should be investigated. If a considerable excess of grout is pumped, the cause should be investigated. It may be due to very soft soils and excessive pumping pressures or the grout flowing into fissures, crevices, or solution channels and cavities in limestone formations. Grout may also be lost in underground structures such as sewer lines. The injection of excess grout may be totally wasteful or damaging to underground or adjacent structures.

Each day, the volume of grout delivered and placed should be checked against the theoretical volume for the linear footage of piles installed. Also, the pile footage filled by each truckload is another useful check. The quantity of grout wasted or spilled must be estimated. For a realistic comparison, the actual yield from the mixer trucks must be determined by periodically emptying a truckload of grout into a hopper of known volume.

6.2.9 Forming Pile Butts. To properly form and protect the pile butt, it is necessary to place a steel sleeve at the top of the pile before that portion of the pile is grouted and the auger is removed. The steel sleeve should extend from the pile cutoff grade or ground surface, whichever is higher, to a point not less than 1 ft (0.3 m) below the pile cutoff grade or ground surface, whichever is lower, and it should be left in place until the grout has hardened. If a steel sleeve is not used, the ground surface adjacent to the pile should be at least 1 ft (0.3 m) higher than the pile cutoff grade, and the hole should be filled with grout to the ground surface. Excess grout should be pumped to displace as much potential laitance as possible.

After the auger is removed, the grout can be dipped out down to the cutoff level. A screen-type dipper should be lowered about 3 ft (1 m) into the fresh grout to screen out any soil clods that may have sloughed off the sides of the hole or dropped off the auger as it came out.

6.2.10 Placing Reinforcing Steel

6.2.10.1 Steel to Resist Bending. Reinforcing steel required to resist bending should not be placed by being pushed down in the grout column if the embedded length of the steel is greater than about 10 ft (3 m). Reinforcing steel must be fabricated into cages with sufficient spacers or spiders to keep the steel properly located within the grout column. The insertion of individual bars should be prohibited. Steel should not be placed after the grout has taken an initial set.

If the required embedment length is longer than about 10 ft (3 m), longitudinal steel should extend the full length of the pile and be placed through special ducts running through the auger flights before the grouting operation begins. The auger must be restrained from rotating during withdrawal, and the steel must be prevented from coming up with the auger as it is withdrawn.

6.2.10.2 Steel to Resist Tension. Reinforcing steel required to resist uplift forces should be full-length. It may be placed through the hollow auger stem before grouting starts, or it may be pushed down the center of the grout column provided (1) the pile is at least 16 in (400 mm) in diameter, (2) the grout is still quite fluid, (3) it (the steel) consists of a single bar or a bundle of bars, (4) it is carefully centered, (5) it is not bent or permitted to bend, and (6) it can be pushed to the bottom of the grout column. If placed through the hollow stem, the steel should be prevented from coming up with the auger. Often, a single high-strength steel bar can be used.

6.2.11 Drop in Grout Level.   Completed piles which are still unset should be checked periodically during and after the installation of adjacent piles to see if the grout level is maintained. If any drop in grout level occurs in a completed pile during the drilling of adjacent piles, the completed pile should be re-jected and replaced. If the grout level subsides when no adjacent piles are being installed, it may be because the fluid grout is pushing out into soft soils. The cause of subsidence should be investigated by means of a test boring. The extent of pile damage should also be investigated. This can be done by core-drilling the pile shaft to a practical depth, by excavating around the pile, or by pulling the pile. If the grout level drops and the pile is salvageable, precau-tions should be taken to prevent contamination of grout at the top of the pile resulting from surface water or sloughing soils. Before additional grout or concrete is placed to bring the butts of satisfactory piles to grade, all laitance and contaminated grout should be removed, and steel dowels should be used at the joint. If the grout has set, it would be preferable to increase the depth of the pile cap rather than build up the pile.

6.2.12 Protecting Pile Butts.   In cold weather, pile butts must be protected from freezing in accordance with Section 5.47.5. Pile butts should be pro-tected from contamination until the grout has set.

6.2.13 Installed Lengths.   The installed length of each auger-grout pile can be determined by knowing the total length of the auger used and observing the depth or elevation to which the auger tip is drilled before grouting starts. It may be convenient to have the leaders marked off in 1-ft (0.5-m) incre-ments, with an index mark on the top sliding drill guide to measure auger penetration. Depths or elevations should be referenced to a fixed datum. Pile lengths can be calculated from tip and specified butt elevations or distances to the tip and butt from a fixed reference.

6.2.14 Payment Quantities.   Auger-grout piles should be paid for in accor-dance with Section 5.57. If grout is placed above the cutoff grade, generally no extra payment should be made for pile lengths above cutoff or for trim-ming pile tops back to the cutoff grade. The contract may provide otherwise.

The contract may provide for payment per cubic yard for the volume of grout pumped in excess of the theoretical volume of the piles. The normal grout quantities that are placed are included in the price for the piles. In such cases, grout-metering devices must be accurate, and the inspector must keep records of the actual volume of grout pumped. Waste grout resulting from spillage or excess pumping once the pile hole is filled should not be included in this pay item.

6.2.15 Records.   Special forms will be required for logging auger-grout piles and recording required data. Data to be recorded include the depths to which the auger is drilled for each pile, the grout volumes pumped, the grouting pressures, the type of reinforcing steel used, and the method used to place the steel. Drilled depths should be referenced to a fixed elevation datum. A record of the theoretical versus actual grout volumes should be kept. Also, any interruption in the installation process should be reported, as well as any changes in observed drilling conditions.

6.3 CAST-IN-SITU PILE

6.3.1 Required Lengths.   Required pile lengths may be specified for each area of similar subsoil conditions. The required driving criteria may also include a minimum penetration resistance. Penetration resistance during driving may include frictional resistance, which could be altered during pile installation by withdrawal of the casing. In some cases the pile-driving logs may give an indication of varying subsoil conditions. If substantial variations are indicated, the cause should be investigated by means of test borings.

6.3.2 Spacing.   Normal pile spacing is from 4 to 5 times the pile diameter. This spacing may have to be increased if the piles are installed in very soft soil or boulder formations unless the piles are driven in a staggered sequence.

6.3.3 Driving Sequence.   If piles have to be driven in a staggered sequence, the concrete or grout in a completed pile should be at least 3 days old for unreinforced piles or 1 day old for reinforced piles before the adjacent piles are driven.

6.3.4 Placing Reinforcing Steel

6.3.4.1 Steel to Resist Bending.   Reinforcing steel required to resist bending should be fabricated into cages of the specified diameter, and there should be sufficient spacers or spiders to center each cage in a pile. If the embedment length is longer than about 10 ft (3 m), the steel should be installed in the casing before concrete or grout is placed, and it should be centered in the casing. The steel cage must be prevented from coming up as the casing is withdrawn. If the embedment length of the cage is not greater than about 10 ft (3 m), the steel may be pushed into the fluid concrete or grout column. Such steel must be carefully centered in the pile and accurately aligned with the pile's longitudinal axis (see Section 5.46).

6.3.4.2 Steel to Resist Tension. Reinforcing steel required to resist uplift forces should be full-length. It may be placed in the center of the casing before concrete or grout is placed, or it may be pushed down the center of the concrete or grout column provided the control provisions for placing steel in this manner are in accordance with Section 6.2.10.2.

6.3.5 Placing Concrete or Grout. After the casing is driven to the required depth, concrete may be placed in accordance with Section 5.47. The concrete must have a sufficiently high slump, usually not less than 6 in (150 mm), so that there is no arching in the casing as the casing is withdrawn. If concrete or grout is placed during the driving operation, it must have a very high slump [10 in or more (250 mm or more)] and contain a retarding admixture so that it will remain fluid until the casing has been withdrawn. Otherwise the grout could adhere to the casing both inside and outside and come up with the casing. The normal slump test is not applicable. The suitable viscosity of the mix is determined by a flow cone test according to specification CRD C-79.* Specified grout strengths will be determined by cube tests according to ASTM C 91[30] and ASTM C 109.[32]

Concrete or grout volumes should be checked as described in Section 5.47.1. It would be advisable to meter the concrete or grout placed in each pile and to check this volume against the theoretical volume for the pile size upon which the design is based. Table C-8 gives data on concrete or grout volumes. If the grout or concrete take is less than the theoretical volume, the pile should be rejected and replaced unless it is proved to be satisfactory by means of an investigation or load test.

6.3.6 Filling the Pile Hole to the Cutoff Grade. To ensure that the pile hole is filled to the cutoff grade, it may be necessary to have a sufficient extra length of casing filled with concrete or grout to fill the space occupied by the steel casing. Alternatively, extra grout or concrete could be added during withdrawal of the casing. Also, the upper portion of the pile hole could be cased off with a steel liner to maintain the hole and prevent soil from caving in on top of the concrete or grout column after the casing is withdrawn and to permit the placement of additional concrete or grout to grade. If the liner is withdrawn, the concrete or grout must be kept sufficiently fluid to prevent it from arching and coming up with the liner. Withdrawal by vibratory means would help prevent this.

When this type of pile is installed, it is often difficult to fill the hole precisely to the required cutoff grade. In most cases excess concrete or grout will be placed, and pile butts must be trimmed back to the required elevation.

*CRD C-79, *Test Method for Flow of Grout Mixtures* (flow cone test), U.S. Corps of Engineers, Waterway Experiment Station, Vicksburg, Miss., December 1977.

6.3.7 Withdrawing the Casing. The driven casing should preferably be withdrawn by vibratory methods to help prevent arching of the concrete or grout in the casing. The casing should be thoroughly cleaned periodically to prevent a buildup of hardened concrete or grout, for this may cause arching and raising of the concrete as the casing is withdrawn. A thorough cleaning should be done at each interruption in the installation schedule, no matter how short.

6.3.8 Protection of the Pile Butt. A short steel sleeve should be placed at the top of the pile to protect the unset concrete or grout at the butt and to ensure proper filling without contamination. This is especially necessary if the cutoff grade is below the ground surface. The sleeve should not be removed until the concrete has set. Pile butts should be protected from contamination until the concrete or grout has hardened. In cold weather, pile butts must be protected from freezing in accordance with Section 5.47.5.

6.3.9 Pile Heave. If ground heave occurs during the driving of adjacent piles (see Section 5.30), all completed piles should be checked for evidence of pile heave. If pile heave is detected, all heaved piles should be rejected and replaced.

6.3.10 Obstructions. If subsurface obstructions including boulders are known to exist, the piles should be installed in a staggered sequence to permit the concrete or grout to harden before adjacent piles are driven. If the ground is heavily obstructed, completed piles should be carefully observed for signs of movement or damage when adjacent piles are driven. If movement or damage is evident, further investigations, such as by excavating or coring, may be required to determine if the piles are satisfactory, or the piles may have to be rejected and replaced (see Section 5.54).

6.3.11 Concrete or Grout Subsidence. When piles are installed in extremely soft soils, the concrete or grout level of completed piles should be checked for subsidence. If the concrete or grout level in a pile has subsided, the cause and possible damage to the pile should be investigated. This can be done by making a test boring alongside the pile, by excavating, or by coring the pile. Before additional concrete or grout is placed to bring the tops of satisfactory piles to the required grade, all laitance and contaminated concrete or grout should be removed, and steel dowels should be inserted in the tops of the piles if the grout or concrete is still unset.

6.3.12 Lateral Support. If, after the casing is withdrawn, a space is left between the pile and the soil, the space should be filled with fluid grout or by washing in sand to reestablish the lateral support of the soil.

6.3.13 Installed Lengths. The installed lengths of cast-in-situ piles can be determined by knowing the length of the drive casing used and observing the depth or elevation to which the bottom end is driven. The casing should be marked off in 5-ft (or 1-m) increments, with incremental marks numbered according to the distance from the bottom. Depths or elevations should be referenced to a fixed datum. Pile lengths can be calculated from pile tip and specified butt elevations or distances to the tip and butt from a fixed reference.

6.3.14 Records. Conventional driving records should be kept (see Section 5.32). Special forms may have to be developed for recording the required data for cast-in-situ piles. The inspector should record the depth to which each pile was installed, and the depth should be referenced to a fixed datum. He should also record the final length of each pile; the installation method used, including how the casing was withdrawn; a description of the reinforcing steel and how it was placed; and the type of grout or concrete used. In addition, the actual volume of grout or concrete placed in each pile should be reported, along with the theoretical volumes.

6.4 PRESSURE INJECTED FOOTING

6.4.1 Required Lengths. The bases for pressure injected footings should be formed in granular materials, which should be of adequate thickness to contain the compaction resulting from forming the bases and to spread the load so as not to overstress underlying soils. The elevations or depths at which pile bases are to be formed will be specified. It is necessary that the vertical location and thickness of the bearing stratum as well as the character and properties of the underlying soils be clearly defined. Additional test borings may be required for this.

6.4.2 Spacing. The normal spacing for pressure injected footings is from 4 to 6 ft (1.2 to 1.8 m). Greater spacing may be required for piles installed with uncased shafts in soft soils or boulder formations unless the piles are installed in a staggered sequence.

6.4.3 Driving the Tube. The drive tube should be driven to the specified depth at which the enlarged base is to be formed. The inspector should observe the driving of the tube in comparison with that of a test pile or a pile installed at a test-boring location. If a radical change is noted, the cause should be investigated by means of a test boring in case pile lengths need to be adjusted. If the plug is driven out during driving, the tube must be withdrawn and then redriven with an adequate plug.

Installing pressure injected footings with crawler-mounted equipment. (*Courtesy of Raymond International Builders, Inc.*)

6.4.4 Concrete.   All concrete should conform to Section 3.3, except that concrete for forming the bases should be of zero slump,[2] and that used for forming compacted uncased shafts should be of 0- to 1-in (25-mm) slump. Zero-slump concrete should contain enough water to ensure hydration of the cement. Concrete used for uncased, high-slump concrete shafts should have a slump of 6 to 8 in (150 to 200 mm).

6.4.5 Hammer Energy.   The weight of the drop hammer must be known to calculate the fall required to deliver the specified energy. To check on the hammer fall and thus the delivered energy, it is necessary to place a mark on the hammer line which will show above the top of the drive tube when the hammer is raised for its full required stroke. The drive tube should be at least as long as the required stroke plus the length of the drop hammer. During its fall, the hammer should not be restrained by the operator, and the hammer line should not be snubbed just at impact. As the hammer falls, it must overhaul the hammer line, and therefore all sheaves and drums must turn freely. The inspector must carefully observe the actions of the rig operator and the operations of the hammer to determine if the delivered energy is being seriously affected.

6.4.6 Formation of the Base.   After being driven to the required depth, the drive tube should be raised not more than about 6 in (150 mm) and restrained from further penetration. The closure plug is then driven out, but a portion of the plug should remain in the drive tube to serve as a seal. If the entire plug is expelled and, as a result, a void is created below the drive tube or soil or water is allowed to enter, the tube should be withdrawn and then redriven with an adequate plug.

For the formation of the enlarged base, batches of zero-slump concrete of the specified volume should be placed in the bottom of the drive tube and rammed out with the drop weight. The volume of typical batches is 5 ft^3 (0.14 m^3). For the design load involved, the specifications will indicate the minimum number of hammer blows of a stated energy required to drive out the last batch of concrete of a stated volume. The minimum total volume of the base may also be specified. Empirical formulas have been derived and proposed relating the pile capacity to various factors, including the hammer energy required to inject the last batch of concrete and the total volume of concrete in the base. Such formulas should be calibrated by means of pile load tests.

During the formation of the base, a sufficient height of dry concrete must be kept in the drive tube at all times to maintain a seal and exclude all water and soil. A mark on the hammer line can be used to monitor the height of the seal in the drive tube. If water or soil enters the tube, the pile must be abandoned and a new one driven. The entry of water will be indicated by a softening of the hammer blows. The inspector should keep a constant record of the quantities of concrete placed in the tube.

The volume of concrete in the bottom of the drive tube (the height of the concrete in the tube) affects the number of blows required to drive out the last batch of base concrete. The contract specifications may limit the height of such concrete. If so, the height should be checked by means of a mark on the hammer line with the hammer at rest at the bottom of the tube. If the specifications do not limit the height of concrete in the tube, the inspector should check with the engineer to establish a suitable height, usually not more than 6 in (150 mm).

If, during an attempt to form the base for any pile, the total volume of concrete placed is more than 50 percent greater than that for a test-pile base, the cause should be investigated. A test boring may reveal a change in subsoil conditions that requires an adjustment in pile lengths. The intrusion of groundwater may soften the concrete, precluding the formation of a normal base. If the base cannot be formed as specified, the contractor may drive through the attempted base to form an acceptable base at a lower depth, providing subsoil data show that a satisfactory bearing stratum exists at that

The drop hammer operates inside the drive tube to form the base and compacted uncased shaft for the pressure injected footing. (*Courtesy of Raymond International Builders, Inc.*)

depth. Possible interference with adjacent pile bases should be considered, and it may be necessary to increase the pile spacing.

6.4.7 Formation of the Shaft

6.4.7.1 Uncased, Compacted Concrete Shaft. The number of hammer blows and the energy required for driving out each batch of concrete in forming the shaft will be specified. The volume of each batch of concrete of 0- to 1-in (25-mm) slump will also be specified. This is generally a maximum of 5 ft³ (0.14 m³). In forming the shaft, the concrete must not be driven out below the bottom of the drive tube.

The concrete in the drive tube should be kept at a sufficient height above the bottom of the tube at all times to maintain an adequate seal. The height can be monitored by means of a mark on the hammer line as the concrete is driven out and the drive tube is raised. If an adequate seal is not maintained, water and soil could enter the tube and contaminate the concrete. If the concrete is driven out below the bottom of the drive tube, water and soil could fill or intrude into the space between the concrete and the bottom of the tube, resulting in a reduction (necking) of the cross section of the shaft or even a complete separation of the concrete shaft. If soil or water enters the drive tube or intrudes into the concrete shaft, the pile should be rejected.

The uncased shaft should be constructed to the cutoff grade without interruption. If the cutoff grade is at or near the ground surface, the compacting energy will have to be reduced. If the design cutoff grade is some distance below the ground surface, adequate measurements must be made to ensure that the shaft has been formed to the required grade. It is advisable to form the shaft higher and trim the butt back later as required. If the shaft is to be formed through unstable or organic soils or through extremely soft soils, a cased shaft is recommended.

6.4.7.2 Uncased, High-Slump Concrete Shaft. Before the drive tube is withdrawn, it should be filled with a sufficient volume of high-slump concrete to fill to the cutoff grade the hole created by the drive tube, including the space occupied by the tube. It will be necessary to use a drive tube of adequate length or to add concrete as the tube is withdrawn. The level of concrete in the tube must be kept above the bottom of the tube as it is withdrawn to maintain a head sufficient to resist hydrostatic and lateral earth pressures and to form a full-size pile shaft.

The concrete slump must be high enough to prevent arching in the tube. If there is any evidence of concrete being raised during tube withdrawal, the pile must be rejected and replaced. If the cutoff grade is below the ground surface, a steel sleeve should be inserted from the ground surface to about 1 ft (0.3 m) below the cutoff grade before the drive tube is withdrawn. This will prevent water and soil from falling in on top of the fresh concrete when the tube is extracted. Alternatively, the hole could be filled to the ground surface and the concrete trimmed back to grade after setting and excavation.

Frequently, the specifications will require a full-length reinforcing cage for this type of shaft. The reinforcement must be set in place before the tube is filled with concrete.

6.4.7.3 Cased Shaft. The steel shell or pipe inserted in the drive tube should be adequately connected to the pile base before the drive tube is withdrawn to ensure a positive seal and a good, sound joint between the base and the shaft. This is usually done by placing a small batch of concrete of 0- to 1-in (25-mm) slump in the shell and tapping it into the base with the drop weight. The inner shell or pipe should be restrained from moving upward as the drive tube is withdrawn. After the drive tube is withdrawn and also before the shell is filled with concrete, the bottom of the shell or pipe should be inspected to determine if any soil or water has entered. If soil has intruded, the pile should be rejected. If only water has entered, it should be removed before the concrete is placed.

Before the shell is filled, its alignment and butt location should be checked. Some correction might easily be made at this stage, and it may be necessary to brace the shell in its proper position until the annular space can be filled. Any annular space between the cased shaft and the soil should be filled with grout or clean sand washed down to reestablish lateral support. Concrete should be placed in the shell or pipe in accordance with Section 5.47.

6.4.8 Reinforcing Steel. Reinforcing steel should be fabricated into cages in accordance with Section 5.46, and as specified. Steel designed to resist uplift loads must be securely anchored into the base to prevent separation of the base and shaft under the service loads. Such steel should be placed in the drive tube before the base formation is completed. U-shaped bars or straps may assist in anchoring the steel to the base. Steel designed to resist bending and shear does not have to be anchored into the base but should be firmly seated on the base.

6.4.8.1 Uncased, Compacted Concrete Shafts. If the steel cage is placed after the base is formed, a small batch of concrete of 0- to 1-in (25-mm) slump should be placed in the tube and tapped down with the drop weight to anchor the cage to the base. The formation of the shaft should be in accordance with Section 6.4.7.1, with the drop hammer operating inside the cage. Care must be exercised to ensure that the cage is not lifted when the drop weight is raised or damaged as the weight falls. If the cage consists of several large-diameter longitudinal bars enclosed in a closely spaced spiral, it may be difficult to ram the concrete out through the steel cage without deforming the cage. In such cases it may be necessary to use a high-slump concrete shaft or a cased shaft. Extra caution must be exercised in forming the upper portions of the pile shaft to ensure that the drop hammer is not raised out of the cage and allowed to damage or dislodge the reinforcement as it drops.

6.4.8.2 Other Shafts. For high-slump concrete shafts and cased shafts, the reinforcing cage should be placed as necessary to resist bending, shear, or uplift forces before concrete is poured.

6.4.9 Heave. Pressure injected footings should not be used under heave conditions unless steps to eliminate heave are taken, such as predrilling or increasing the pile spacing (see Section 5.30). If heave measurements indicate that the tops of pressure injected footings have heaved, such piles must be rejected and replaced because of the possible separation of base and shaft.

6.4.10 Pile Butts. When uncased shafts are formed, it is difficult to form the shafts precisely to the cutoff grade. The tops of the pile shafts should be at or above the required elevation and trimmed back if necessary.

6.4.11 Installed Lengths. The installed length of a pressure injected footing can be determined from the elevation or depth to which the bottom of the drive tube is driven, with reference to a fixed datum, and the cutoff elevation or depth, referenced to the same datum. To facilitate taking measurements, the drive tube should be marked off in 1-ft (or 0.25-m) increments, and each 5-ft (or 1-m) mark should be numbered with the distance from the bottom.

6.4.12 Pay Quantities.   Payment for pressure injected footings will generally be on a lump-sum basis for a stated number of piles, with payment for added piles on a unit-price basis. The inspector should check the contract for actual payment provisions. If payment is based on installed lengths, the pay lengths should be those measured from the depth to which the drive tube is driven to the cutoff grade. No extra payment should be made for bases, regardless of size, or for trimming off pile butts.

6.4.13 Load Tests.   Pressure injected footings are generally designed to carry high loads, and the actual capacity is a function of many variables such as the density, thickness, and physical properties of the granular stratum in which the base is formed, the type and bearing capacity of the underlying soils, the proper shape and formation of the base, the degree of compaction of the surrounding soils, the dynamic energy applied in forming the base, and the integrity of the pile shaft and its connection with the base. The method of installation and the final product are sensitive to the actions of the rig operator. Load tests should be conducted to verify installation criteria and methods.

If the results of closely spaced, reliable test borings are not available, the actual capacities of the piles should be checked by means of periodic proof load tests. Piles to be tested should be selected at random by the engineer from among those installed.

6.4.14 Records.   In addition to keeping the normal records for payment quantities, the inspector should keep an accurate record of the length of each pile, the volume of concrete in each base, the height of concrete in the tube when the final batch of base concrete is injected, the number of hammer blows and the energy required to compact the last batch of concrete in forming the base, and the elevation at which each base was formed. This would be the elevation of the bottom of the drive tube. The inspector should also record the number of hammer blows used to compact each batch of concrete used in forming the uncased shaft. He should check the contract and specifications for any other data to be recorded.

6.5 ENLARGED-TIP PILE

6.5.1 Required Lengths.   The required pile length or the elevation to which the enlarged tip is to be driven may be specified. The development of high capacity for this type of pile requires that the tip be driven into a stratum of granular soil which can be compacted by the displacement action of the enlarged tip. The bearing stratum must be of adequate thickness and underlain by satisfactory competent soils. More closely spaced test borings may be required to define the type, thickness, and vertical position of the bearing stratum and the adequacy of the underlying soils. If sufficient and reliable subsoil information is available to establish the required elevations of pile tips, the final penetration resistance may be correlated with that of test piles.

6.5.2 Spacing.   The center-to-center spacing of enlarged-tip piles should be at least 2 times the average tip diameter or diagonal dimension.

6.5.3 Tip Fabrication.   The precast concrete tips should be properly designed and constructed to withstand driving stresses without damage, and they must conform with the requirements of the plans and specifications. For inspection details see Section 3.2 for plant-produced tips or Section 3.3 for tips made at the jobsite.

6.5.4 Tip-to-Shaft Construction.   The pipe or shell should be attached to the tip so as to prevent the entry of soil or water. Joints between the tip and any type of pile shaft must be capable of resisting all driving and service load stresses, including bending and tension. For short piles the joint may be subjected to bending from lateral loads resulting from ground movements or construction activity (see Section 5.51).

6.5.5 Shaft Construction.   The precast concrete tip is generally attached to the bottom of a pile shell or pipe shaft, but it could be attached to a timber pile or a steel H pile or formed at the end of a precast concrete pile.[75] The applicable control provisions for the type of pile shaft used (see Chapters 3 and 5) must be enforced.

6.5.6 Uncased Shafts.   The use of uncased cast-in-place concrete shafts with enlarged precast concrete tips should not be permitted. The chances of installing an adequate foundation are quite remote. If such shafts are permitted, all the applicable control provisions of Sections 6.3 and 6.4 and this section must be strictly enforced.

6.5.7 Heave.   If ground or pile heave occurs (see Section 5.30), check levels should be taken on the tops of all driven piles until driving progresses beyond the heave range. For cased cast-in-place concrete shafts, levels should be taken on telltale pipes bearing on the pile tips to check on possible separation of tip and shaft.

Heaved piles may be redriven as necessary provided the joints between the tips and shafts have not separated. If a joint cannot take the tension resulting from heave, and if check levels indicate possible joint separation, the pile joint should be investigated, and if separation has occurred, the pile should be rejected and replaced.

6.5.8 Relaxation.   If relaxation occurs (see Section 5.29), and if pile tips are not driven to hard material, consideration should be given to changing the pile type or assigning a lower design capacity to each pile.

6.5.9 Reinforcing Steel.   If internal reinforcing steel is required for cased concrete shafts, it should be placed in accordance with Section 5.46. If such steel is required to resist uplift loads, it must be positively connected to the precast tip so as to transfer the tensile forces.

6.5.10 Concrete.   Concrete for cased cast-in-place shafts should conform with the control provisions of Sections 3.3 and 5.47.

6.5.11 Lateral Support.   The annular space between the soil and the pile shaft created by the enlarged tip must be backfilled to provide lateral support for the pile. The natural sloughing off or caving of soils may not be sufficient to restore lateral support. Grout can be pumped into the annular space or clean sand washed down if the space remains open. If the space closes and there is a possibility of voids below, the area around each pile shaft should be tamped and backfilled as necessary. In extreme cases, it may be necessary to remove the upper sloughed-in soil in order to place the backfill properly. These generally involve high-capacity foundation units that require full lateral support for stability.

6.5.12 Installed Lengths.   The installed length of the pile shaft can be determined in accordance with Section 5.57. To this length may be added the length or height of the enlarged tip. However, if the measured length of the pile shaft includes a portion recessed into the tip, the amount of recess should not be included in the length of the precast tip to be added.

6.5.13 Pay Quantities.   Payment for enlarged-tip piles may be on a lump-sum basis or for actual lengths installed. The inspector should check the contract for actual payment provisions. If payment is based on pile length, the pay length may not include the length of the precast tip. Tips may be paid for separately at a stated unit price.

6.5.14 Load Tests.   Enlarged-tip piles are generally designed to carry high loads, and the actual capacity depends upon several factors such as the density, thickness, and physical properties of the bearing stratum, the degree of compaction of the soil resulting from driving the tip into it, the type and bearing capacity of the underlying soil, and the degree to which lateral soil support is reestablished. Load tests should be conducted to verify installation criteria methods.

If final penetration resistances vary, and if the results of closely spaced, reliable test borings are not available, the capacity of the piles should be checked by means of periodic proof load tests. Piles to be tested should be selected at random by the engineer from among those installed.

6.5.15 Records. In addition to keeping the normal records for payment quantities, the inspector should keep an accurate record of the installed length of each pile, including the elevation to which each enlarged tip was driven. Such elevations must be referenced to a permanent datum. Driving records should be prepared which would include the details on each pile installed, including the size of the tip and the final penetration resistance (see Section 5.32).

7

Pile Load Testing

Piles are load-tested so that design data can be developed, or so that installation criteria can be established, or so that the design and the installation criteria can be verified, or so that the required capacity of a pile can be confirmed, or for a combination of some of these reasons. Load-test programs to develop design data, including the selection of the pile type, are conducted before the foundation is designed and often involve several pile types. Tests to establish or verify the installation criteria or to verify the design capacities are usually conducted just before the installation of production piles gets under way. Tests to confirm a pile's capacity may be made at any time during the project. Piles may be tested individually or in groups.

Generally, it is the contractor's responsibility to set up and conduct the pile load tests. This could include setting up the necessary instrumentation, or that could be the responsibility of the inspection agency. Since critical decisions are often made on the basis of load-test results, careful planning, reliable equipment and instrumentation, the proper setup and conduct, and accurate recording and reporting of the data are essential.[68] The results of pile load tests are applicable only to similar types of piles installed with the same equipment and methods as used for the test pile, or with comparable equipment and methods, and under essentially similar subsoil conditions.

7.1 GENERAL

Piles can be tested in compression (bearing), in tension (uplift), laterally, or under combined loading. Although the actual details for conducting the pile load tests may be specified, compression tests are usually governed by ASTM D 1143,[41] uplift tests by ASTM D 3689,[43] and lateral tests by ASTM D 3966.[44] These standards cover all aspects of pile load testing except the interpretation

170

of the test results. If ASTM standards are referenced, the year designation must be specified, since such standards are subject to change.

Although the project specifications may reference these ASTM standards for pile testing, some modifications or additional requirements may be included in the specifications. Also, since these standards contain optional procedures, the specifications should be checked for options to be used. In some cases, the contractor may propose using certain options subject to the engineer's approval.

7.2 TEST-PILE DATA

The pile to be tested should be properly identified (see Section 5.5) and adequately described as to material, type, size, length, weight, and date installed (and concreted if applicable). The elevation of the pile butt should be referenced to a fixed and permanent datum.

7.3 DRIVING RECORD

A complete record of the installation of the test pile should be made, including the driving log; descriptions of the hammer, hammer cushion (cap block), pile cushion (if used), drive cap, follower (if used), and drill or jet (if used); and a record of the depths predrilled or jetted (see Section 5.32). Any interruptions or unusual occurrences during pile installation should be clearly and completely described.

7.4 LOAD REACTION

If reaction piles or other types of soil or rock anchors are used, they should be described as to type, size, and lengths. Each reaction pile or anchor should have a unique designation. The depth of each anchor, the driving log for each reaction pile, and the location of each reaction pile or anchor with reference to the test pile should be reported. For lateral and uplift tests, the reaction should be adequately described as to type and dimensions.

7.5 TEST-BORING DATA

The location of the closest boring with reference to the test pile should be recorded. The boring must be identified, and the boring log should accompany the load-test report. Ground surface elevations for all test borings must be shown and referenced to the same datum used for the pile tests.

7.6 INSTRUMENTATION FOR
MEASURING PILE HEAD MOVEMENTS

The movements of the pile butt under a load can be measured by dial gauges, by a wire and scale system, or by a remotely stationed engineer's level or transit reading a scale attached to the pile or a target rod held on the pile. Both a primary and secondary measuring system should be used to assure a check on all readings and the continuity of readings in case one of the systems malfunctions or requires resetting. All instruments must be properly mounted and installed, and they must function accurately. For tests on pile groups the instrumentation or reference points will normally be on the pile cap instead of on the test pile as described below. Instruments and their supporting systems should be protected from wind, extreme temperature variations, and accidental disturbance.

In addition to the standard measurement of pile butt movements in the direction of the applied loads, the specifications may require special measurements. These would include measurements of lateral movements for compression and uplift tests or measurements of rotational, fixed-head, vertical, or side movements for lateral tests. Suitable instrumentation must be mounted to measure these movements.

7.6.1 Dial Gauges. For bearing and uplift tests, at least two dial gauges should be used, and they should be mounted on opposite sides of the pile. The use of four dial gauges spaced equally around the pile is recommended. All gauges must be spaced equidistantly from the center of the pile. The required sensitivity of the gauges may be specified, but normally readings to 0.01 in (0.2 mm) are sufficient. Gauges should be mounted so as to measure movements at the sides of the pile near the butt in relation to an independent reference system. Gauges should not be mounted to bear on the test plate on top of the pile unless the plate is welded to the pile or instrumentation is provided to measure the movement of the plate in relation to the pile as test loads are applied. Dial gauge stems must be accurately aligned with the direction of the load and bear against a smooth surface such as glass or polished stainless steel.

7.6.2 Wire and Scale. The scale should preferably be mounted on a mirror which in turn is fixed to the side of the pile. Consistent readings are thus assured by lining up the wire with its image. Piano wire should be used. It should be stretched across the face of the scale about 1 in (25 mm) away and supported independently of the test setup. The wire must be kept taut at all times so that when it is plucked, it returns to its original position. This can be done with a turnbuckle but not necessarily with a weighted end passing over a pulley. A wire and scale system is not affected by temperature changes.

Any weighted box or platform can serve as a reaction to the test loads applied with a hydraulic jack. (*Courtesy of Raymond International Builders, Inc.*)

7.6.3 Level or Transit. The engineer's level or transit should be stationed a sufficient distance from the test pile so as not to be influenced by pile or ground movement during testing. If readings are taken on a scale, it should be fixed to the side of the test pile. If a target rod is used, readings should be taken on a fixed point on the side of the test pile. Readings may be taken on the test plate if it is welded to the pile or on a steel pin embedded in the top of the pile and free from the test plate. Readings should be referenced to a fixed benchmark, or the instrument can be mounted on a fixed object, such as a pile, for consistent readings.

7.7 TEST LOADS AND REACTIONS

For bearing tests, loads can be applied directly to the test pile or pile group with objects of known weight, or they can be applied with a hydraulic jack ram acting against a suitable reaction such as a weighted platform or a steel frame tied to reaction piles or other types of ground anchors. For tests on batter piles, the load is usually applied with a hydraulic jack. Loads for uplift tests can be applied with a hydraulic jack or with a crane of suitable capacity. If a jack is used, the load reaction can be adjacent piles or adequate cribbing. For lateral load tests, the load can be applied with a hydraulic jack or some type of suitable pulling system. The reaction can be cribbing, a weighted platform, or an adjacent pile. If adjacent piles are used, the piles can be tested laterally by pushing them apart or pulling them together. The ASTM load-test standards[41,43,44] illustrate various testing setups.

7.7.1 Direct Load. The amount of load applied to the pile can be checked by the volume and unit-weight method for the material involved. If necessary, test-load material can actually be weighed beforehand to determine the load being applied. The weight of the test load should be known within an accuracy of 10 percent. Sometimes standard test weights are available. The weight of any test beam, platform, box, or tank bearing on the test pile should be included in the first load increment. The test load must be balanced on the pile and allowed to act without restraint.

7.7.2 Hydraulic Jack. The jacking system should be calibrated to an accuracy of at least 5 percent. A calibration certificate should be submitted for each complete jacking system, including the ram, pump, and pressure gauge. If multiple jack rams are used, they should be of equal piston size, connected via a manifold to a single pump and gauge, and, if possible, calibrated as a single system. If this is impractical because of the total jacking capacity or the limitations of available testing equipment, each jack ram should be calibrated separately with the pump and gauge. Adjustment factors may have to be applied for the complete system. Calibrations should be furnished for both increasing and decreasing loads.

Anchor piles tied to the test frame provide a reaction for the test loads applied with the hydraulic jack. (*Courtesy of Raymond International Builders, Inc.*)

7.7.3 Load Cell. A load cell may be used to determine the amount of test load being applied. Load cells must be properly designed and constructed, and they must be accurately calibrated for both increasing and decreasing loads to within an accuracy of 2 percent. The effects of possible eccentric loading should be reflected in the calibration. This can be done by intentionally applying eccentric loads during calibration. Load cells should be equipped with properly designed and machined spherical bearing plates.

7.7.4 Dynamometer. If a pulling system is used for uplift or lateral loading, a calibrated dynamometer should be installed in the system. Calibrations should be within an accuracy of 10 percent. If the load is applied with multiple-part reeving, the location of the dynamometer within the system should be carefully recorded along with a correlation of the dynamometer readings and the actual loads applied.

7.8 REACTION SYSTEM

The minimum distances between the test pile and the anchor piles or supports for the reaction load will generally be specified. It is recommended that arrangements be made to take readings of the movements of anchor piles or other load reaction systems during the test. This can be done with suitably mounted dial gauges or with a surveying instrument reading scales attached to the reaction system or reading a target rod held on fixed points.

7.9 TEST-PILE INSTRUMENTATION

The specifications may require that special instrumentation such as electric strain gauges or telltales (strain rods) be placed in or on the test piles to determine pile tip movements or deflections along the pile or the distribution of loads or bending moments during testing. The installation of telltales is generally performed by the contractor, whereas specialists are often employed to install electric strain gauges and set up the measuring system. All instrumentation should be installed according to the specifications and the manufacturer's recommendations. Telltales must be allowed to operate without restraint, and all instruments must be adequately protected, especially during driving if they are installed before the pile is driven.

Figure 7-1 illustrates the installation of several telltales terminating at various points along the pile and extending to the top of the pile. Alternatively, the telltales could be brought out through the sides of the pile near its top, or provisions could be made for taking measurements on the telltales through windows or slots cut in the sides of the pile. Telltales mounted along the sides

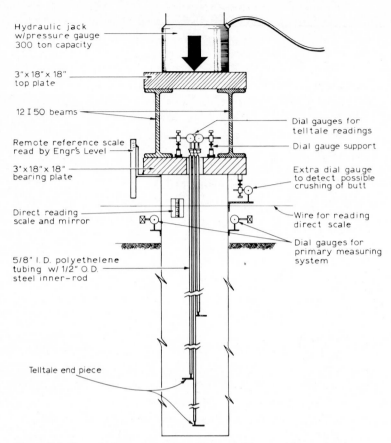

Hydraulic jack
w/pressure gauge
300 ton capacity

3"x 18"x 18"
top plate

12 I 50 beams

Remote reference scale
read by Engr's Level

3"x18"x 18"
bearing plate

Direct reading
scale and mirror

5/8" I.D. polyethelene
tubing w/ 1/2" O.D.
steel inner-rod

Telltale end piece

Dial gauges for
telltale readings

Dial gauge support

Extra dial gauge
to detect possible
crushing of butt

Wire for reading
direct scale

Dial gauges for
primary measuring
system

Figure 7-1 Test-pile instrumentation. (*Courtesy of Raymond International Builders, Inc.*)

of the pile are readily accessible for such measurements. If several telltales are used, data for determining load distribution can be collected.

Telltale readings should generally be referenced to the top of the pile so that a direct measurement of elastic shortening under the load can be obtained. Alternatively, they can be referenced to the same reference system used for measuring pile settlement. A telltale to the pile tip will give a direct measurement of the tip settlement under test loads. This is valuable information for evaluating pile performance.

With electric strain gauges, the complete stress history of a pile can be developed if the gauges are mounted before the pile is driven and readings are taken before and after driving in addition to during testing. Residual stresses resulting from driving can be determined and considered in evaluating the load-test results.

For lateral tests, the measurement of slope along the pile axis may be required. In such cases it will be necessary to install in or on the pile a duct or tube to accommodate a slope-measuring device. The specifications will indicate how far below the ground surface slope measurements are to be made. This will generally be limited to the upper third or 10 to 15 ft (3 to 4.5 m) of the pile.

7.10 TESTING ARRANGEMENT

Steel test plates having a minimum thickness of 2 in (50 mm) should be used on top of the test pile, the jack ram, and the load cell (if used). All compression and tension loads must be applied directly along the longitudinal axis of the test pile. Eccentric loading must be avoided by means of an accurate alignment of the load and the pile. For lateral tests, the load must be applied in line with the central longitudinal axis of the pile. The load generally acts in a direction perpendicular to the pile axis. For group tests the loads should act on the center of the group. This requires very careful positioning and alignment of all applied loads, loading devices, and special equipment such as load cells.

7.11 TESTING PROCEDURES

The overall testing procedures, including the rate of load application, holding times, etc., may be specified in detail or by reference to an ASTM standard. If ASTM standards are referenced, the standard procedure or one of the available optional procedures should be specified. The project specifications may modify or deviate from the ASTM standard on certain requirements, in which case the project specifications must be followed unless rescinded or revised by the engineer. The engineer may also approve special procedures proposed by the contractor, especially for proof testing.

There are many different types of testing procedures, and so before testing begins, there should be a clear understanding among all parties concerned as to what procedures will be used. The inspector should be familiar with the requirements of those testing procedures.

7.11.1 Compression Tests.   Loading procedures for compression (bearing) tests on piles are covered by ASTM D 1143.[41] The standard procedure is the maintained-load method, but the quick-load[60] and constant rate of penetration methods,[121] which are commonly used, are included as optional procedures, as are other options. Some loading procedures are not applicable to all subsoil conditions.

7.11.2 Uplift Tests.   Loading procedures for tension (uplift) tests on piles are covered by ASTM D 3689.[43] The maintained-load method is the standard procedure, but other optional procedures are included.

Combined compression and lateral load test. Note the use of the plate and roller assembly. (*Courtesy of Raymond International Builders, Inc.*)

7.11.3 Lateral Tests.   Loading procedures for lateral load tests on piles are covered by ASTM D 3966.[44] In addition to the standard maintained-loading procedures, there are several optional procedures, including surge loading, reverse loading, and reciprocal loading.

Also, the lateral load capacity of a pile or pile group may be determined under combined loading to simulate in-service loading conditions. Lateral loads are applied while the permanent dead load is acting on the test pile or pile group. Suitable devices, such as a steel rollers and plates assembly or antifriction plates, must be used to permit the test pile or group to respond freely to the lateral test loads. There should be no evidence that the test pile or group is being restrained by the compression load.

The specifications may require that the lateral load tests be conducted on fixed-head piles to simulate in-service conditions. The required degree of fixity may also be specified, or the method to be used may be detailed on the plans. ASTM D 3966 also covers tests on fixed-head piles, including the apparatus to be used.

The specifications may call for measurements of the rotation of free-head test piles. The attachment of suitable pile extensions may be required to permit the measurement of rotational movements with dial gauges. Measurements of rotations could also be made with a sensitive graduated spirit level on top of the pile.

7.12 CONCRETE STRENGTH

For tests on cast-in-place concrete piles, the concrete must be of sufficient age (strength) to carry the test loads without failure or excessive creep. Standard concrete cylinders can be tested at approximately the same age as the pile, but they may show strengths greater than that of the concrete in the pile. This is normal and results from the slower curing of the cast-in-place concrete, especially when it is confined in a steel shell or completely submerged. Sufficient time must be allowed between concreting and load testing to avoid excessive creep of uncured concrete. Type III cement can be used in concrete for test piles to achieve high strength at an early age.

7.13 SOIL FREEZE

If test piles are driven in soils which could exhibit freeze or setup (see Section 5.28), a sufficient time should elapse between pile driving and testing to permit the soil to regain its shear strength. The length of time necessary for the soil to set up could vary from a few hours to 30 days or longer. Prior experience in the area would serve as a guide. If there is a potential for soil freeze and test results are not up to expectations, the pile should be retested after additional time has elapsed.

7.14 SPECIAL TESTING METHODS

The specifications may require that a special method be used to test the pile, such as casing off, cyclic loading, or failure loading. A special testing method may be necessary for achieving specific objectives or developing special data.

7.14.1 Casing Off.   For this procedure, the upper portion of the pile is installed through a casing so that it is isolated from the surrounding soil. This is done for various reasons, such as to develop bearing capacity data on underlying soils or to eliminate from the test results the frictional support of the cased-off soil. The cased-off soil may be overburden soil through which the test piles are driven, or it may be soil which eventually would exert negative friction loading on the pile. The outer casing should have a suitable diameter, and it should be installed to the proper depth and thoroughly cleaned out. It may be necessary to insert support members at regular intervals along the pile length within the casing to eliminate buckling under the load. Such supports should not restrain the pile from axial movement under the load.

7.14.2 Cyclic Loading.   To develop information on load distribution and transfer or on the behavior of the pile under various load levels, or to obtain the load-settlement data for the interpretation of test results, or to get data for plotting elastic (net) load-movement curves, it may be necessary to have specifications which require that the pile be loaded and unloaded in cycles. The load level for each cycle and the number of loading cycles at each load level will be specified. The proposed design load should be one of the cycled load levels.

7.14.3 Ultimate Loading.   The specifications may require that the ultimate capacity of the pile-soil system be determined by carrying the test to failure as evidenced by progressive movement of the pile under a constant load. This may be difficult to accomplish for point-bearing piles. To determine the actual failure load, it would be necessary to have a close estimation of the ultimate capacity of the pile-soil system so that sufficient testing capacity is furnished. The contractor may qualify this requirement by limiting the testing capacity that he will furnish. In some cases, the pile may fail structurally before the ultimate capacity of the soil is reached.

7.15 RECORDING DATA

A complete and accurate record should be made of all time-load-movement data. Each dial gauge, scale, or measuring point should be accurately identified and marked so that confusion or error in observing and recording data can be avoided. Extreme care must be exercised to ensure that all readings are made accurately. If multiple gauges, scales, or measuring points are involved, and especially if tests are conducted within a short period of time, it may be necessary to have more than one inspector reading and recording data. Electric strain gauge readings may be recorded manually or on tape.

The readings to be taken and recorded will depend on the test procedures used and the specification requirements. These may include supplementary measurements such as measurements of the movements of the pile butt in directions other than that of the applied load or measurements of rotational movements for lateral tests. Other data to be recorded could be telltale, electric strain gauge, or slope indicator readings. In addition, the recording of movements of the reference system used for measurements, of the test reaction system, and of the test plate in relation to the pile top may be required. Periodic readings should be taken and recorded so that any movement of the reaction and reference systems can be determined.

Dial gauges for measuring pile butt settlements under the test loads are mounted on brackets welded to the side of the pile. (*Courtesy of Raymond International Builders, Inc.*)

Telltale readings should generally be referenced to the top of the pile so that direct measurements of the elastic-plastic shortening of the pile under a load can be obtained. If they are referenced to the independent reference system used for measuring pile butt movements, sufficient accurate data must be recorded so that the elastic-plastic shortening of the pile can be computed. Electric strain gauge and slope indicator readings may be taken by specialists.

The specifications may determine when various readings are to be taken and recorded. If they do not, and if the procedures are not governed by an ASTM standard, a reasonable and practical program should be established for recording sufficient data so that the time-load-movement performance of the pile can be determined.

If it is necessary during the test to reset gauges or scales, a complete record of exactly what was done should be made, and there should be a clear explanation of the relationships between the old readings and the new readings. This is most important for maintaining the continuity of the data. Any adjustments made to the field data should be thoroughly explained.

7.16 INTERPRETATION OF LOAD-TEST RESULTS

In most cases the inspector will not be involved with the interpretation of the load-test results. However, he should be familiar with the acceptance criterion, which should be specified in advance so that all parties concerned, including the contractor, will know what constitutes a satisfactory test. A crite-

Instrumentation for measuring pile movements. (*Courtesy of Raymond International Builders, Inc.*)

rion may require that the inspector plot the load-movement data as they are developed in the field to ensure that sufficient data are recovered for the application of the criterion.

Most of the pile load testing conducted at the start of or during pile installation is for proof testing or for establishing the installation criteria. Under such conditions, the test load is generally carried to only twice the proposed working load. The acceptance criterion for such tests often involves a definition of what constitutes the "failure" load. Generally, the allowable working load is half the arbitrary "failure" load as defined by the acceptance criterion, but other safety factors may be specified depending on the acceptance criterion used. If actual failure of the pile-soil system occurs as evidenced by a progressive movement of the pile under a constant load, or if the pile fails structurally, a greater factor of safety should be applied in determining the allowable working load.

7.16.1 Compression Tests.   There are several acceptance criteria in use involving an arbitrary definition of the failure load.[71,72] Some are based on a maximum permissible gross or net pile settlement as measured at the pile butt. The gross settlement is the movement of the pile butt under the full test load, and the net settlement is the distance the pile has permanently moved

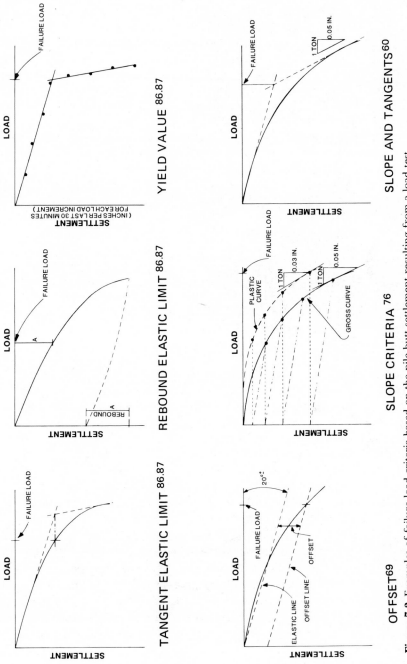

Figure 7-2 Examples of failure-load criteria based on the pile butt settlement resulting from a load test.

183

after it has rebounded upon removal of the test load. The permissible gross or net pile settlement may depend on the structure involved.

The gross settlement permitted may be that measured after the theoretical elastic shortening of the pile is deducted. The permissible net settlement may be a fixed distance, such as $\frac{1}{2}$ in (12 mm), or a function of the total test load, such as 0.01 in per ton (0.03 mm per kilonewton) of load applied.

The failure load may be defined by a maximum permissible slope of the gross or net load-settlement curve[76] (see Figure 7-2). For example, the maximum slope could be 0.05 in per ton (0.14 mm/kN) on the gross curve or 0.03 in per ton (0.09 mm/kN) on the net or plastic curve. To apply this criterion to the net curve would require cyclic loading to determine a sufficient number of points for defining the curve. The total acceptance criterion could include a maximum permissible slope combined with a maximum permissible gross settlement under the proposed working load.

The acceptance criterion could be based on the offset method, which defines the failure load.[69] The elastic shortening of the pile, considered as a point-bearing, free-standing column, is computed and plotted on the load-settlement curve, with the elastic shortening line passing through the origin. An offset line is drawn parallel to the elastic line. The offset is usually 0.15 in (4 mm) plus a quake factor, which is a function of the pile tip diameter. For normal-size piles this factor could be 1 percent of the pile tip diameter in inches (millimeters). The intersection of the offset line with the gross load-settlement curve determines the "failure" load. The load-settlement curve should be plotted with data resulting from holding each load increment, including the full test load, for no longer than 1 h. The coordinate scales should be chosen so that the elastic line plots about 20° from the load axis, as shown in Figure 7-2. This criterion tends to be conservative and is more applicable to friction piles.

Some definitions of the failure load are based upon the performance of the pile during the test—for example, "that load that shows a settlement on the curve equal to the rebound after application and removal of the full test load" (rebound elastic limit[86,87]), or "that load for which the settlement is twice the settlement under 90 percent of the load," or "that load determined by the intersection of the two straight portions of a curve resulting from the plotting of the load versus the settlement under that load during the last 30 min for which it was held" (yield value[86,87]). Some of these are illustrated in Figure 7-2.

There are several definitions of the arbitrary "failure" load which are rather indeterminate, such as "where the load-settlement curve shows a 'break,' " or "where the settlement is disproportionate to the load," or "the point of intersection of tangents drawn to two parts of the load-settlement curve" (see Figure 7-2). These become vague when there is no clear break in the load-settlement curve.

7.16.2 Uplift Tests. The acceptance criterion for uplift tests should be specified. Not many criteria have been proposed. The acceptance criterion may be based on a gross (or net) upward movement of the pile butt, or on the slope of the load-movement curve, or on an offset method. The offset could equal the theoretical elastic lengthening of the pile plus a stated distance, such as 0.10 in (2.5 mm). Generally, if the pile-soil system behaves elastically under the proposed test load, the test will be considered satisfactory. If upward movement of the pile is progressive under a constant load, the actual ultimate uplift capacity of the pile is determined, and a suitable factor of safety must be applied to establish the working load.

7.16.3 Lateral Tests.   The acceptance criterion for lateral load tests will be as specified and may be based on the gross movement of the pile butt under the proposed working load or total test load or on the net movement. There are no established acceptance criteria for lateral load tests. In general, if the pile exhibits elastic behavior during the test, the test is considered satisfactory. For lateral tests, the amount of lateral movement under the design load should be an important consideration, and the permissible amount will depend upon the structure involved. The amount of permanent lateral deflection of the pile butt (net movement after removal of the test load) may also be critical, and the permissible amount may depend upon the structure. If failure occurs, the allowable working load should not be greater than one-third the failure load.

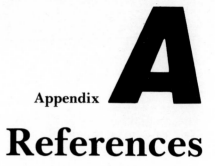

Appendix

References

1. *Recommended Practice for Selecting Proportions for Normal and Heavyweight Concrete*, ACI 211.1, 1981.*

2. *Recommended Practice for Selecting Proportions for No Slump Concrete*, ACI 211.3, 1975, rev. 1980.*

3. *Admixtures for Concrete*, ACI 212.1R, 1981.*

4. *Guide for Use of Admixtures in Concrete*, ACI 212.2R, 1981.*

5. *Recommended Practice for Evaluation of Compression Test Results of Field Concrete*, ACI 214, 1977.*

6. *Selection and Use of Aggregates for Concrete*, ACI 221R, 1961.*

7. *Recommended Practice for Measuring, Mixing, Transporting and Placing Concrete*, ACI 304, 1973, reaffirmed 1978.*

8. *Placing Concrete by Pumping Methods*, ACI 304.2R, 1971.*

9. *Hot-Weather Concreting*, ACI 305R, 1977.*

10. *Cold-Weather Concreting*, ACI 306R, 1978.*

11. *Building Code Requirements for Reinforced Concrete*, ACI 318, 1977.*

12. *Recommendations for Design, Manufacture and Installation of Concrete Piles*, ACI 543R, 1974, reaffirmed 1980.*

13. *Subsurface Investigation for Design and Construction of Foundations of Buildings*, ASCE Manual of Engineering Practice, no. 56, American Society of Civil Engineers, New York, 1976.

14. *Specification for General Requirements for Rolled Steel Plates, Shapes, Sheet Piling, and Bars for Structural Use*, ASTM A 6, 1980.†

15. *Specification for Structural Steel*, ASTM A 36, 1977.†

16. *Specification for Cold-Drawn Steel Wire for Concrete Reinforcement*, ASTM A 82, 1979.†

17. *Specification for Welded and Seamless Steel Pipe Piles*, ASTM A 252, 1980.†

18. *Methods and Definitions for Mechanical Testing of Steel Products*, ASTM A 370, 1977.†

19. *Specification for Uncoated Seven-Wire Stress-Relieved Strand for Prestressed Concrete*, ASTM A 416, 1980.†

20. *Specification for Uncoated Stress-Relieved Wire for Prestressed Concrete*, ASTM A 421, 1980.†

*Available from American Concrete Institute, P.O. Box 4754, Detroit, Mich. 48219.
†Available from American Society for Testing and Materials, 1916 Race St., Philadelphia, Pa. 19103.

21. *Specification for High-Strength Low-Alloy Columbian Vanadium Steel of Structural Quality*, ASTM A 572, 1979.†

22. *Specification for Deformed and Plain Billet-Steel Bars for Concrete Reinforcement*, ASTM A 615, 1980.†

23. *Specification for Rail-Steel Deformed and Plain Bars for Concrete Reinforcement*, ASTM A 616, 1979.†

24. *Specification for Axle-Steel Deformed and Plain Bars for Concrete Reinforcement*, ASTM A 617, 1979.†

25. *Specification for Low-Alloy Steel Deformed Bars for Concrete Reinforcement*, ASTM A 706, 1980.†

26. *Specification for Uncoated High-Strength Steel Bars for Prestressing Concrete*, ASTM A 722, 1975.†

27. *Methods of Making and Curing Concrete Test Specimens in the Field*, ASTM C 31, 1980.†

28. *Specification for Concrete Aggregates*, ASTM C 33, 1981.†

29. *Method of Test for Compressive Strength of Cylindrical Concrete Specimens*, ASTM C 39, 1980.†

30. *Specification for Masonry Cement*, ASTM C 91, 1978.†

31. *Specification for Ready Mixed Concrete*, ASTM C 94, 1981.†

32. *Test Method for Compressive Strength of Hydraulic Cement Mortars (Using 2-in. or 50-mm Cube Specimens)*, ASTM C 109, 1980.†

33. *Method of Test for Slump of Portland Cement Concrete*, ASTM C 143, 1978.†

34. *Specification for Portland Cement*, ASTM C 150, 1981.†

35. *Methods of Sampling Fresh Concrete*, ASTM C 172, 1977.†

36. *Specification for Molds for Forming Concrete Test Cylinders Vertically*, ASTM C 470, 1979.†

37. *Method of Tests for Penetration Resistance of Hardened Concrete*, ASTM C 803, 1979.†

38. *Test Method for Penetration of Bituminous Materials*, ASTM D 5, 1978.†

39. *Specification for Round Timber Piles*, ASTM D 25, 1979.†

40. *Specification for Asphalt Cement for Use in Pavement Construction*, ASTM D 946, 1980.†

41. *Method of Testing Piles under Static Axial Compressive Load*, ASTM D 1143, 1981.†

42. *Specification for Pressure Treatment of Timber Products*, ASTM D 1760, 1980.†

43. *Method for Testing Individual Piles under Static Axial Tensile Load*, ASTM D 3689, 1978.†

44. *Method of Testing Piles under Lateral Loads*, ASTM D 3966, 1981.†

45. *All Timber Products—Preservative Treatment by Pressure Processes*, AWPA C1, 1981.‡

46. *Piles—Preservative Treatment by Pressure Processes*, AWPA C3, 1981.‡

47. *Standard for Pressure Treated Material in Marine Construction*, AWPA C18, 1977.‡

48. *Standard for the Purchase of Treated Wood Products*, AWPA M1, 1976.‡

49. *Standard for Inspection of Treated Timber Products*, AWPA M2, 1981.‡

50. *Standard for the Care of Preservative Treated Wood Products*, AWPA M4, 1980.‡

51. *Brands Used on Forest Products*, AWPA M6, 1975.‡

52. *Standards for Water-Borne Preservatives*, AWPA P5, 1981.‡

53. "Recommended Practice for Design, Manufacture, and Installation of Prestressed Concrete Piling," *Journal of the Prestressed Concrete Institute*, vol. 22, no. 2, March–April 1977.

†Available from American Society for Testing and Materials, 1916 Race St., Philadelphia, Pa. 19103.

‡Available from American Wood-Preserver's Association, 1625 Eye St., N.W., Washington, D.C. 20006.

54. H. T. Arni, "Impact and Penetration Tests of Portland Cement Concrete," *Highway Research Record,* no. 378, Transportation Research Board, Washington, 1972.

55. C. E. Bastian, "The Effect of Vibrations on Freshly Placed Concrete," *Foundation Facts,* vol. 6, no. 1, 1970.

56. Delmar L. Bloem, "Concrete Strength in Structures," *Journal of the American Concrete Institute,* vol. 65, March 1968.

57. Delmar L. Bloem, "Concrete Strength Measurement—Cores vs. Cylinders," *Proceedings,* vol. 65, American Society for Testing and Materials, Philadelphia, 1965.

58. Bengt B. Broms, "Allowable Bearing Capacity of Initially Bent Piles," *Journal of the Soil Mechanics and Foundations Division,*§ vol. 89, no. SM5, September 1963.

59. R. N. Bruce, Jr., and D. C. Hebert, "Splicing of Precast Prestressed Concrete Piles: Part I— Review and Performance of Splices," *Journal of the Prestressed Concrete Institute,* vol. 19, no. 5, September–October 1974.

60. H. D. Butler and H. E. Hoy, *The Texas Quick-Load Method for Foundation Load Testing,* User's Manual IP 77.8, Department of Transportation, Federal Highway Administration, Washington, 1976.

61. Richard H. Campbell and Robert E. Tobin, "Core and Cylinder Strengths of Natural and Lightweight Concrete," *Journal of the American Concrete Institute,* vol. 64, April 1967.

62. R. D. Chellis, *Pile Foundations,* 2d ed., McGraw-Hill, New York, 1961.

63. Dunstan D. S. Chen, James V. Toto, and I. H. Wong, "Field Evaluation of Hammer Efficiency and Pile Driving Criteria," in F. M. Fuller (ed.), *Symposium on Deep Foundations,* American Society of Civil Engineers, New York, 1980.

64. H. W. Chung, "How Good Is Good Enough—A Dilemma in Acceptance Testing of Concrete," *Journal of the American Concrete Institute,* vol. 75, August 1978.

65. F. M. Clemente, Jr., "Downdrag on Bitumen Coated Piles in a Warm Climate," *Proceedings of the Tenth International Conference on Soil Mechanics and Foundation Engineering,* International Society of Soil Mechanics and Foundation Engineering, Stockholm, 1981.

66. William A. Corden, "Minimum Strength Specifications Can Be Practical," *Journal of the American Concrete Institute,* vol. 66, July 1969.

67. A. E. Cummings, "Dynamic Pile Driving Formulas," *Journal of the Boston Society of Civil Engineers,* vol. 23, January 1940.

68. M. T. Davisson, "Static Measurements of Pile Behavior," in H. Fang and T. D. Dismuke (eds.), *Design and Installation of Pile Foundations and Cellular Structures,* Envo Publishing, Lehigh Valley, Pa., 1970.

69. M. T. Davisson, "Pile Load Capacity," *Proceedings—Design, Construction and Performance of Deep Foundations,* American Society of Civil Engineers Seminar, University of California, Berkeley, August 1975.

70. T. D. Dismuke, "Behavior of Steel Piles During Installation and Service," in R. Lundgren (ed.), *Behavior of Deep Foundations,* STP 670, American Society for Testing and Materials, Philadelphia, 1979.

71. Bengt H. Fellenius, "Test Loading of Piles and New Proof Testing Procedure," *Journal of the Geotechnical Engineering Division,*§ vol. 101, no. GT9, September 1975.

72. Bengt H. Fellenius, "The Analysis of Results from Routine Pile Load Tests," *Ground Engineering,* vol. 13, no. 6, September 1980.

73. Kaare Flaate, "An Investigation of the Validity of Three Pile-Driving Formulae in Cohesionless Material," Publication 56, Norwegian Geotechnical Institute, Oslo, 1964.

§Published by the American Society of Civil Engineers.

74. W. K. Fleming and Z. J. Sliwinski, "The Use and Influence of Bentonite in Bored Pile Construction," Report PG3, Construction Industry Research and Information Association, London, September 1977.

75. F. M. Fuller, "Methods and Equipment for the Installation of Piles in Foreign Countries," in H. Fang and T. D. Dismuke (eds.), *Design and Installation of Pile Foundations and Cellular Structures,* Envo Publishing, Lehigh Valley, Pa., 1970.

76. F. M. Fuller and H. E. Hoy, "Pile Load Tests Including Quick-Load Test Method, Conventional Methods and Interpretations," *Highway Research Record,* no. 333, Transportation Research Board, Washington, 1970.

77. G. G. Goble, K. Fricke, and G. E. Likins, Jr., "Driving Stresses in Concrete Piles," *Journal of the Prestressed Concrete Institute,* vol. 21, no. 1, January–February 1976.

78. G. G. Goble, G. E. Likins, Jr., and F. Rausche, "Bearing Capacity of Piles from Dynamic Measurements," *Final Report,* Department of Civil Engineering, Case Western Reserve University, Cleveland, March 1975.

79. George G. Goble, Frank Rausche, and Garland E. Likins, Jr., "The Analysis of Pile Driving—A State-of-the-Art," in H. Bredenberg (ed.), *Proceedings of the International Seminar on the Application of Stress-Wave Theory on Piles,* A. A. Balkema, Rotterdam, June 1980.

80. G. G. Goble and F. Rausche, "Wave Equation Analysis of Pile Driving, WEAP Program," *User's Manual,* vols. 1–4, Report FHWA-IP-76-14.1, National Technical Information Service, Springfield, Va., July 1976.

81. C. J. Gravare, G. G. Goble, F. Rausche, and G. E. Likins, Jr., "Pile Driving Construction Control by the Case Method," *Ground Engineering,* vol. 13, no. 2, March 1980.

82. Lawrence A. Hansen and W. L. Schroeder, "Penetration Resistance for Driven Piling," *Journal of the Construction Division,*§ vol. 103, no. CO3, September 1977.

83. Peter Hewlett and Roger Rixom, "Superplasticized Concrete," *Journal of the American Concrete Institute,* vol. 74, May 1977.

84. Teddy J. Hirsch, Larry Carr, and Lee L. Lowery, Jr., "Pile Driving Analysis—Wave Equation," *User's Manual, TTI Program,* vols. 1–4, Report FHWA-IP-76-13.4, National Technical Information Service, Springfield, Va., April 1976.

85. T. J. Hirsch, L. L. Lowery, H. M. Coyle, and C. H. Samson, Jr., "Pile Driving Analysis by One-Dimensional Wave Theory: State of the Art," *Highway Research Record,* no. 333, Transportation Research Board, Washington, 1970.

86. W. S. Housel, "Field and Laboratory Determination of the Bearing Capacity of Hardpan for Design of Deep Foundations," ASTM Conference, Atlantic City, June 1956, American Society for Testing and Materials, Philadelphia.

87. W. S. Housel, "Pile Load Capacity: Estimates and Test Results," *Journal of the Soil Mechanics and Foundations Division,*§ vol. 92, no. SM4, July 1966.

88. M. J. Hvorslev, *Subsurface Exploration and Sampling of Soils for Civil Engineering Purposes,* American Society of Civil Engineers, New York, 1949.

89. S. M. Johnson, "Determining the Capacity of Bent Piles," *Journal of the Soil Mechanics and Foundations Division,*§ vol. 88, no. SM6, December 1962.

90. Earle Klohn, Jr., "Pile Heave and Redriving," *Journal of the Soil Mechanics and Foundations Division,*§ vol. 87, no. SM4, August 1961.

91. Shu-t'ien Li, V. Ramakrishman, and J. E. Russell, "Advances in Nondestructive Testing of Concrete," *Highway Research Record,* no. 378, Transportation Research Board, Washington, 1972.

§Published by the American Society of Civil Engineers.

92. V. M. Malhotra, *Testing Hardened Concrete: Nondestructive Methods,* American Concrete Institute, Detroit, 1976.

93. V. Mohan Molhotra, "In-Place Evaluation of Concrete," *Journal of the Construction Division,*§ vol. 101, no. CO2, June 1975.

94. V. M. Malhotra, "Contract Strength Requirements—Cores versus In Situ Evaluation," *Journal of the American Concrete Institute,* vol. 74, April 1977.

95. Bryant Mather and William O. Tynes, "Investigation of Compressive Strength of Molded Cylinders and Drilled Cores of Concrete," *Journal of the American Concrete Institute,* vol. 57, January 1961.

96. E. T. Mosley, "The Practical Application of the Wave Equation," *Proceedings of the Soil Mechanics and Foundation Engineering Conference,* University of Kansas, Lawrence, 1971.

97. E. T. Mosley and T. Raamot, "Pile Driving Formulas," *Highway Research Record,* no. 333, Transportation Research Board, Washington, 1970.

98. Dixon O'Brien, Jr., "So What Is New in Testing and Inspection?" *Concrete International,* November 1981.

99. Roy F. Olson and Kaare S. Flaate, "Pile-Driving Formulas for Friction Piles in Sand," *Journal of the Soil Mechanics and Foundations Division,*§ vol. 93, no. SM6, November 1967.

100. J. D. Parsons and S. D. Wilson, "Safe Loads on Dog-Leg Piles," *Transactions,*§ vol. 121, 1956.

101. Walter H. Price, "Factors Influencing Concrete Strength," *Journal of the American Concrete Institute,* vol. 48, February 1951.

102. T. Raamot, "Analysis of Pile Driving by the Wave Equation," *Foundation Facts,* vol. 3, no. 1, 1967.

103. George E. Ramey and Roy C. Johnson, Jr., "Relative Accuracy and Modification of Some Dynamic Pile Capacity Prediction Equations," *Ground Engineering,* vol. 12, no. 6, September 1979.

104. Frank Rausche, Fred Moses, and George G. Goble, "Soil Resistance Predictions from Pile Dynamics," *Journal of the Soil Mechanics and Foundations Division,*§ vol. 98, no. SM9, September 1972.

105. F. Rausche and G. G. Goble, "Performance of Pile Driving Hammers," *Journal of the Construction Division,*§ vol. 98, no. CO2, September 1972.

106. F. Rausche and G. G. Goble, "Determinations of Pile Damage by Top Measurements," in R. Lundgren (ed.), *Behavior of Deep Foundations,* STP 670, American Society for Testing and Materials, Philadelphia, 1979.

107. Lymon C. Reese, "Construction of Drilled Shafts," *Proceedings of the Joint Conference Association of Drilled Shaft Contractors and the Sociedad Mexicana de Mecanica de Suelos,* Sociedad Mexicana de Mecanica de Suelos, Mexico City, June 1976.

108. D. M. Rempe, "Mechanics of Diesel Pile Driving," Ph.D. thesis, University of Illinois, Urbana, 1975.

109. D. M. Rempe and M. T. Davisson, "Performance of Diesel Pile Hammers," *Proceedings of the Ninth International Conference on Soil Mechanics and Foundation Engineering,* International Society of Soil Mechanics and Foundation Engineering, Tokyo, 1977.

110. A. Samarin and P. Meynink, "Use of Combined Ultrasonic and Rebound Hammer Method for Determining Strength of Concrete Structural Members," *Concrete International,* March 1981.

111. E. A. L. Smith, "Pile Driving Analysis by the Wave Equation," *Transactions,*§ vol. 127, pt. I, 1962.

§Published by the American Society of Civil Engineers.

112. John R. Smith, "Testing Hardened Concrete," *Journal of the American Concrete Institute,* vol. 74, June 1977.

113. R. K. Snow, "Raycrete 800—A Proven Mix," *Foundation Facts,* vol. 11, no. 1, 1976.

114. T. Sorenson and B. Hansen, "Pile Driving Formulae—An Investigation Based on Dimensional Considerations and a Statistical Analysis," *Proceedings of the Fourth International Conference on Soil Mechanics and Foundation Engineering,* International Society of Soil Mechanics and Foundation Engineering, London, 1957.

115. M. G. Spangler and Harry F. Mumma, "Pile Test Loads Compared with Bearing Capacity Calculated by Formulas," *Proceedings of the Highway Research Board,* vol. 37, Transportation Research Board, Washington, 1958.

116. F. Tavenas and R. Audy, "Limitations of the Driving Formulas for Predicting the Bearing Capacities of Piles in Sand," *Canadian Geotechnical Journal,* vol. 9, no. 1, February 1972.

117. S. Thorburn and J. Q. Thorburn, "Review of Problems Associated with the Construction of Cast-in-Place Concrete Piles," Report PG2, Construction Industry Research and Information Association, London, January 1977.

118. H. Van Koten, "The Determination of the Forms and Sizes of Discontinuities in Foundation Piles by Means of Sonic Testing," Report B1-77-111, Institute TNO for Building Materials and Building Structures, Delft, The Netherlands, December 1977.

119. A. J. Weltman, "Integrity Testing of Piles: A Review," Report PG4, Construction Industry Research and Information Association, London, September 1977.

120. A. J. Weltman and J. A. Little, "A Review of Bearing Pile Types," Report PGI, Construction Industry Research and Information Association, London, January 1977.

121. Thomas Whitaker and Robert W. Cooke, "A New Approach to Pile Testing," *Proceedings of the Fifth International Conference on Soil Mechanics and Foundation Engineering,* International Society of Soil Mechanics and Foundation Engineering, Paris, 1961.

122. R. J. Woodward, Jr., W. S. Gardner, and D. Greer, *Drilled Pier Foundations,* McGraw-Hill, New York, 1972.

123. Nai C. Yang, "Relaxation of Piles in Sand and Inorganic Silt," *Journal of the Soil Mechanics and Foundations Division,*§ vol. 96, no. SM2, March 1970.

124. Ronald F. Zollo and Edwin F. Heyer, "Rx—Treated Lumber and Metal—Corrosion Ailments," *Civil Engineering,* August 1982.

§Published by the American Society of Civil Engineers.

Appendix **B**

Hammer Data

Table B-1 SPECIFICATIONS—STEAM, AIR, OR HYDRAULIC PILE HAMMERS[a]

Make and Model[b]	Maximum Rated Energy,[c] ft·lbf (kJ)[l]	Type[d]	Ram Weight, lb (kg)	Total Weight,[e] lb (kg)	Stroke,[f] in (mm)	Boiler Capacity,[g] hp (kW)	Air Consumption,[h] scfm (m³/s)	Operating Pressure at Hammer,[i] lb/in² (kPa)	Hose Size and Number,[j] in (mm)	Operating Speed,[k] blows/min
Conmaco[m]										
50-K[n]	15,000 (20.3)	SA	5,000 (2,268)	9,700 (4,400)	36 (910)	81 (800)	565 (0.27)	80 (550)	2 (50)	60
50-C[n]	15,000 (20.3)	SA	5,000 (2,268)	10,600 (4,808)	36 (910)	81 (800)	565 (0.27)	80 (550)	2 (50)	60
65-K	19,500 (26.4)	SA	6,500 (2,948)	11,200 (5,080)	36 (910)	94 (900)	625 (0.29)	100 (690)	2 (50)	60
65-C	19,500 (26.4)	SA	6,500 (2,948)	12,100 (5,488)	36 (910)	94 (900)	625 (0.29)	100 (690)	2 (50)	60
80-K	26,000 (35.3)	SA	8,000 (3,629)	16,700 (7,575)	39 (990)	121 (1,200)	880 (0.42)	85 (590)	2.5 (65)	50
80-C[o]	26,000 (35.3)	SA	8,000 (3,629)	17,280 (7,838)	39 (990)	75 (700)	730 (0.34)	85 (590)	2.5 (65)	50
100-K	32,500 (44.1)	SA	10,000 (4,536)	18,700 (8,482)	39 (990)	145 (1,400)	1,002 (0.47)	100 (690)	2.5 (65)	50
100-C[o]	32,500 (44.1)	SA	10,000 (4,536)	19,280 (8,745)	39 (990)	85 (800)	820 (0.39)	100 (690)	2.5 (65)	50
140-D	36,000 (48.8)	D	14,000 (6,350)	31,200 (14,152)	15.5 (390)	211 (2,100)	1,425 (0.67)	140 (970)	3 (75)	103
115-K	37,375 (50.7)	SA	11,500 (5,216)	20,250 (9,185)	39 (990)	161 (1,600)	1,060 (0.50)	120 (830)	2.5 (65)	50
115-C[o]	37,375 (50.7)	SA	11,500 (5,216)	20,830 (9,448)	39 (990)	99 (1,000)	910 (0.43)	120 (830)	2.5 (65)	50
160-D	41,280 (56.0)	D	16,000 (7,257)	35,400 (16,057)	15.5 (390)	237 (2,300)	1,550 (0.73)	160 (1,100)	3 (75)	103

Table B-1 SPECIFICATIONS—STEAM, AIR, OR HYDRAULIC PILE HAMMERS[a] (Continued)

Make and Model[b]	Maximum Rated Energy,[c] ft·lbf (kJ)[l]	Type[d]	Ram Weight, lb (kg)	Total Weight,[e] lb (kg)	Stroke,[f] in (mm)	Boiler Capacity,[g] hp (kW)	Air Consumption,[h] scfm (m³/s)	Operating Pressure at Hammer,[i] lb/in² (kPa)	Hose Size and Number,[j] in (mm)	Operating Speed,[k] blows/min
Conmaco[m] (*continued*)										
140	42,000 (56.9)	SA	14,000 (6,350)	30,750 (13,948)	36 (910)	177 (1,700)	1,161 (0.55)	110 (760)	3 (75)	60
160	48,750 (66.1)	SA	16,250 (7,371)	33,200 (15,059)	36 (910)	198 (1,900)	1,275 (0.60)	120 (830)	3 (75)	60
200	60,000 (81.4)	SA	20,000 (9,072)	44,560 (20,212)	36 (910)	217 (2,100)	1,634 (0.77)	120 (830)	3 (75)	60
300	90,000 (122.0)	SA	30,000 (13,608)	55,390 (25,124)	36 (910)	248 (2,400)	1,833 (0.87)	150 (1,030)	3 (75)	55
5300	150,000 (203.4)	SA	30,000 (13,608)	62,000 (28,123)	60 (1,520)	234 (3,500)	2,148 (1.01)	160 (1,100)	4 (100)	46
5700	350,000 (474.5)	SA	70,000 (31,751)	152,000 (68,946)	60 (1,520)	616 (6,000)	4,502 (2.12)	160 (1,100)	2 at 4 (2 at 100)	42
6850	510,000 (691.5)	SA	85,000 (38,555)	173,600 (78,744)	72 (1,830)	806 (7,900)	5,889 (2.78)	180 (1,240)	6 (150)	40
Menck[m]										
MH 48	35,400 (48.0)	DH	5,510 (2,500)	12,790 (5,800)	35 (900)	NA	NA	1,600 (11,000)	2 at 1.25 (2 at 32)	48
MH 57	42,040 (57.0)	DH	6,610 (3,000)	14,990 (6,800)	35 (900)	NA	NA	1,820 (12,500)	2 at 1.25 (2 at 32)	48
MRBS 500	45,200 (61.3)	SA	11,020 (5,000)	15,210 (6,900)	49 (1,250)	90 (900)	1,100 (0.50)	140 (1,000)	2.5 (65)	48
MH 68	50,150 (68.0)	DH	7,720 (3,500)	17,640 (8,000)	35 (900)	NA	NA	2,110 (14,500)	2 at 1.25 (2 at 32)	48
MH 80	59,000 (80.0)	DH	9,260 (4,200)	21,830 (9,900)	35 (900)	NA	NA	2,470 (17,000)	2 at 1.50 (2 at 40)	48

Model									
MRBS 750	67,810 (91.9)	SA	16,500 (7,500)	25,520 (11,570)	49 (1,250)	185 (1,800)	1,590 (0.75)	110 (800)	3 (75)	50
MH 96	70,800 (96.0)	DH	11,020 (5,000)	25,350 (11,500)	35 (900)	NA	NA	2,830 (19,500)	2 at 1.50 (2 at 40)	48
MH 120	88,510 (120.0)	DH	13,890 (6,300)	33,520 (15,200)	35 (900)	NA	NA	2,320 (16,000)	2 at 1.50 (2 at 40)	44
MRBS 850	93,300 (126.5)	SA	18,960 (8,600)	29,760 (13,500)	59 (1,500)	150 (1,500)	1,950 (0.92)	140 (1,000)	3 (75)	45
MH 145	106,950 (145.0)	DH	16,540 (7,500)	39,690 (18,000)	35 (900)	NA	NA	2,760 (19,000)	2 at 2 (2 at 50)	42
MH 165	121,700 (165.0)	DH	19,000 (8,600)	45,200 (20,500)	35 (900)	NA	NA	3,190 (22,000)	2 at 2 (2 at 50)	42
MRBS 1500	135,620 (183.9)	SA	33,000 (15,000)	51,800 (23,500)	49 (1,250)	200 (2,000)	3,180 (1.50)	110 (800)	4 (100)	50
MHU 195	143,820 (195.0)	DH	22,000 (10,000)	48,500 (22,000)	35 (900)	NA	NA	3,000 (21,000)	2 at 2 (2 at 50)	36
MH 195	143,820 (195.0)	DH	22,000 (10,000)	52,900 (24,000)	35 (900)	NA	NA	3,560 (24,500)	2 at 2 (2 at 50)	38
MRBS 1800	189,850 (257.4)	SA	38,600 (17,500)	64,600 (29,300)	59 (1,500)	295 (2,900)	3,700 (1.75)	140 (1,000)	4 (100)	44
MHU 300	221,270 (300.0)	DH	37,000 (16,800)	74,200 (33,650)	35 (900)	NA	NA	3,000 (21,000)	2 at 2.5 (2 at 64)	42
MRBS 2500	226,030 (306.5)	SA	55,100 (25,000)	74,900 (34,000)	49 (1,250)	500 (4,900)	5,300 (2.50)	110 (800)	2 at 3 (2 at 75)	50
MHU 400	295,020 (400.0)	DH	51,800 (23,500)	92,200 (41,800)	35 (900)	NA	NA	3,100 (22,000)	2 at 3 (2 at 75)	42
MRBS 3000	325,490 (441.3)	SA	66,100 (30,000)	108,000 (49,000)	59 (1,500)	510 (5,000)	6,000 (2.83)	140 (1,000)	5 (125)	42
MRBS 4000	361,650 (490.3)	SA	88,200 (40,000)	160,900 (73,000)	49 (1,250)	800 (7,800)	8,475 (4.00)	110 (800)	2 at 4 (2 at 100)	40
MHU 600	442,540 (600.0)	DH	74,200 (33,650)	137,100 (62,200)	35 (900)	NA	NA	3,250 (23,000)	2 at 3 (2 at 75)	42
MRBS 4600	499,100 (676.7)	SA	101,400 (46,000)	176,400 (80,000)	59 (1,500)	830 (8,100)	9,900 (4.67)	140 (1,000)	6 (150)	42

Table B-1   SPECIFICATIONS—STEAM, AIR, OR HYDRAULIC PILE HAMMERS[a] (Continued)

Make and Model[b]	Maximum Rated Energy,[c] ft·lbf (kJ)[i]	Type[d]	Ram Weight, lb (kg)	Total Weight,[e] lb (kg)	Stroke,[f] in (mm)	Boiler Capacity,[g] hp (kW)	Air Consumption,[h] scfm (m³/s)	Operating Pressure at Hammer,[i] lb/in² (kPa)	Hose Size and Number,[j] in (mm)	Operating Speed,[k] blows/min
Menck[m] (continued)										
MRBS 7000	614,800 (833.6)	SA	154,300 (70,000)	302,000 (137,000)	49 (1,250)	1,400 (13,700)	14,830 (7.00)	110 (800)	2 at 6 (2 at 150)	40
MHU 900	663,810 (900.0)	DH	112,400 (51,000)	213,600 (96,900)	35 (900)	NA	NA	3,250 (23,000)	2 at 4 (2 at 100)	42
MRBS 8000	867,960 (1,176.8)	SA	176,400 (80,000)	330,700 (150,000)	59 (1,500)	1,380 (13,500)	15,900 (7.50)	140 (1,000)	8 (200)	38
MHU 1700	1,253,860 (1,700.0)	DH	211,200 (95,800)	400,100 (181,500)	35 (900)	NA	NA	3,400 (24,000)	2 at 4 (2 at 100)	30
MRBS 12500	1,582,220 (2,145.2)	SA	275,600 (125,000)	540,100 (245,000)	69 (1,750)	2,400 (23,500)	26,500 (12.50)	170 (1,200)	2 at 6 (2 at 150)	36
MKT[m]										
5	1,000 (1.4)	DA	200 (91)	1,500 (680)	7 (180)	NA	250 (0.12)	100 (690)	1.25 (32)	300
6	2,500 (3.4)	DA	400 (181)	2,900 (1,315)	8.75 (222)	NA	400 (0.19)	100 (690)	1.25 (32)	275
7	4,150 (5.6)	DA	800 (363)	5,000 (2,268)	9.5 (240)	65 (600)	450 (0.21)	100 (690)	1.5 (40)	225
9B3	8,750 (11.9)	DA	1,600 (726)	7,000 (3,175)	17 (430)	85 (800)	600 (0.28)	100 (690)	2 (50)	145
S3	9,000 (12.2)	SA	3,000 (1,361)	9,030 (4,096)	36 (910)	50 (500)	400 (0.19)	80 (550)	1.5 (40)	60
10B3	13,100 (17.8)	DA	3,000 (1,361)	10,850 (4,921)	19 (480)	104 (1,000)	750 (0.35)	100 (690)	2.5 (65)	105
C5	14,210[p] (19.3)	C	5,000 (2,268)	11,880 (5,389)	18 (460)	NA	585 (0.28)	115 (790)	2.5 (65)	110

C5	16,210[o] (22.0)	C	5,000 (2,268)	11,880 (5,389)	18 (460)	60 (600)	NA	115 (790)	2.5 (65)	110
S5	16,250 (22.0)	SA	5,000 (2,268)	12,460 (5,652)	39 (990)	85 (800)	600 (0.28)	80 (550)	2 (50)	60
11B3	19,150 (26.0)	DA	5,000 (2,268)	14,000 (6,350)	19 (480)	126 (1,200)	900 (0.42)	100 (690)	2.5 (65)	95
C826	21,210[p] (28.8)	C	8,000 (3,629)	17,750 (8,051)	18 (460)	NA	875 (0.41)	125 (860)	2.5 (65)	95
C826	24,375[q] (33.1)	C	8,000 (3,629)	17,750 (8,051)	18 (460)	60 (600)	NA	125 (860)	2.5 (65)	95
S8	26,000 (35.3)	SA	8,000 (3,629)	18,300 (8,301)	39 (990)	120 (1,200)	850 (0.40)	80 (550)	2.5 (65)	55
MS350	30,800 (41.8)	SA	7,716 (3,500)	11,925 (5,409)	48 (1,220)	50 (500)	760 (0.36)	105 (720)	2.5 (65)	40
S10	32,500 (44.1)	SA	10,000 (4,536)	22,380 (10,151)	39 (990)	130 (1,300)	1,000 (0.47)	80 (550)	2.5 (65)	55
S14	37,500 (50.8)	SA	14,000 (6,350)	31,700 (14,379)	32 (810)	155 (1,500)	NA	100 (690)	3 (75)	60
MS500	44,000 (59.7)	SA	11,000 (4,990)	16,925 (7,677)	48 (1,220)	65 (650)	1,060 (0.50)	115 (790)	2.5 (65)	40
S20	60,000 (81.4)	SA	20,000 (9,072)	38,650 (17,531)	36 (910)	190 (1,900)	NA	150 (1,030)	3 (75)	60
Raymond[m]										
1	15,000 (20.3)	SA	5,000 (2,268)	11,000 (4,990)	36 (910)	40 (440)	665 (0.31)	80 (550)	1.5 (40)	60
15M[r]	15,000 (20.3)	D	5,000 (2,268)	10,305 (4,674)	18 (460)	60 (900)	1,340 (0.63)	120 (830)	2 (50)	90
1-S	19,500 (26.4)	SA	6,500 (2,948)	12,500 (5,670)	36 (910)	40 (480)	713 (0.34)	104 (720)	1.5 (40)	58
65C	19,500 (26.4)	D	6,500 (2,948)	14,675 (6,656)	16 (410)	70 (1,000)	1,473 (0.70)	120 (830)	2 (50)	110

Table B-1   SPECIFICATIONS—STEAM, AIR, OR HYDRAULIC PILE HAMMERS[a] (Continued)

Make and Model[b]	Maximum Rated Energy,[c] ft·lbf (kJ)[l]	Type[d]	Ram Weight, lb (kg)	Total Weight,[e] lb (kg)	Stroke,[f] in (mm)	Boiler Capacity,[g] hp (kW)	Air Consumption,[h] scfm (m³/s)	Operating Pressure at Hammer,[i] lb/in² (kPa)	Hose Size and Number,[j] in (mm)	Operating Speed,[k] blows/min
Raymond[m] (continued)										
65CH	19,500 (26.4)	DH	6,500 (2,948)	14,615 (6,629)	16 (410)	NA	NA	5,000 (34,470)	1 (25)	136
1/0	24,374 (33.1)	SA	7,500 (3,402)	16,100 (7,303)	39 (990)	50 (670)	998 (0.47)	110 (760)	2 (50)	52
80C	24,450 (33.2)	D	8,000 (3,629)	17,885 (8,113)	16.5 (420)	80 (1,160)	1,710 (0.81)	120 (830)	2.5 (65)	105
80CH	24,450 (33.2)	DH	8,000 (3,629)	17,780 (8,065)	16.5 (420)	NA	NA	5,000 (34,470)	1 (25)	120
2/0	32,500 (44.1)	SA	10,000 (4,536)	18,550 (8,414)	39 (990)	55 (770)	1,140 (0.54)	110 (760)	2 (50)	50
125CX	40,625 (55.1)	D	15,000 (6,804)	32,800 (14,878)	15 (380)	150 (2,260)	NA	120 (830)	3 (75)	120
3/0	40,625 (55.1)	SA	12,500 (5,670)	21,225 (9,628)	39 (990)	70 (960)	NA	120 (830)	2.5 (65)	48
150C	48,750 (66.1)	D	15,000 (6,804)	32,500 (14,742)	18 (460)	150 (2,260)	NA	120 (830)	3 (75)	105
4/0	48,750 (66.1)	SA	15,000 (6,804)	23,800 (10,796)	39 (990)	85 (1,160)	NA	120 (830)	2.5 (65)	46
5/0	56,875 (77.1)	SA	17,500 (7,938)	26,450 (11,998)	39 (990)	100 (1,360)	NA	135 (930)	3 (75)	44
22X	56,900 (77.2)	SA	22,050 (10,002)	31,750 (14,402)	31 (790)	100 (1,450)	NA	135 (930)	3 (75)	58
30X	75,000 (101.7)	SA	30,000 (13,608)	52,000 (23,587)	30 (760)	200 (2,740)	NA	135 (930)	3 (75)	70
8/0	81,250 (110.2)	SA	25,000 (11,340)	34,000 (15,422)	39 (990)	140 (1,930)	NA	135 (930)	3 (75)	38

198

Model									
40X	100,000 (135.6)	SA	40,000 (18,144)	62,000 (28,123)	30 (760)	250 (3,220)	NA	135 (930)	3 (75)	64
60X	150,000 (203.4)	SA	60,000 (27,216)	85,000 (38,555)	30 (760)	300 (3,900)	NA	165 (1,140)	4 (100)	60
Vulcan™									
DGH-900	4,000 (5.4)	D	900 (408)	5,000 (2,268)	10 (250)	75 (700)	580 (0.27)	78 (540)	1.5 (40)	238
2	7,260 (9.8)	SA	3,000 (1,361)	6,700 (3,039)	29 (740)	49 (500)	336 (0.16)	80 (550)	1.5 (40)	70
30C	7,260 (9.8)	D	3,000 (1,361)	7,036 (3,191)	12.5 (320)	70 (700)	488 (0.23)	120 (830)	1.5 (40)	133
1 and 106ˢ	15,000 (20.3)	SA	5,000 (2,268)	9,700 (4,400)	36 (910)	81 (800)	565 (0.27)	80 (550)	2 (50)	60
50C	15,100 (20.5)	D	5,000 (2,268)	11,782 (5,344)	15.5 (390)	125 (1,200)	880 (0.42)	120 (830)	2 (50)	117
65C	19,200 (26.0)	D	6,500 (2,948)	14,886 (6,752)	15.5 (390)	152 (1,500)	991 (0.47)	150 (1,030)	2 (50)	115
06 and 106ˢ	19,500 (26.4)	SA	6,500 (2,948)	11,200 (5,080)	36 (910)	94 (900)	625 (0.29)	100 (690)	2 (50)	60
65CA	19,580 (26.6)	D	6,500 (2,498)	16,385 (7,432)	16.5 (420)	160 (1,600)	1,142 (0.54)	95 (660)	2.5 (65)	107
0	24,375 (33.1)	SA	7,500 (3,402)	16,250 (7,371)	39 (990)	128 (1,300)	841 (0.40)	80 (550)	2.5 (65)	50
80C	24,450 (33.2)	D	8,000 (3,629)	17,885 (8,113)	16.5 (420)	180 (1,800)	1,245 (0.59)	120 (830)	2.5 (65)	109
08	26,000 (35.3)	SA	8,000 (3,629)	16,750 (7,598)	39 (990)	125 (1,200)	880 (0.42)	83 (570)	2.5 (65)	50
0R	30,225 (41.0)	SA	9,300 (4,218)	18,050 (8,187)	39 (990)	140 (1,400)	1,020 (0.48)	100 (690)	2.5 (65)	50
010	32,500 (44.1)	SA	10,000 (4,536)	18,750 (8,505)	39 (990)	150 (1,500)	1,002 (0.47)	105 (720)	2.5 (65)	50
140C	36,000 (48.8)	D	14,000 (6,350)	27,984 (12,693)	15.5 (390)	211 (2,100)	1,425 (0.67)	140 (970)	3 (75)	101

Table B-1 SPECIFICATIONS—STEAM, AIR, OR HYDRAULIC PILE HAMMERS[a] (Continued)

Make and Model[b]	Maximum Rated Energy,[c] ft·lbf (kJ)[l]	Type[d]	Ram Weight, lb (kg)	Total Weight,[e] lb (kg)	Stroke,[f] in (mm)	Boiler Capacity,[g] hp (kW)	Air Consumption,[h] scfm (m³/s)	Operating Pressure at Hammer,[i] lb/in² (kPa)	Hose Size and Number,[j] in (mm)	Operating Speed,[k] blows/min
Vulcan[m] (*continued*)										
012	39,000 (52.9)	SA	12,000 (5,443)	20,750 (9,412)	39 (990)	175 (1,700)	1,075 (0.51)	125 (860)	2.5 (65)	50
014	42,000 (56.9)	SA	14,000 (6,350)	27,500 (12,474)	36 (910)	200 (2,000)	1,161 (0.55)	110 (760)	3 (75)	59
016	48,750 (66.1)	SA	16,250 (7,371)	33,340 (15,123)	36 (910)	150 (1,500)	1,275 (0.60)	120 (830)	3 (75)	58
200C	50,200 (68.1)	D	20,000 (9,072)	42,315 (19,194)	15.5 (390)	300 (3,000)	2,002 (0.94)	142 (980)	4 (100)	98
020	60,000 (81.4)	SA	20,000 (9,072)	43,785 (19,861)	36 (910)	200 (2,000)	1,634 (0.77)	120 (830)	3 (75)	59
030	90,000 (122.0)	SA	30,000 (13,608)	55,410 (25,134)	36 (910)	250 (2,500)	1,833 (0.87)	150 (1,030)	3 (75)	54
400C	113,448 (153.8)	D	40,000 (18,144)	92,300 (41,867)	16.5 (420)	750 (7,400)	5,281 (2.49)	150 (1,030)	6 (150)	102
340	120,000 (162.7)	SA	40,000 (18,144)	98,140 (44,516)	36 (910)	500 (4,900)	3,400 (1.60)	120 (830)	2 at 3 (2 at 75)	62
530	150,000 (203.4)	SA	30,000 (13,608)	57,680 (26,163)	60 (1,520)	300 (2,900)	2,076 (0.98)	150 (1,030)	3 (75)	42
600C	179,130 (242.9)	D	60,000 (27,216)	120,000 (54,431)	18 (460)	900 (8,800)	6,530 (3.08)	160 (1,100)	3 at 4 (3 at 100)	90
360	180,000 (244.1)	SA	60,000 (27,216)	124,830 (56,622)	36 (910)	650 (6,400)	4,652 (2.20)	130 (900)	2 at 4 (2 at 100)	60
540	204,500 (277.3)	SA	40,900 (18,552)	102,980 (46,711)	60 (1,520)	500 (4,900)	3,755 (1.77)	130 (900)	3 at 4 (3 at 100)	48
560	312,500 (423.7)	SA	62,500 (28,350)	134,060 (60,809)	60 (1,520)	750 (7,400)	5,410 (2.55)	150 (1,030)	3 at 4 (3 at 100)	47

5100	500,000 (677.9)	SA	100,000 (45,359)	60 (1,520)	219,000 (99,337)	1,300 (13,000)	9,326 (4.40)	150 (1,030)	3 at 4 (3 at 100) 48
5150	750,000 (1,016.9)	SA	150,000 (68,039)	60 (1,520)	275,000 (124,738)	1,700 (16,700)	11,399 (5.38)	175 (1,210)	2 at 6 (2 at 150) 46
5250	1,250,000 (1,694.8)	SA	250,000 (133,398)	60 (1,520)	470,000 (213,188)	2,000 (19,600)	13,846 (6.53)	200 (1,380)	2 at 6 (2 at 150) 38
6300	1,800,000 (2,440.5)	SA	300,000 (136,078)	72 (1,830)	575,000 (260,816)	3,000 (29,400)	21,061 (9.94)	175 (1,210)	2 at 6 (2 at 150) 38

[a] Specifications are often subject to change without notice.

[b] Some models are no longer manufactured but may still be in use. Different model numbers may be shown for hammers that are essentially the same but that have slightly different characteristics.

[c] Energy ratings are fixed by ram weight and stroke and, in addition for double-acting, differential, and compound hammers, by piston areas and operating pressures. The energy for all types of hammers can be varied by adjusting the stroke and to some degree by adjusting the operating pressure. Strokes can be adjusted by changing slide bars to vary the wedge location, by using a multiple-wedge slide bar to activate a movable valve trip, or by using a special control device to vary the stroke within set limits.

[d] SA = single-acting, DA = double-acting, D = differential, C = compound, H = hydraulic.

[e] Includes the weight of the base.

[f] Maximum or normal stroke. For double-acting, differential, and compound hammers, an equivalent stroke can be computed from the energy and ram weight. For many hammers, the stroke can be varied.

[g] Except for Raymond hammers, the boiler capacity is based on a steam consumption at 212°F of 34.5 lb/h being equal to 1 (boiler) horsepower (16.4 kg/h at 100°C = 10 kW). For Raymond hammers, the boiler capacity is based on 10 ft² (1 m²) of heating surface per horsepower.

[h] Except for Raymond hammers, air consumption is based on adiabatic compression. Unless the air is reheated before entering the hammer, the actual consumption will be greater. The compressor capacity should be from 30 to 50 percent greater than the air consumption shown depending on operational conditions at the site. For Raymond hammers, the theoretical air consumption is based on steam consumption, assuming that there is equivalent volumetric throughput at the normal working pressure in the hammer, that the steam is saturated, and that the air temperature in the hammer is 100°F (38°C).

[i] Pressure at the boiler should be from 15 to 25 lb/in² (100 to 170 kPa) higher to provide for line losses.

[j] Piping should be of the next larger size. The use of two or more hoses increases pressure and temperature losses.

[k] For the stroke shown. The operating speed depends on several factors, such as penetration resistance, cushion material, operating pressure, stroke, pile material, and hammer rebound. The speeds given are for hard driving under ideal conditions. Delivered energy is not a function of operating speed.

[l] Except for Menck hammers, the SI values are approximate. They have been rounded off to reflect a degree of precision comparable to that of the inch-pound values. For Menck hammers the inch-pound values are approximate.

[m] *Conmaco:* Conmaco, Inc., P.O. Box 5097, Kansas City, Kan. 66119. *Menck:* International Construction Equipment, Inc., 301 Warehouse Dr., Matthews, N.C. 28105. *MKT:* MKT Geotechnical Systems, Box 793, Dover, N.J. 07801. *Raymond:* Raymond International Builders, Inc., P.O. Box 22718, Houston, Tex. 77227. *Vulcan:* Vulcan Iron Works Inc., 2909 Riverside Dr., Chattanooga, Tenn. 37406.

[n] K models have keyed hammer columns; C models have cable columns.

[o] Hammers have short cylinders.

[p] When operated by compressed air.

[q] When operated by steam.

[r] Internal hammer used with special Raymond mandrel.

[s] For model 106 the ram weight can be changed from 5000 to 6500 lb (2268 to 2948 kg) by adding two 750-lb (340-kg) weights which fit inside cylinders formed in the ram.

Table B-2   SPECIFICATIONS—DIESEL PILE HAMMERS[a]

Make and Model[b]	Range of Rated Energy,[c] ft · lbf (kJ)[h]	Type[d]	Piston Weight, lb (kg)	Total Weight,[e] lb (kg)	Stroke,[f] in (mm)	Operating Speed,[g] blows/min
Berminghammer[i]						
B-200	9,000– 18,000	SA	2,000	5,500	122	40– 60
	(12.2– 24.4)		(907)	(2,495)	(3,100)	
B-225[j]	14,500– 29,000	SA	3,031	6,945	118	40– 60
	(19.7– 39.3)		(1,373)	(3,150)	(3,000)	
B-300[j]	17,000– 34,000	SA	3,727	7,795	130	40– 60
	(23.1– 46.1)		(1,690)	(3,536)	(3,300)	
B-400	23,000– 46,000	SA	5,000	12,325	129	40– 60
	(31.2– 62.4)		(2,268)	(5,590)	(3,280)	
B-500	39,500– 79,000	SA	6,900	16,000	156	35– 60
	(53.6–107.1)		(3,130)	(7,257)	(3,960)	
Delmag[i]						
D2	1,815	SA	484	792	51	60– 70
	(2.5)		(220)	(360)	(1,300)	
D4	3,630	SA	836	1,360	61	50– 60
	(4.9)		(380)	(620)	(1,550)	
D5	9,100	SA	1,100	2,730	98	42– 60
	(12.3)		(500)	(1,238)	(2,500)	
D8-22	9,500– 18,000	SA	1,765	4,760	123	38– 52
	(12.9– 24.4)		(800)	(2,159)	(3,120)	
D12	22,500	SA	2,755	6,050	98	40– 60
	(30.5)		(1,250)	(2,744)	(2,500)	
D15	27,100	SA	3,305	6,600	98	40– 60
	(36.7)		(1,500)	(2,994)	(2,500)	
D22	39,700	SA	4,850	11,200	98	42– 60
	(53.8)		(2,200)	(5,080)	(2,500)	
D22-02	24,500– 48,500	SA	4,850	11,400	120	38– 54
	(33.2– 65.8)		(2,200)	(5,171)	(3,050)	
D22-13	24,500– 48,500	SA	4,850	11,400	120	38– 52
	(33.2– 65.8)		(2,200)	(5,171)	(3,050)	
D30	23,800– 54,250	SA	6,615	12,300	98	39– 60
	(32.3– 73.6)		(3,000)	(5,579)	(2,500)	
D30-02	33,700– 66,100	SA	6,615	13,150	120	38– 54
D30-13	(45.7– 89.6)		(3,000)	(5,965)	(3,050)	
D36-02	38,000– 83,100	SA	7,935	17,700	126	37– 53
D36-13	(51.5–112.7)		(3,600)	(8,029)	(3,250)	
D36	38,000– 83,100	SA	7,935	17,700	126	37– 53
	(51.5–112.7)		(3,600)	(8,029)	(3,250)	
D44	43,500– 87,000	SA	9,480	22,300	110	37– 56
	(59.0–118.0)		(4,300)	(10,115)	(2,790)	
D46-02	48,400–105,000	SA	10,140	19,900	128	37– 53
D46-13	(65.6–142.4)		(4,600)	(9,026)	(3,250)	
D55	62,010–117,000	SA	12,125	26,300	116	36– 47
	(84.1–158.6)		(5,500)	(11,930)	(2,950)	
D62-02	78,000–162,000	SA	14,000	27,900	138	35– 50
	(105.8–219.6)		(6,350)	(12,655)	(3,510)	

Table B-2   SPECIFICATIONS—DIESEL PILE HAMMERS[a] **(Continued)**

Make and Model[b]	Range of Rated Energy,[c] ft · lbf (kJ)[h]	Type[d]	Piston Weight, lb (kg)	Total Weight,[e] lb (kg)	Stroke,[f] in (mm)	Operating Speed,[g] blows/min
Delmag[i]						
(continued)						
D62-12	82,600–165,000	SA	14,600	28,000	138	34– 50
	(112.0–223.7)		(6,622)	(12,700)	(3,510)	
D80-12	90,000–225,000	SA	19,510	35,900	138	35– 50
	(122.0–305.1)		(8,850)	(16,284)	(3,510)	
D100	138,000–300,000	SA	23,000	42,000	156	32– 50
	(187.1–406.8)		(10,433)	(19,051)	(3,960)	
FEC[i]						
1200	9,000– 22,500	SA	2,645	6,549	129	40– 60
	(12.2– 30.5)		(1,200)	(2,966)	(3,280)	
1500	10,840– 27,100	SA	3,305	7,225	132	40– 60
	(14.7– 36.7)		(1,500)	(3,277)	(3,350)	
2500	21,000– 52,500	SA	5,500	12,100	124	40– 60
	(28.5– 71.2)		(2,500)	(5,490)	(3,150)	
3000	25,200– 63,000	SA	6,615	13,200	126	40– 60
	(34.2– 85.4)		(3,000)	(5,987)	(3,200)	
ICE[i]						
105[k]	3,750– 7,500	DA	1,445	3,885	53.8	95– 98
	(5.1– 10.2)		(655)	(1,762)	(1,370)	
180[k]	4,050– 8,100	DA	1,725	4,645	55.7	90– 95
	(5.5– 11.0)		(782)	(2,107)	(1,410)	
312[k]	9,000– 18,000	DA	3,857	10,375	46.4	100–105
	(12.2– 24.4)		(1,750)	(4,706)	(1,180)	
440[k]	9,050– 18,100	DA	4,000	9,839	54	88– 92
	(12.3– 24.5)		(1,814)	(4,463)	(1,370)	
520[k]	15,000– 30,000	DA	5,070	13,845	62.2	80– 84
	(20.3– 40.7)		(2,300)	(6,280)	(1,580)	
640	40,000	DA	6,000	15,565	80	74– 77
	(54.2)		(2,722)	(7,060)	(2,030)	
660	25,000– 50,000	DA	7,500	24,480	80	84– 88
	(33.9– 67.8)		(3,402)	(11,104)	(2,030)	
1070	35,000– 70,000	DA	10,000	21,500	84	64– 68
	(47.5– 94.9)		(4,536)	(9,752)	(2,130)	
Kobe[i]						
K-13	19,398– 25,388	SA	2,870	8,000	106	40– 60
	(26.3– 34.4)		(1,300)	(3,630)	(2,700)	
K-22	34,665– 46,245	SA	4,850	11,700	112	39– 60
	(47.0– 62.7)		(2,200)	(5,310)	(2,850)	
K-25	39,386– 52,588	SA	5,510	13,100	112	39–60
	(53.4– 71.3)		(2,500)	(5,940)	(2,850)	
K-32	50,449– 67,266	SA	7,050	16,500	112	39– 60
	(68.4– 91.2)		(3,200)	(7,480)	(2,850)	
K-35	55,170– 73,609	SA	7,720	18,700	112	39– 69
	(74.8– 99.8)		(3,500)	(8,480)	(2,850)	

Table B-2   SPECIFICATIONS—DIESEL PILE HAMMERS[a] (Continued)

Make and Model[b]	Range of Rated Energy,[c] ft · lbf (kJ)[h]	Type[d]	Piston Weight, lb (kg)	Total Weight,[e] lb (kg)	Stroke,[f] in (mm)	Operating Speed,[g] blows/min
Kobe[i]						
(continued)						
K-42	66,233– 88,286 (89.8–119.7)	SA	9,260 (4,200)	23,300 (10,570)	112 (2,850)	39– 60
K-45	70,953– 94,629	SA	9,920	25,600	112	39– 60
KB-45	(96.2–128.3)		(4,500)	(11,610)	(2,850)	
KB-60	94,629–126,123	SA	13,230	37,500	112	35– 60
	(128.3–171.0)		(6,000)	(17,000)	(2,850)	
KB-80	126,123–168,164	SA	17,640	45,200	112	35– 60
	(171.0–228.0)		(8,000)	(20,500)	(2,850)	
Mitsubishi[i]						
M-14S	15,430– 26,300 (20.9– 35.7)	SA	3,090 (1,400)	7,280 (3,300)	102 (2,600)	42– 60
MH-15	16,530– 28,200 (22.4– 38.3)	SA	3,310 (1,500)	8,380 (3,800)	102 (2,600)	42– 60
MB-22	24,250– 41,400 (32.9– 56.1)	SA	4,850 (2,200)	11,680 (5,300)	102 (2,600)	42– 60
M-23	25,350– 43,300 (34.4– 58.6)	SA	5,070 (2,300)	11,240 (5,100)	102 (2,600)	42– 60
MH-23	27,560– 47,000 (37.4– 63.7)	SA	5,510 (2,500)	13,230 (6,000)	102 (2,600)	42– 60
M-33	36,380– 62,100 (49.3– 84.1)	SA	7,280 (3,300)	16,980 (7,700)	102 (2,600)	42– 60
MH-35	38,580– 65,800 (52.3– 89.2)	SA	7,720 (3,500)	18,520 (8,400)	102 (2,600)	42– 60
M-43	47,400– 80,900 (64.3–109.6)	SA	9,480 (4,300)	22,710 (10,300)	102 (2,600)	42– 60
MB-43	49,600– 84,600 (67.3–114.7)	SA	9,920 (4,500)	24,690 (11,200)	102 (2,600)	42– 60
MH-45	50,270– 85,800	SA	10,050	24,600	102	42– 60
MH-45B	(68.2–116.3)		(4,560)	(11,160)	(2,600)	
MB-70	79,370–135,400	SA	15,870	40,790	102	42– 60
MH-72B	(107.6–183.6)		(7,200)	(18,500)	(2,600)	
MH-80	88,180–150,400 (119.6–204.0)	SA	17,640 (8,000)	42,330 (19,200)	102 (2,600)	42– 60
MKT[i]						
DA-15C[l]	6,600– 8,200 (9.0– 11.1)	DA	1,100 (500)	4,825 (2,190)	90 (2,290)	78– 82
DA-15	6,600– 8,300 (9.0– 11.3)	DA	1,100 (500)	5,000 (2,270)	90 (2,290)	78– 82
DE-10	6,600– 8,800 (9.0– 11.9)	SA	1,100 (500)	3,100 (1,400)	96 (2,440)	40– 50
DA-15C[l]	6,600– 9,350[m] (9.0– 12.7)	SA SA	1,100 (500)	4,825 (2,190)	126 (3,200)	40– 50
DE-20	12,000– 16,000 (16.3– 21.7)	SA	2,000 (905)	5,375 (2,440)	96 (2,440)	40– 50

Table B-2 SPECIFICATIONS—DIESEL PILE HAMMERS[a] (Continued)

Make and Model[b]	Range of Rated Energy,[c] ft · lbf (kJ)[h]	Type[d]	Piston Weight, lb (kg)	Total Weight,[e] lb (kg)	Stroke,[f] in (mm)	Operating Speed,[g] blows/min
MKT[i]						
(continued)						
DE-20B/30B/	12,000– 17,000[m]	SA	2,000	6,450	120	40– 50
33[n]	(16.3– 23.1)		(905)	(2,925)	(3,050)	
DA-35B[l]	15,600– 21,000	DA	2,800	10,800	90	78– 82
DA-35C[l]	(21.2– 28.5)		(1,270)	(4,900)	(2,290)	
DE-30	16,800– 22,400	SA	2,800	8,125	96	40– 50
	(22.8– 30.4)		(1,270)	(3,685)	(2,440)	
DA-35B[l]	16,800– 23,800[m]	SA	2,800	10,800	126	40– 50
DA-35C[e]	(22.8– 32.3)		(1,270)	(4,900)	(3,200)	
DE-30B/	16,800– 23,800[m]	SA	2,800	7,250	120	40– 50
33/20B[n]	(22.8– 32.3)		(1,270)	(3,290)	(3,050)	
DA-45[l]	18,500– 30,700	DA	4,000	14,200	92	78– 82
	(25.1– 41.6)		(1,815)	(6,440)	(2,340)	
DE-33/20B/	19,800– 28,050[m]	SA	3,300	7,750	96	40– 50
30B[n]	(26.9– 38.0)		(1,497)	(3,515)	(2,440)	
DE-40	24,000– 32,000	SA	4,000	9,825	96	40– 50
	(32.5– 43.4)		(1,815)	(4,455)	(2,440)	
DA-45[l]	24,000– 34,000[m]	SA	4,000	14,200	126	40– 50
	(32.5– 46.1)		(1,815)	(6,440)	(3,200)	
DA-55B[l]	31,200– 38,200	DA	5,000	17,000	92	78– 82
DA-55C[l]	(42.3– 51.8)		(2,270)	(7,710)	(2,340)	
DA-55B[l]	30,000– 42,500[m]	SA	5,000	17,000	126	40– 50
DA-55C[l]	(40.7– 57.6)		(2,270)	(7,710)	(3,200)	
DE-50B	30,000– 42,500[m]	SA	5,000	12,000	126	40– 50
	(40.7– 57.6)		(2,270)	(5,445)	(3,200)	
DE-50B/70B[j]	30,000– 42,500[m]	SA	5,000	12,700	126	40– 50
	(40.7– 57.6)		(2,270)	(5,760)	(3,200)	
DE-70B/50B[j]	42,000– 59,500[m]	SA	7,000	14,700	126	40– 50
	(56.9– 80.7)		(3,175)	(6,670)	(3,200)	
DE-110	66,000– 93,500[m]	SA	11,000	24,150	126	40– 50
	(89.4–126.6)		(5,000)	(10,950)	(3,200)	
Vulcan[i]						
1C-30	24,000	SA	3,000	7,500	120	50– 60
	(32.5)		(1,361)	(3,402)	(3,050)	
01N100	24,600	SA	3,000	7,645	98	50– 60
N-33	(33.4)		(1,361)	(3,468)	(2,490)	
04N100	32,549	SA	3,960	9,845	97.6	50– 60
N-46	(44.1)		(1,796)	(4,466)	(2,480)	
03N100	43,400	SA	5,280	12,760	97.6	50– 60
N-60	(58.8)		(2,395)	(5,788)	(2,480)	

[a]Specifications are often subject to change without notice.

[b]Some models are no longer manufactured but may still be in use. Different model numbers may be shown for hammers that are essentially the same but that have slightly different characteristics.

[c]Energy ratings are based on the piston (ram) weight and maximum stroke for single-acting hammers or on

the equivalent stroke for double-acting (closed-top) hammers except as noted. Energy can be reduced by abnormal preignition. Energy can be varied by adjusting the fuel pump settings and by controlling the throttle.

[d]SA = single-acting (open-top), DA = double-acting (closed-top).

[e]Total weights are with anvils but without drive caps.

[f]Maximum stroke for single-acting hammers. Equivalent stroke for double-acting hammers. The length of the stroke will vary directly with the driving resistance, the fuel setting, the pile type and size, and other factors.

[g]The operating speed will vary inversely with the length of the stroke. Delivered energy is not a function of operating speed.

[h]For the Berminghammer, ICE, MKT, and Vulcan hammers, the SI values are approximate. They have been rounded off to reflect a degree of precision comparable to that of the inch-pound values. For the other hammers the inch-pound values are approximate.

[i]*Berminghammer:* Berminghammer Corporation Limited, Wellington Street Marine Terminal, Hamilton, Ont., Canada L8L 4Z9. *Delmag:* Pileco Inc., P.O. Box 16099, Houston, Tex. 77022. *FEC:* The Foundation Equipment Corp., 100 Elizabeth St., Newcomerstown, Ohio 43832. *ICE:* International Construction Equipment, Inc., 301 Warehouse Dr., Matthews, N.C. 28105. *Kobe:* L. B. Foster Company, 4825 N. Scott St., Schiller Park, Ill. 60176. *Mitsubishi:* International Construction Equipment, Inc., 301 Warehouse Dr., Matthews, N.C. 28105. *MKT:* MKT Geotechnical Systems, Box 793, Dover, N.J. 07801. *Vulcan:* Vulcan Iron Works Inc., 2909 Riverside Dr., Chattanooga, Tenn. 37406.

[j]Can be fitted with two pistons, each having a different weight.

[k]Formerly Linkbelt and Syntron.

[l]Convertible from the double-acting mode to the single-acting mode and vice versa.

[m]Based on an 8.5-ft (2590-mm) stroke.

[n]Can be fitted with three pistons, each having a different weight.

Table B-3 SPECIFICATIONS—VIBRATORY PILE DRIVERS^a

Make and Model^b	Eccentric Moment, lbf · in (N · m)^g	Dynamic Force,^{c} ton (kN)	Drive	Steady-State Frequency, cycles/min	Output,^{d} hp (kW)	Vibrating Weight,^{e} lb (kg)	Total Operating Weight,^{f} lb (kg)
Foster^h							
1000	1,000	36.4	Hydraulic	1,600	120	3,400	5,200
	(113)	(323)			(90)	(1,540)	(2,360)
1200	1,200	38.3	Hydraulic	1,500	70	6,320	6,700
	(136)	(341)			(52)	(2,865)	(3,040)
1700	1,740	48.4	Hydraulic	1,400	147	7,200	12,900
	(197)	(431)			(110)	(3,265)	(5,850)
1800	1,800	65.4	Hydraulic	1,600	175	6,175	10,900
	(203)	(582)			(130)	(2,800)	(4,945)
4000	4,000	111.3	Hydraulic	1,400	299	9,440	18,800
	(452)	(990)			(223)	(4,280)	(8,530)
4030 DM	4,000^i	127.8^i	Hydraulic	1,500	350	8,700	17,600
	(452)	(1,137)			(261)	(3,945)	(7,985)
4150	4,166	134.4	Hydraulic	1,500	350	10,516	15,895
	(471)	(1,196)			(261)	(4,770)	(7,210)
ICE^h							
116	600	21.8	Hydraulic	1,600	94	2,500	4,200
	(68)	(194)			(70)	(1,135)	(1,905)
216	1,000	36.4	Hydraulic	1,600	115	2,700	4,825
	(113)	(324)			(85)	(1,225)	(2,190)
416	1,800	65.4	Hydraulic	1,500	200	7,175	13,100
	(203)	(582)			(150)	(3,255)	(5,940)
812	4,000	145.3	Hydraulic	1,600	400	10,500	15,600
	(452)	(1,293)			(300)	(4,765)	(7,075)
1412	10,000	204.5	Hydraulic	1,200	550	13,400	20,400
	(1,130)	(1,819)			(410)	(6,080)	(9,255)
MKT^h							
V-5	1,000	36.4	Hydraulic	1,600	79	4,000	6,800
	(113)	(324)			(59)	(1,815)	(3,090)
V-10	1,152	56.0	Hydraulic	1,850	110	8,100	10,000
	(130)	(498)			(82)	(3,675)	(4,535)
V-14	1,442	70.1	Hydraulic	1,850	140	8,300	10,500
	(163)	(624)			(104)	(3,765)	(4,765)
V-16	1,800	78.3	Hydraulic	1,750	200	7,600	12,000
	(203)	(697)			(149)	(3,450)	(5,445)
V-18	2,400	98.5	Hydraulic	1,700	248	11,100	15,400
	(271)	(876)			(185)	(5,035)	(6,985)
V-20	2,600	100.0	Hydraulic	1,650	310	9,000	12,500
	(294)	(890)			(231)	(4,080)	(5,670)
V-36	5,309	193.0	Hydraulic	1,600	550	13,350	18,800
	(600)	(1,717)			(410)	(6,055)	(8,530)
PTC^h							
3H^j	266	15.1	Hydraulic	2,000	25	1,540	1,590
	(30)	(134)			(19)	(700)	(720)
13H1	1,106	42.3	Hydraulic	1,640	133	2,000	4,100
	(125)	(376)			(99.4)	(910)	(1,860)
14H^j	1,239	39.6	Hydraulic	1,500	70	2,870	6,700
	(140)	(352)			(52)	(1,300)	(3,040)
14H2	1,239	39.6	Hydraulic	1,500	120	2,870	5,510
	(140)	(352)			(90)	(1,300)	(2,500)
2-40^{j,k}	1,770	30.4	Electric	1,100	100	8,110	10,200
	(200)	(271)			(75)	(3,680)	(4,625)

Table B-3   SPECIFICATIONS—VIBRATORY PILE DRIVERS[a] *(Continued)*

Make and Model[b]	Eccentric Moment, lbf · in (N · m)[g]	Dynamic Force,[c] ton (kN)	Drive	Steady-State Frequency, cycles/min	Output,[d] hp (kW)	Vibrating Weight,[e] lb (kg)	Total Operating Weight,[f] lb (kg)
PTC[h]							
(continued)							
20A3	1,770	30.4	Electric	1,100	80	4,630	9,920
	(200)	(271)			(60)	(2,100)	(4,500)
20H4	1,770	56.6	Hydraulic	1,500	165	9,300	12,900
	(200)	(503)			(123)	(4,220)	(5,850)
20H6	1,770	64.4	Hydraulic	1,600	185	3,970	7,720
	(200)	(572)			(138)	(1,800)	(3,500)
25H1	2,213	70.7	Hydraulic	1,500	249	4,630	7,715
	(250)	(629)			(186)	(2,100)	(3,500)
2-75[j,k,l]	3,540	52.3	Electric	1,020	150	9,740	15,500
	(400)	(465)			(112)	(4,420)	(7,030)
40A2[l]	3,540	54.9	Electric	1,045	150	5,730	18,080
	(400)	(488)			(110)	(2,600)	(8,200)
40-H	3,540	113.1	Hydraulic	1,500	330	8,700	21,500
	(400)	(1,006)			(246)	(3,945)	(9,750)
50H1	4,425	141.4	Hydraulic	1,500	482	7,050	16,980
	(500)	(1,258)			(355)	(3,200)	(7,700)
50H2	4,425	156.9	Hydraulic	1,580	476	9,920	17,640
	(500)	(1,396)			(355)	(4,500)	(8,000)
100H1	8,850	152.1	Hydraulic	1,110	650	8,820	19,860
	(1,000)	(1,353)			(485)	(4,000)	(9,000)
Resonant[h]							
RDU 400 S[m]	98.6 (11.3)	69 (613)	Internal-combustion engine	4,800– 7,200	400 (300)	2,000 (910)	20,000 (9,100)
RDU 400 T[n]	128 (14.7)	95 (845)	Internal-combustion engine	4,800– 7,200	400 (300)	2,000 (910)	20,000 (9,100)

[a]Specifications are often subject to change without notice.

[b]Some models are no longer manufactured but may still be in use. Different model numbers may be shown for drivers that are essentially the same but that have slightly different characteristics.

[c]At the maximum frequency shown when a 2000-lb (900-kg) pile is being driven in granular soil.

[d]At the oscillator.

[e]With standard head and clamp but without pile.

[f]Can be increased by adding static weights.

[g]Except for PTC drivers, the SI values are approximate. They have been rounded off to reflect a degree of precision comparable to that of the inch-pound values. For the PTC drivers, the inch-pound values are approximate.

[h]*Foster:* L. B. Foster Company, 4825 N. Scott St., Schiller Park, Ill. 60176. *ICE:* International Construction Equipment, Inc., 301 Warehouse Dr., Matthews, N.C. 28105. *MKT:* MKT Geotechnical Systems, Box 793, Dover, N.J. 07801. *PTC:* Pileco Inc., P.O. Box 16099, Houston, Tex. 77022. *Resonant:* Hawker Siddeley Canada Ltd., P.O. Box 4200, Vancouver, B.C., Canada VGB 4K6.

[i]Eccentric moment can be changed to 3000 lbf · in (339 N · m), and thus the dynamic force is decreased to 95.9 ton (853 kN).

[j]Model numbers assigned by L. B. Foster.

[k]Force and frequency can be varied by changing the sprocket ratio.

[l]Can be used in tandem or twin-tandem. For tandem use, the tabulated values for dynamic force, eccentric moment, and output are 2 times greater. For twin-tandem use, these values are 4 times greater.

[m]With steel rollers.

[n]With tungsten rollers.

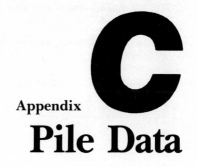

Appendix **C**

Pile Data

Table C-1   DIMENSIONS AND WEIGHTS OF HP SHAPES

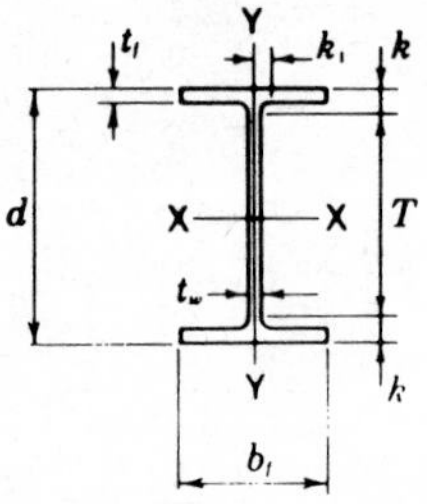

HP SHAPES
Dimensions

Designation	Area A	Depth d		Web Thickness t_w		$\frac{t_w}{2}$	Flange Width b_f		Flange Thickness t_f		T	k	k_1
	In.²	In.		In.		In.	In.		In.		In.	In.	In.
HP 14x117	34.4	14.21	14¼	0.805	13/16	7/16	14.885	14⅞	0.805	13/16	11¼	1½	1 1/16
x102	30.0	14.01	14	0.705	11/16	3/8	14.785	14¾	0.705	11/16	11¼	1⅜	1
x 89	26.1	13.83	13⅞	0.615	5/8	5/16	14.695	14¾	0.615	5/8	11¼	1 5/16	15/16
x 73	21.4	13.61	13⅝	0.505	1/2	1/4	14.585	14⅝	0.505	1/2	11¼	1 3/16	7/8
HP 13x100	29.4	13.15	13⅛	0.765	3/4	3/8	13.205	13¼	0.765	3/4	10¼	1 7/16	1
x 87	25.5	12.95	13	0.665	11/16	3/8	13.105	13⅛	0.665	11/16	10¼	1⅜	15/16
x 73	21.6	12.75	12¾	0.565	9/16	5/16	13.005	13	0.565	9/16	10¼	1¼	15/16
x 60	17.5	12.54	12½	0.460	7/16	1/4	12.900	12⅞	0.460	7/16	10¼	1⅛	7/8
HP 12x 84	24.6	12.28	12¼	0.685	11/16	3/8	12.295	12¼	0.685	11/16	9½	1⅜	1
x 74	21.8	12.13	12⅛	0.605	5/8	5/16	12.215	12¼	0.610	5/8	9½	1 5/16	15/16
x 63	18.4	11.94	12	0.515	1/2	1/4	12.125	12⅛	0.515	1/2	9½	1¼	7/8
x 53	15.5	11.78	11¾	0.435	7/16	1/4	12.045	12	0.435	7/16	9½	1⅛	7/8
HP 10x 57	16.8	9.99	10	0.565	9/16	5/16	10.225	10¼	0.565	9/16	7⅝	1 3/16	13/16
x 42	12.4	9.70	9¾	0.415	7/16	1/4	10.075	10⅛	0.420	7/16	7⅝	1 1/16	3/4
HP 8x 36	10.6	8.02	8	0.445	7/16	1/4	8.155	8⅛	0.445	7/16	6⅛	15/16	5/8

SOURCE: Courtesy of American Institute of Steel Construction.

Table C-2   SIZES AND WEIGHTS OF WELDED AND SEAMLESS STEEL PIPE PILES*

Outside Diameter, in	Nominal Thickness, in	Weight per Linear Foot (Plain Ends), lb	Outside Diameter, in	Nominal Thickness, in	Weight per Linear Foot (Plain Ends), lb
6	0.134	8.40	10¾	0.203	22.88
	0.141	8.80		0.219	24.60
	0.156	9.74		0.230	25.84
	0.164	10.28		0.250	28.04
	0.172	10.70		0.279	31.20
				0.307	34.24
8	0.141	11.80		0.344	38.20
	0.172	14.36		0.365	40.48
				0.438	48.19
8⅝	0.109	9.95		0.500	54.74
	0.141	12.74			
	0.172	15.20	12	0.134	17.04
	0.188	16.90		0.141	17.81
	0.203	18.26		0.150	18.92
	0.219	19.64		0.164	20.78
	0.250	22.36		0.172	21.71
	0.277	24.70		0.179	22.60
	0.312	27.74		0.188	23.72
	0.322	28.55		0.203	25.57
	0.344	30.40		0.219	27.56
	0.375	33.04		0.230	28.98
	0.438	38.26		0.250	31.87
	0.500	43.39		0.281	35.17
				0.312	38.95
10	0.109	11.51			
	0.120	12.62	12¾	0.109	14.77
	0.134	14.17		0.134	18.12
	0.141	14.81		0.141	18.94
	0.150	15.73		0.150	20.12
	0.164	17.27		0.164	22.10
	0.172	18.04		0.172	23.09
	0.179	18.81		0.179	24.07
	0.188	19.65		0.188	25.16
	0.203	21.25		0.203	27.20
	0.219	22.85		0.219	29.28
	0.230	24.00		0.230	30.75
	0.250	26.03		0.250	33.38
				0.281	37.45
10¾	0.109	12.43		0.312	41.51
	0.120	13.58		0.330	43.77
	0.134	15.25		0.344	45.55
	0.141	15.93		0.375	49.56
	0.150	16.93		0.438	57.53
	0.164	18.59		0.500	65.44
	0.172	19.42			
	0.179	20.24	14	0.134	19.92
	0.188	21.15		0.141	20.82

Table C-2 SIZES AND WEIGHTS OF WELDED AND SEAMLESS STEEL PIPE PILES*
(Continued)

Outside Diameter, in	Nominal Thickness, in	Weight per Linear Foot (Plain Ends), lb	Outside Diameter, in	Nominal Thickness, in	Weight per Linear Foot (Plain Ends), lb
14	0.150	22.11	18	0.281	53.22
	0.164	24.29		0.312	59.03
	0.172	25.38		0.344	64.82
	0.179	26.47		0.375	70.59
	0.188	27.66		0.438	82.06
	0.203	29.93		0.469	87.77
	0.219	32.20		0.500	93.45
	0.230	33.82			
	0.250	36.71	20	0.141	29.83
	0.281	41.21		0.172	36.40
	0.312	45.68		0.188	39.67
	0.344	50.14		0.219	46.21
	0.375	54.57		0.250	52.73
	0.438	63.37		0.281	59.23
	0.469	67.78		0.312	65.71
	0.500	72.00		0.344	72.16
				0.375	78.60
16	0.134	22.79		0.438	91.41
	0.141	23.82		0.469	97.78
	0.150	25.31		0.500	104.13
	0.164	27.80			
	0.172	29.06	22	0.172	40.07
	0.179	30.30		0.188	43.68
	0.188	31.66		0.219	50.88
	0.203	34.27		0.250	58.07
	0.219	36.87		0.281	65.24
	0.230	38.74		0.312	72.38
	0.250	42.05		0.375	86.61
	0.281	47.22		0.438	100.75
	0.312	52.36		0.469	107.79
	0.344	57.48		0.500	114.81
	0.375	62.58			
	0.438	72.72	24	0.172	43.74
	0.469	77.75		0.188	47.68
	0.500	82.77		0.219	55.56
				0.250	63.41
18	0.141	26.82		0.281	71.25
	0.172	32.73		0.312	79.06
	0.188	35.67		0.375	94.62
	0.219	41.54		0.438	110.10
	0.230	43.65		0.469	117.81
	0.250	47.39		0.500	125.49

*Sizes and weights smaller or greater than those listed may be furnished by special agreement between the manufacturer and the purchaser.

SOURCE: Courtesy of American Society for Testing and Materials.

Table C-3 CONCRETE CONTENTS—STEP-TAPER SHELLS

Section Number	Nominal Diameter, in	Concrete Content, yd^3/ft
000	$8\frac{5}{8}$	0.013
00	$9\frac{1}{2}$	0.016
0	$10\frac{3}{8}$	0.019
1	$11\frac{3}{8}$	0.023
2	$12\frac{3}{8}$	0.027
3	$13\frac{3}{8}$	0.032
4	$14\frac{3}{8}$	0.038
5	$15\frac{3}{8}$	0.043
6	$16\frac{3}{8}$	0.049
7	$17\frac{3}{8}$	0.056
8	$18\frac{3}{8}$	0.063

Table C-4 CONCRETE CONTENTS—CONSTANT-SECTION CORRUGATED SHELLS

Outside Diameter, in	Concrete Content,* yd^3/ft
$8\frac{5}{8}$	0.0141
$10\frac{5}{8}$	0.0218
$12\frac{1}{4}$	0.0274
14	0.0364
$16\frac{1}{8}$	0.0486
$19\frac{1}{8}$	0.0694

*Based on 16 gauge.

Table C-5 CONCRETE CONTENTS—MONOTUBE PILES

Type and Taper, in/ft	Tapered Sections			Concrete Content, yd^3
	Dimensions			
	Point, in	Butt, in	Length, ft	
F	8½	12	25	0.43
0.14	8	12	30	0.55
	8½	14	40	0.95
	8	16	60	1.68
	8	18	75	2.59
J	8	12	17	0.32
0.25	8	14	25	0.58
	8	16	33	0.95
	8	18	40	1.37
Y	8	12	10	0.18
0.40	8	14	15	0.34
	8	16	20	0.56
	8	18	25	0.86

Type	Extensions	Concrete Content, yd^3/ft
	Outside Diameter, in	
N-12	12	0.026
N-14	14	0.035
N-16	16	0.045
N-18	18	0.058

Table C-6 CONCRETE CONTENTS—STEEL PIPE PILES

Outside Diameter, in*	Nominal Wall Thickness, in*†	Concrete Content, yd^3/ft	Outside Diameter, in*	Nominal Wall Thickness, in*†	Concrete Content, yd^3/ft
8	0.125	0.0121	8⅝	0.277	0.0132
	0.134	0.0120		0.312	0.0129
	0.141	0.0120		0.322	0.0129
	0.164	0.0118		0.344	0.0127
	0.172	0.0118		0.375	0.0125
	0.179	0.0117		0.438	0.0121
	0.188	0.0117		0.500	0.0117
	0.219	0.0115	10	0.125	0.0192
8⅝	0.125	0.0141		0.134	0.0191
	0.141	0.0140		0.141	0.0190
	0.172	0.0138		0.150	0.0189
	0.188	0.0137		0.164	0.0188
	0.203	0.0136		0.172	0.0188
	0.219	0.0135		0.179	0.0187
	0.250	0.0133		0.188	0.0187

Table C-6   CONCRETE CONTENTS—STEEL PIPE PILES (Continued)

Outside Diameter, in*	Nominal Wall Thickness, in*†	Concrete Content, yd³/ft	Outside Diameter, in*	Nominal Wall Thickness, in*†	Concrete Content, yd³/ft
10	0.203	0.0185	12¾	0.219	0.0306
	0.219	0.0184		0.230	0.0305
	0.230	0.0183		0.250	0.0303
	0.250	0.0182		0.281	0.0300
				0.312	0.0296
10¾	0.125	0.0222		0.330	0.0295
	0.134	0.0221		0.375	0.0291
	0.141	0.0221		0.500	0.0279
	0.150	0.0220			
	0.164	0.0219	14	0.125	0.0381
	0.172	0.0218		0.134	0.0380
	0.179	0.0218		0.141	0.0380
	0.188	0.0217		0.150	0.0379
	0.203	0.0216		0.164	0.0377
	0.219	0.0214		0.172	0.0376
	0.230	0.0213		0.179	0.0375
	0.250	0.0212		0.188	0.0375
	0.279	0.0209		0.203	0.0373
	0.307	0.0208		0.219	0.0371
	0.344	0.0205		0.230	0.0370
	0.365	0.0203		0.250	0.0368
	0.438	0.0197		0.281	0.0364
	0.500	0.0192		0.312	0.0361
				0.344	0.0358
12	0.125	0.0278		0.375	0.0355
	0.134	0.0277		0.438	0.0348
	0.141	0.0277		0.500	0.0341
	0.150	0.0276			
	0.164	0.0275	16	0.125	0.0501
	0.172	0.0274		0.134	0.0499
	0.179	0.0273		0.141	0.0499
	0.188	0.0272		0.150	0.0498
	0.203	0.0271		0.164	0.0496
	0.219	0.0270		0.172	0.0495
	0.230	0.0269		0.179	0.0494
	0.250	0.0267		0.188	0.0493
	0.281	0.0264		0.203	0.0491
	0.312	0.0261		0.219	0.0489
	0.330	0.0259		0.230	0.0487
				0.250	0.0485
12¾	0.125	0.0315		0.281	0.0481
	0.134	0.0314		0.312	0.0477
	0.141	0.0314		0.344	0.0473
	0.150	0.0313		0.375	0.0470
	0.164	0.0311		0.469	0.0458
	0.172	0.0310		0.500	0.0396
	0.179	0.0310			
	0.188	0.0309	18	0.141	0.0634
	0.203	0.0307		0.172	0.0630

Table C-6   CONCRETE CONTENTS—STEEL PIPE PILES *(Continued)*

Outside Diameter, in*	Nominal Wall Thickness, in*†	Concrete Content, yd³/ft	Outside Diameter, in*	Nominal Wall Thickness, in*†	Concrete Content, yd³/ft
18	0.188	0.0627	22	0.172	0.0947
	0.219	0.0623		0.188	0.0945
	0.230	0.0621		0.219	0.0939
	0.250	0.0619		0.250	0.0934
	0.281	0.0614		0.281	0.0928
	0.312	0.0610		0.312	0.0923
	0.344	0.0605		0.375	0.0912
	0.375	0.0601		0.438	0.0901
	0.438	0.0592		0.469	0.0896
	0.469	0.0588		0.500	0.0891
	0.500	0.0584	24	0.172	0.1130
20	0.141	0.0785		0.188	0.1127
	0.172	0.0780		0.219	0.1121
	0.188	0.0778		0.250	0.1116
	0.219	0.0773		0.281	0.1110
	0.250	0.0768		0.312	0.1104
	0.281	0.0763		0.375	0.1092
	0.312	0.0758		0.438	0.1080
	0.344	0.0753		0.469	0.1074
	0.375	0.0749		0.500	0.1069
	0.438	0.0739			
	0.469	0.0734			
	0.500	0.0729			

*Other diameters and wall thicknesses may be available.

†The minimum wall thickness per ASTM A-252 equals 0.875 times the nominal wall thickness.

Table C-7 CONCRETE CONTENTS—DRILLED-AUGERED PILES

Auger Diameter, in	Concrete Content,* yd³/ft
8	0.014
10	0.022
12	0.032
14	0.044
16	0.057
18	0.072
20	0.089
22	0.108
24	0.128
26	0.150
28	0.174
30	0.200
32	0.228
34	0.257
36	0.288

*Includes a 10% allowance for overbreaks and auger wobble. Does not include any enlarged base.

Table C-8 CONCRETE CONTENTS—CAST-IN-SITU PILES

Diameter,* in	Concrete Content, yd³/ft
10	0.020
11	0.024
12	0.029
13	0.034
14	0.040
15	0.045
16	0.052
17	0.058
18	0.065
19	0.073
20	0.081
21	0.089
22	0.098
23	0.107
24	0.116

*Diameter of closure plate if oversize. Otherwise, diameter of drive tube or casing.

Inspection Forms

D.1 EQUIPMENT RECORDS

VIBRATORY PILE DRIVING EQUIPMENT DATA   RIG : 1 2 3

PROJECT :_____	SHEET NO.____ OF _____
LOCATION :_____	DATE _____
OWNER : _____	TIME _____
ENGINEER :_____	BY _____
CONTRACTOR:_____	OPERATOR

DRIVER MAKE : _____

DRIVER MODEL NO. :_____

RATING : _____

TOTAL WEIGHT : _____

OSCILLATOR :   LENGTH : _____

                      WEIGHT : _____

                      TYPE : _____

FOLLOWER :   LENGTH : _____

                      WEIGHT : _____

                      TYPE : _____

CLAMP :   LENGTH: _____

                      WEIGHT: _____

                      TYPE : _____

ADAPTER :   LENGTH : _____

                      WEIGHT: _____

                      TYPE : _____

SPECIAL ADAPTER: LENGTH:_____

                      WEIGHT: _____

                      TYPE   _____

GEAR RATIO : _____

LEADS   NO: _____YES: _____ft.___WEIGHT:_____

RIG :   CRANE MODEL : _____

                      CAPACITY, TONS: _____

                      BOOM LENGTH: _____

                      COUNTERWEIGHT : _____

_____

_____

_____

SKETCHES OF EQUIPMENT

NO FOLLOWER   WITH FOLLOWER   OTHER

Figure D-1 Inspection form for recording data for vibratory pile-driving equipment. (*Courtesy of M. T. Davisson.*)

GENERAL RIG INFORMATION RECORD

RIG NUMBER

Date _____

STS Rig Inspector _____   STS Job No: _____

Project _____
Location _____
Owner _____
Const. Manager _____
Engineer _____
Pile Contractor _____
Inspector _____

Hammer Make & Model _____
Hammer Type _____
Ram   Weight _____
Hammer Stroke or Bounce Chamber Press. Required _____
Hammer Energy Rating _____
Hammer Speed Rating _____

(See attached sketch for hammer position and slide bar measurements)

Crane Make & Model _____
Length & Type of Leads _____

Type of Drivehead or Helmet _____
Weight of Helmet and/or Anvil _____
Hammer Cushion Composition _____
Hammer Cushion Dimensions _____
Pile Cushion Composition & Dimensions _____
Type of Follower or Mandrel _____
Flower/ Mandrel Dimensions & Weight _____

Required Air/Steam Pressure at Hammer/Source_____
Location of Pressure Gage & Hose Size _____
Boiler or Air Compressor Type & Size _____
Boiler or Air Compressor Capacity _____
Boiler or, Air Compressor Location _____

Drill and/or Jet Type _____
Drill Jet Diameter & Length _____
Jet Pump Type & Size _____
Hose Size & Length _____

STS CONSULTANTS LTD.

Figure D-2 Inspection form for recording general pile-driving equipment data. (*Courtesy of STS Consultants Ltd.*)

D.2 RECORDS FOR CONVENTIONAL PILE DRIVING

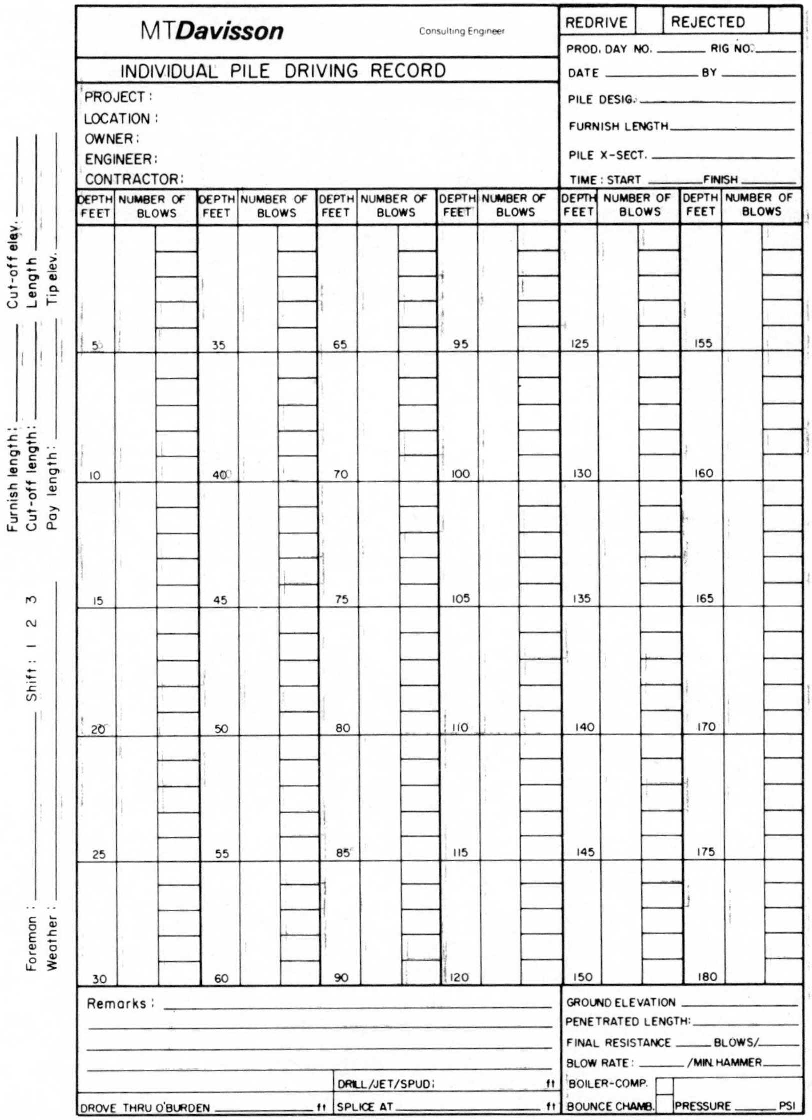

MTDavisson Consulting Engineer

INDIVIDUAL PILE DRIVING RECORD

PROJECT:
LOCATION:
OWNER:
ENGINEER:
CONTRACTOR:

REDRIVE | REJECTED
PROD. DAY NO. ______ RIG NO. ______
DATE ______ BY ______
PILE DESIG. ______
FURNISH LENGTH ______
PILE X-SECT. ______
TIME: START ______ FINISH ______

Cut-off elev. ______
Length ______
Tip elev. ______
Furnish length: ______
Cut-off length: ______
Pay length: ______
Shift: 1 2 3
Foreman: ______
Weather: ______

DEPTH FEET	NUMBER OF BLOWS	DEPTH FEET	NUMBER OF BLOWS	DEPTH FEET	NUMBER OF BLOWS	DEPTH FEET	NUMBER OF BLOWS	DEPTH FEET	NUMBER OF BLOWS	DEPTH FEET	NUMBER OF BLOWS
5		35		65		95		125		155	
10		40		70		100		130		160	
15		45		75		105		135		165	
20		50		80		110		140		170	
25		55		85		115		145		175	
30		60		90		120		150		180	

Remarks: ______

GROUND ELEVATION ______
PENETRATED LENGTH: ______
FINAL RESISTANCE ______ BLOWS/______
BLOW RATE: ______ /MIN. HAMMER ______
DRILL/JET/SPUD: ______ ft
BOILER-COMP.
DROVE THRU O'BURDEN ______ ft
SPLICE AT ______ ft
BOUNCE CHAMB.
PRESSURE ______ PSI

Figure D-3 Individual pile-driving record form. (*Courtesy of M. T. Davisson.*)

DELTA TESTING AND INSPECTION, INC.   Sheet No._____ of _____

Pile Driving Record Sheet

Job No._____   Pile No._____

Project _____   Type of Pile _____

Recorder _____

Date _____   Time Started _____   Time Finished _____

Type Hammer _____   Wt. of Ram _____   Stroke _____   Energy _____
                                                                                                    FT. LBS.

Pile Marking   [scale 0 — 10 — 20]   LENGTH

	MARINE USE		LAND USE	
	Length in Leads _____		Length in Leads _____
	Total Cut Off _____		Total Cut Off _____
	Water Elevation _____		Cut Off Elevation _____
	Dept of Water _____		Natural Ground
	Cut Off Elevation _____		Elevation _____

PILE FT. MARK	BLOWS PER FOOT	REMARKS	PILE FT. MARK	BLOWS PER FOOT	REMARKS	PILE FT. MARK	BLOWS PER FOOT	REMARKS	PILE FT. MARK	BLOWS PER FOOT	REMARKS	PILE FT. MARK	BLOWS PER FOOT	REMARKS	
1			31			61			91			121			
2			32			62			92			122			
3			33			63			93			123			
4			34			64			94			124			
5			35			65			95			125			
6			36			66			96			126			
7			37			67			97			127			
8			38			68			98			128			
9			39			69			99			129			
10			40			70			100			130			
11			41			71			101			131			
12			42			72			102			132			
13			43			73			103			133			
14			44			74			104			134			
15			45			75			105			135			
16			46			76			106			136			
17			47			77			107			137			
18			48			78			108			138			
19			49			79			109			139			
20			50			80			110			140			
21			51			81			111			141			
22			52			82			112			142			
23			53			83			113			143			
24			54			84			114			144			
25			55			85			115			145			
26			56			86			116			146			
27			57			87			117			147			
28			58			88			118			148			
29			59			89			119			149			
30			60			90			120			150			

REMARKS

Piles Pre-Drilled to Elev. _____   Diameter of Drill _____

Piles Jetted to Elev. _____   Size Jet _____   Pump Size _____

Pump Manufacturer _____

Pump Model No. _____

Figure D-4 Individual pile-driving record form. (*Courtesy of Delta Testing and Inspection, Inc.*)

PROJECT Nª _____   SEQUENCE Nª _____

PILE Nª _____

PILE DRIVING LOG

STEEL PILE, TYPE _____ DRIVING DATE _____

SITE _____

DETAIL _____

1 ST SEGMENT : LENGTH_____ , MARKING_____ ,   SIZE _____
      (SHOE INCLUDED)

2 ND SEGMENT : _____ , _____ ,   WEIGHT _____

3 RD SEGMENT : _____ , _____ ,   STEEL YIELD _____

4 TH SEGMENT : _____ , _____ ,

         TOTAL _____

HAMMER TYPE _____

MISC.   NOTES _____
(BATTER, LOCATION,
  PREBORING,   _____
  WEATHER, ETC.)

CHECK LIST

☐   SPLICES SQUARE   PILE HEAD ELEVATION   _____

☐   CUSHION PAD   PILE END ELEVATION   _____

☐   ROCKSHOE WITH PIN   PILE CUT OFF ELEVATION   _____

☐   VISUAL INSPECTION   GROUND ELEVATION   _____

HEIGHT OF FALL, ENERGY	BLOWS	SUM OF BLOWS	PENETRA-TION	DEPTH OF PILE END (SHOE INCLUDED)	NOTES — TIME OF START AND FINISH, PAUSES, RELOCATION, PREBORING, CHANGE OF CUSHION PAD, SPLICING, ETC. ALL RELATED TO DEPTH OF PILE END.	REFUSAL BLOWS	PENE-TRATION
					RETAPPING		
					DATE:		
						BLOWS	PENE-TRATION
			FINAL DEPTH OF PILE END AFTER REFUSAL				
				TECHNICIAN :			

Figure D-5 Individual pile-driving record form. (*Courtesy of Bengt H. Fellenius.*)

PILE DRIVING RECORD

Job No. _____　　Project _____　　Date _____

Contractor _____　　Location _____　　Inspector _____

Structure _____　　Pile Group _____　　Pile Number _____

Pile Type: _____

Mandrel: YES/NO

Tip Diam. _____ in.

Butt Diam. _____ in.

Driving Cap: _____

Ground Surface El. _____

Pre-excavation: { JETTING / AUGERING / ROTARY DRILLING

Hole Diam. _____ in.

Hole Depth: _____ ft

El. of Pre-excavation: _____

Hammer Type: _____

Rated Energy: _____ ft-lb/blow

Blows Per Minute: _____

Steam/Air Pressure _____ psi

Pile Tip El. _____

Ft	No. of Blows	Cum. Blows	Ft	No. of Blows	Cum. Blows	Ft	No. of Blows	Cum. Blows	Ft	No. of Blows	Cum. Blows	Ft	No. of Blows	Cum. Blows
1			21			41			61			81		
2			22			42			62			82		
3			23			43			63			83		
4			24			44			64			84		
5			25			45			65			85		
6			26			46			66			86		
7			27			47			67			87		
8			28			48			68			88		
9			29			49			69			89		
10			30			50			70			90		
11			31			51			71			91		
12			32			52			72			92		
13			33			53			73			93		
14			34			54			74			94		
15			35			55			75			95		
16			36			56			76			96		
17			37			57			77			97		
18			38			58			78			98		
19			39			59			79			99		
20			40			60			80			100		

REMARKS: Alignment, plumbness, water, cleanness, concreting, delays and unusual driving.

_____

_____

_____

MCCLELLAND
ENGINEERS

Figure D-6 Individual pile-driving record form. (*Courtesy of McClelland Engineers, Inc.*)

PILE DRIVING RECORD

Job No. _____

Date _____ Project _____ Pile Length _____

Weather _____ Location _____ Waste _____

Report _____ Owner _____ Pay Length _____

Sheet _____ Contractor _____ Cut-Off Elev. _____

Column No _____ Foreman _____ Tip Elev. _____

Pile No. _____ Pile Capacity & Type _____ Stroke _____

Ground Elev. _____ Hammer _____ Energy _____

DEVIATION ► | N | E | S | W | Signature (Inspector) _____

DEPTH	BLOWS	REMARKS	DEPTH	BLOWS	REMARKS	DEPTH	BLOWS	REMARKS
1			36			71		
2			37			72		
3			38			73		
4			39			74		
5			40			75		
6			41			76		
7			42			77		
8			43			78		
9			44			79		
10			45			80		
11			46			81		
12			47			82		
13			48			83		
14			49			84		
15			50			85		
16			51			86		
17			52			87		
18			53			88		
19			54			89		
20			55			90		
21			56			91		
22			57			92		
23			58			93		
24			59			94		
25			60			95		
26			61			96		
27			62			97		
28			63			98		
29			64			99		
30			65			100		
31			66			101		
32			67			102		
33			68			103		
34			69			104		
35			70			105		

Raamot Associates, P.C.   Consulting Engineers

Figure D-7 Individual pile-driving record form. (*Courtesy of Raamot Associates, P.C.*)

RAYMOND INTERNATIONAL BUILDERS, INC.
Pile Driving Log

Owner: **Deseret Generation and Transmission Cooperative**   Location: **Vernal, Utah**

Project: **Moon Lake Station - Unit No. 1**   Rig No._____ Shift (1)_____

Pile No. _____ Col. No._____   Shift (2)_____

Structure: _____   Pile Type: **Step-Taper**

Drawing No.: _____   Mandrel Type (Wt.)_____

Date Driven: _____   Hammer: **65-C**

Date Concreted: _____   Speed: **Rated 100-110**

Production Day No._____   Observed: _____

Cut-off Elev.:_____ Predrill Depth: _____   Energy: **19,500 ft. lbs.**

Length of Pile:_____ Auger Size:_____   Air Pressure, p.s.i.:

Tip Elev.:_____ Time: Start_____ Finish_____   Rated Min. **120 p.s.i.**

Weather: _____   Observed: _____

Depth Pile Ft.	Blows per Foot		Depth Pile Ft.	Blows per Foot		Depth Pile Ft.	Blows per Foot
0-1			21			41	
2			22			42	
3			23			43	
4			24			44	
5			25			45	
6			26			46	
7			27			47	
8			28			48	
9			29			49	
10			30			50	
11			31			51	
12			32			52	
13			33			53	
14			34			54	
15			35			55	
16			36			56	
17			37			57	
18			38			58	
19			39			59	
20			40			60	

Checked for Heave _____

REMARKS:

Logger _____

Figure D-8 Individual pile-driving record form. (*Courtesy of Raymond International Builders, Inc.*)

RAYMOND INTERNATIONAL BUILDERS, INC.

Pile Driving Log

Owner: Arkansas Power & light Co.   Location: Newark, Arkansas

Project: Independence Steam Electric Station   Job No. WP-1971-KC

Date_____ Time_____   Weather _____   Rig No._____ Day/Night

Driving Sequence _____   Hammer _____   Pile Type _____

Drawing No._____   Energy _____   Point Dia._____

Pier No._____ Pile No._____   _____   Butt Dia. _____

Cut Off Elev.: _____   _____   Length of Pile _____

Pay Length _____   Predrill Depth _____

Tip Elev. _____   Auger Size _____

L Pile Ft.	Blows per Foot	L Pile Ft.	Blows per Foot	L Pile Ft.	Blows per Foot	L Pile Ft.	Blows per Foot
0-1		23		45		67	
2		24		46		68	
3		25		47		69	
4		26		48		70	
5		27		49		71	
6		28		50		72	
7		29		51		73	
8		30		52		74	
9		31		53		75	
10		32		54		76	
11		33		55		77	
12		34		56		78	
13		35		57		79	
14		36		58		80	
15		37		59		81	
16		38		60		82	
17		39		61		83	
18		40		62		84	
19		41		63		85	
20		42		64		86	
21		43		65		87	
22		44		66		88	

Checked for Heave _____

Amount of Heave _____

Retapped _____

Blows per inch

1_____ _____
2_____ _____
3_____ _____
4_____ _____
5_____ _____
6_____ _____
7_____ _____
8_____ _____
9_____ _____
10_____ _____
11_____ _____
12_____ _____

Final driving resistance

blows per inch _____

Remarks:

Logger _____

Figure D-9 Individual pile-driving record form. (*Courtesy of Raymond International Builders, Inc.*)

INDIVIDUAL PILE DRIVING RECORD

Project _____

Location _____

Owner _____

Const. Manager _____

Arch/Engineer _____

Pile Contractor _____ Foreman _____

Inspector _____ Job No _____

PILE DESIGNATION _____

LOCATION _____

PILE TYPE _____

PILE X-SECT. _____

PILE TIP/PLATE DIA. _____ in

PRE-DRILL/JET LENGTH _____ ft.

HAMMER _____ RIG No _____

RATED ENERGY _____ ft.—lbs.

(ALSO SEE GENERAL RIG INFORMATION SHEET FOR HAMMER/CUSHION DATA)

DEPTH (FT.)	NO. OF BLOWS	DEPTH (FT.)	NO. OF BLOWS	DEPTH (FT.)	NO. OF BLOWS	DEPTH (FT.)	NO. OF BLOWS	DEPTH (FT.)	NO. OF BLOWS	DEPTH (FT.)	NO. OF BLOWS	DEPTH (FT.)	NO. OF BLOWS	DEPTH (FT.)	NO. OF BLOWS
0		15		30		45		60		75		90		105	
1		16		31		46		61		76		91		106	
2		17		32		47		62		77		92		107	
3		18		33		48		63		78		93		108	
4		19		34		49		64		79		94		109	
5		20		35		50		65		80		95		110	
6		21		36		51		66		81		96		111	
7		22		37		52		67		82		97		112	
8		23		38		53		68		83		98		113	
9		24		39		54		69		84		99		114	
10		25		40		55		70		85		100		115	
11		26		41		56		71		86		101		116	
12		27		42		57		72		87		102		117	
13		28		43		58		73		88		103		118	
14		29		44		59		74		89		104		119	
15		30		45		60		75		90		105		120	

STATUS OF PILE DRIVING	END OF DRIVE	RETAP 1	RETAP 2
PENETRATION RATE (BLOWS PER)			
CORRESPONDING HAMMER STROKE OR B.C. PRESS.			
PILE DEPTH BELOW REF. ELEVATION (FT)			
APPROX. REFERENCE ELEVATION (FT)			
TIP ELEVATION (FT)			
FURNISH LENGTH OF PILE (FT)			
HAMMER WARM UP STATUS			
PILE BUTT END CONDITION			
HAMMER ALIGNMENT			
ACCEPTANCE STATUS			

GROUND ELEVATION _____ FT

CUT-OFF ELEV. _____ FT; LENGTH _____ FT

PILE HEAVE OR SETTLEMENT _____ IN.

PLUMBNESS Δ/L _____ %

DEVIATION FROM ALIGNMENT _____ IN.

DEPTH (FT.)	NUMBER OF BLOWS PER INCH				STATUS	DATE
	1ST 3 INCH	2ND 3 INCH	3RD 3 INCH	4 TH 3 INCH		

COMMENTS : ① _____

_____

_____

SPLICE LOCATIONS F. T.	FT	DATE CONCRETED

RIG TIME INFORMATION					CORRES. DEPTH FT.	BLOW RATE PER MIN.
STATUS	DATE	START	STOP	Net Min.		
					CORRES. DEPTH FT.	AIR/STEAM PRESSURE (PSI)

STS CONSULTANTS LTD.

Figure D-10 Individual pile-driving record form. (*Courtesy of STS Consultants Ltd.*)

PILE NO. _____

RECORD NO._____

PILE INSPECTION RECORD

Project Name _____ Project No. _____

Ground Elev. _____

FEET	BLOWS	REMARKS	FEET	BLOWS	REMARKS
0-1			40-41		
2			42		
3			43		
4			44		
5			45		
6			46		
7			47		
8			48		
9			49		
10			50		
11			51		
12			52		
13			53		
14			54		
15			55		
16			56		
17			57		
18			58		
19			59		
20			60		
21			61		
22			62		
23			63		
24			64		
25			65		
26			66		
27			67		
28			68		
29			69		
30			70		
31			71		
32			72		
33			73		
34			74		
35			75		
36			76		
37			77		
38			78		
39			79		
39-40			79-80		

PILE TYPE:_____

PILE LOCATION:_____

PILE CAPACITY:_____

LENGTH AS CAST:_____

DATE DRIVEN:_____

TIME DRIVEN:_____

HAMMER:_____

ENERGY:_____

PLUMBNESS:_____

HEAVE:_____

CUT-OFF ELEV.:_____

LENGTH CUT OFF:_____

FINISHED TIP ELEV.:_____

PAY LENGTH:_____

PILE APPROVED: _____ DATE:_____

PILE REJECTED:_____

INSPECTOR:_____

NOTES:

WOODWARD–CLYDE CONSULTANTS

Figure D-11 Individual pile-driving record form. (*Courtesy of Woodward-Clyde Consultants.*)

BLOW COUNT / STROKE PILE DRIVING RECORD

SAXIMETER NO. _____

PILE NO. _____ DRIVING ORDER NO. _____ DATE _____

PROJECT _____ LOCATION _____

PILE TYPE/SIZE _____ LENGTH _____ BATTER _____

ELEVATION: GROUND _____ PILE TIP _____ CUTOFF _____

HAMMER TYPE/SIZE _____ THROTTLE SETTING _____

CAP/HELMET/CUSHION _____

CONTRACTOR _____ FOREMAN _____ OBSERVER _____

Depth ft	Blows/foot	Stroke	Depth ft	Blows/foot	Stroke	Depth ft	Blows/foot	Stroke	Depth ft	Blows/foot	Stroke
0-1			25-26			50-51			75-76		
1-2			26-27			51-52			76-77		
2-3			27-28			52-53			77-78		
3-4			28-29			53-54			78-79		
4-5			29-30			54-55			79-80		
5-6			30-31			55-56			80-81		
6-7			31-32			56-57			81-82		
7-8			32-33			57-58			82-83		
8-9			33-34			58-59			83-84		
9-10			34-35			59-60			84-85		
10-11			35-36			60-61			85-86		
11-12			36-37			61-62			86-87		
12-13			37-38			62-63			87-88		
13-14			38-39			63-64			88-89		
14-15			39-40			64-65			89-90		
15-16			40-41			65-66			90-91		
16-17			41-42			66-67			91-92		
17-18			42-43			67-68			92-93		
18-19			43-44			68-69			93-94		
19-20			44-45			69-70			94-95		
20-21			45-46			70-71			95-96		
21-22			46-47			71-72			96-97		
22-23			47-48			72-73			97-98		
23-24			48-49			73-74			98-99		
24-25			49-50			74-75			99-100		

REMARKS: _____ TIME OF START _____ STOP _____

DEPTH	MIN.	INTERRUPTION REASON

Figure D-12 Pile-driving record form for use with the Saximeter. (*Courtesy of Pileco Inc.*)

DELTA TESTING AND ▋ INSPECTION, INC.

P. O. BOX 19172 • NEW ORLEANS, LA. 70179 • PHONE 486-5595

REPORT NO. _____   SHEET _____ OF _____

DTI 34   **PILE DRIVING RECORD**   DATE:

PROJECT	CONTRACTOR	ARCHITECT	ENGINEER	ORDER NO.

NUMBER OF BLOWS															
PILE NO.															
TIP. IN.															
BUTT. IN.															
LENGTH FT.															

PENETRATION IN FEET

REMARKS 1. TYPE HAMMER: _____

   2. TYPE PILE: _____

   3. DWG NO.: _____

INSPECTOR: _____

WORK TIME _____ to _____

TRAVEL TIME: _____

MILEAGE: _____

SUBSISTENCE: _____

Figure D-13 Pile-driving record form for logging several piles. (*Courtesy of Delta Testing and Inspection, Inc.*)

DELTA TESTING AND ▌ INSPECTION, INC.

P. O. BOX 19172 • NEW ORLEANS, LA. 70179 • PHONE 486-5595

DTI 34   **PILE DRIVING RECORD**   Date:

PROJECT	CONTRACTOR	ARCHITECT	ENGINEER	ORDER NO.

NUMBER OF BLOWS

FOOTING NO.	Pile #	Pile #	Pile #	Pile #	Pile #	Pile #	Pile #
PENETRATION	Tip In.	Tip In.	Tip In.	Tip In.	Tip In.	Tip In.	Tip In.
IN FEET	Butt In.	Butt In.	Butt In.	Butt In.	Butt In.	Butt In.	Butt In.
	Lngth. Ft.	Lngth. Ft.	Lngth. Ft.	Lngth. Ft.	Lngth. Ft.	Lngth. Ft.	Lngth. Ft.

Inspector:

Figure D-14 Pile-driving record form for logging several piles. (*Courtesy of Delta Testing and Inspection, Inc.*)

JOB NO. _____	**PILE DRIVING RECORD**					SHEET __ OF__		
JOB NAME_____	**RAAMOT ASSOCIATES**					DATE _____		

REPORT NO.								
COLUMN NO.								
PILE NUMBER								
LENGTH IN LEADS								
WASTE								
PAY LENGTH								
CUT-OFF ELEVATION								
TIP ELEVATION								
DEVIATION NORTH-SOUTH								
DEVIATION EAST-WEST								

COMMENTS:

HAMMER _____

ENERGY _____

STROKE _____

PILE TYPE _____

CAPACITY _____

PROFESSIONAL ENGINEER:

_____

NO. _____

1								
2								
3								
4								
5								
6								
7								
8								
9								
10								
11								
12								
13								
14								
15								
16								
17								
18								
19								
20								
21								
22								
23								
24								
25								
26								
27								
28								
29								
30								
31								
32								
33								
34								
35								
36								
37								
38								
39								
40								

Figure D-15 Pile-driving record form for logging several piles. (*Courtesy of Raamot Associates, P.C.*)

RAYMOND INTERNATIONAL BUILDERS, INC.

JOB NO._____ PILE DRIVING LOGS DATE_____

PROJECT: _____ OWNER: _____
PILE TYPE: _____ HAMMER SIZE: _____

DEPTH-ft.	PILE NO._____ PIER NO._____ C.O. EL._____ TIP EL._____ LENGTH_____ft. DRILLED_____ft.	DEPTH-ft.	PILE NO._____ PIER NO._____ C.O. EL._____ TIP EL._____ LENGTH_____ft. DRILLED_____ft.	DEPTH-ft.	PILE NO._____ PIER NO._____ C.O. EL._____ TIP EL._____ LENGTH_____ft. DRILLED_____ft.	DEPTH-ft.	PILE NO._____ PIER NO._____ C.O. EL._____ TIP EL._____ LENGTH_____ft. DRILLED_____ft.
1	51	1	51	1	51	1	51
2	52	2	52	2	52	2	52
3	53	3	53	3	53	3	53
4	54	4	54	4	54	4	54
5	55	5	55	5	55	5	55
6	56	6	56	6	56	6	56
7	57	7	57	7	57	7	57
8	58	8	58	8	58	8	58
9	59	9	59	9	59	9	59
10	60	10	60	10	60	10	60
11	61	11	61	11	61	11	61
12	62	12	62	12	62	12	62
13	63	13	63	13	63	13	63
14	64	14	64	14	64	14	64
15	65	15	65	15	65	15	65
16	66	16	66	16	66	16	66
17	67	17	67	17	67	17	67
18	68	18	68	18	68	18	68
19	69	19	69	19	69	19	69
20	70	20	70	20	70	20	70
21	71	21	71	21	71	21	71
22	72	22	72	22	72	22	72
23	73	23	73	23	73	23	73
24	74	24	74	24	74	24	74
25	75	25	75	25	75	25	75
26	76	26	76	26	76	26	76
27	77	27	77	27	77	27	77
28	78	28	78	28	78	28	78
29	79	29	79	29	79	29	79
30	80	30	80	30	80	30	80
31	81	31	81	31	81	31	81
32	82	32	82	32	82	32	82
33	83	33	83	33	83	33	83
34	84	34	84	34	84	34	84
35	85	35	85	35	85	35	85
36	86	36	86	36	86	36	86
37	87	37	87	37	87	37	87
38	88	38	88	38	88	38	88
39	89	39	89	39	89	39	89
40	90	40	90	40	90	40	90
41	91	41	91	41	91	41	91
42	92	42	92	42	92	42	92
43	93	43	93	43	93	43	93
44	94	44	94	44	94	44	94
45	95	45	95	45	95	45	95
46	96	46	96	46	96	46	96
47	97	47	97	47	97	47	97
48	98	48	98	48	98	48	98
49	99	49	99	49	99	49	99
50	100	50	100	50	100	50	100

INSPECTOR

Figure D-16 Pile-driving record form for logging several piles. (*Courtesy of Raymond International Builders, Inc.*)

234

D.3 RECORDS FOR VIBRATORY PILE DRIVING

PILE PENETRATION RATE DATA

SHEET _____ OF _____
DATE : _____
PILE NO: _____ RIG NO : _____

PROJECT : _____
LOCATION : _____
OWNER : _____
ENGINEER : _____

BY : _____
WEATHER : _____
TEMP : _____ °F

DEPTH Feet	TIME Minutes	RPM or FREQ.	VAC. In. Hg.	No. Eng	DEPTH Feet	TIME Minutes	RPM or FREQ.	VAC. In. Hg.	No. Eng	DEPTH Feet	TIME Minutes	RPM or FREQ.	VAC. In. Hg.	No. Eng
					61					106				
0														
5					65					110				
10														
15														
					70					115				
20														
25														
30					75					120				
35					80					125				
40					85					130				
45					90					135				
50					95					140				
55					100					145				
60					105					150				

REMARKS : _____
_____
_____

Figure D-17 Individual pile-driving record form for vibratory driving. (*Courtesy of M. T. Davisson.*)

PROJECT : ______
LOCATION : ______
OWNER : ______
ENGINEER ______
CONTRACTOR: ______

VIBRATORY PILE DRIVING LOG SHEET

DAY : M T W T F S S
RIG : 1 2 3
SHIFT : 1 2 3

SHEET ____ OF ____
DATE : ______
BY : ______
WEATHER : ______
TEMP : ______ °F

NOTE : See Vibratory Pile Driving Equipment Data Sheet No. ______ , & Pile Plan No.

TIME OF DAY	PILE DESIG.	TYPE OF PILE & POINT	INTERLOCK	LENGTH OF PILE FURNISH-ED, ft	NO ENGS.	POWER-SETTINGS		DEPTH DRIVEN BELOW GROUND, ft	RATE OF PENETR. in/sec	PULLING	DRIVING TIME, mins.	GROUND SURFACE ELEV. ft	Stopwatch	Energy	FREQ-UENCY CPS		REMARKS: Out of plumb, collapse, damage, troubles, obstructions, non-routine features, test, etc.
						VACUUM IN. Hg	R.P.M.						______	HP			

Figure D-18 Form for daily summary of piles installed with a vibratory driver. (*Courtesy of M. T. Davisson.*)

D.4 PILE INSPECTION REPORTS

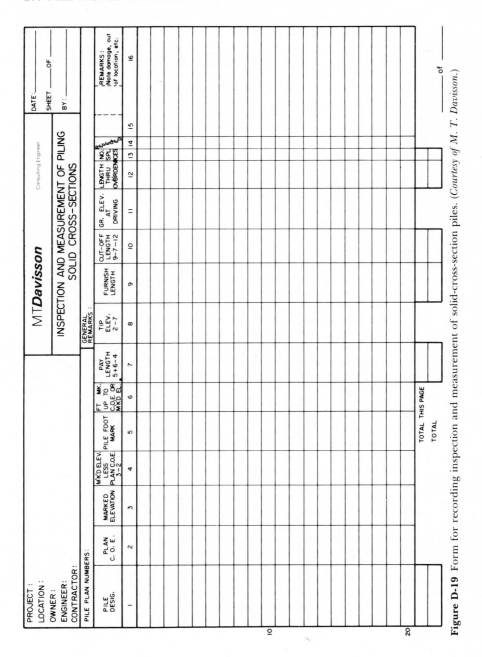

Figure D-19 Form for recording inspection and measurement of solid-cross-section piles. (*Courtesy of M. T. Davisson.*)

	MT***Davisson***									DATE:
PROJECT:							Consulting Engineer			
LOCATION:										SHEET ___ OF ___
OWNER:										
ENGINEER:		INSPECTION AND MEASUREMENT OF PILING								BY:
CONTRACTOR:		CAST-IN-PLACE								

PILE PLAN NUMBERS:

GENERAL REMARKS:

PILE DESIG.	PILE FOOT MARK	DIST. FT MARK TO TOP	TOTAL EXTERIOR FOOTAGE 2+3	INSIDE LGTH. PLUS PLATE	TOP TO C.O.E. UP + DN. (-)	PAY LENGTH 5+6	FURNISH LENGTH	CUT-OFF LENGTH 8-7-13	PLAN C.O.E.	TIP ELEV.	GR. ELEV. AT DRIVING	LENGTH THRU OVALDENCES 12-10	NO. SPL.	REMARKS: Note debris, water, collapse, etc.
1	2	3	4	5	6	7	8	9	10	11	12	13	14 15 16	17
10														
20					TOTAL THIS PAGE									
					TOTAL									___ of ___

Figure D-20 Form for recording inspection and measurement of cast-in-place concrete piles. (*Courtesy of M. T. Davisson.*)

PROJECT :
LOCATION :
OWNER :
ENGINEER :
CONTRACTOR :

MT**Davisson** Consulting Engineer

INSPECTION OF CONCRETING OF PILING

DATE : ______
SHEET ____ OF ____
BY : ______
CREW NO : ______

PILE PLAN NUMBERS :

GENERAL REMARKS: Weather, Delays, etc.

TICKET NO.	CU YD.	TIME WATER ADDED	TIME OF PLACING CONC.	SLUMP	NO. OF CYL.	AIR T °F	CONC T °F	INSP. DATE	PILE DESIG.	√	LENGTH	LENGTH UNPLACED	LENGTH PLACED	THEOR. LENGTH OR YARDAGE	REMARKS :	REJECTED

______ of ______

Figure D-21 Form for recording inspection of concreting of cast-in-place piles. (*Courtesy of M. T. Davisson.*)

INDIVIDUAL PILE CONDITION AND CONCRETING RECORD

PROJECT :_____   STS CONSULTANTS LTD.

LOCATION :_____   JOB NUMBER _____

OWNER :_____   STS INSPECTOR _____

CONSTR. MANAGER :_____   CONCRETING CREW NO. _____

ARCH./ENGINEER :_____   CREW FOREMAN_____

PILING SUBCONTRACTOR:_____   PILE DESIGNATION _____

PILE CONDITION OBSERVATIONS

DATE _____   Amount of Bottom Visable _____

TIME OF CONDITION OBSERVATION _____   Direction, Nature of Pile Sweep_____

ACCEPTANCE STATUS_____   Depth of Spider Penetration if Bottom not Visable ____ft.

COMMENTS:_____   Damage and Debris Observations_____

_____   Amount of Water in Pile_____

_____   Taped Inside Length of Pile _____ft.

CONCRETING OBSERVATIONS

	Truck Status per Pile	1st Truck	2nd Truck
DATE_____	Truck Ticket Number		
WEATHER_____	Yards on Truck Before Pour		
AIR TEMPERATURE_____	Length Unplaced Concrete		
ACCEPTANCE STATUS_____	Length Placed Concrete		
COMMENTS_____	Theor. Length or Yardage		
_____	Concreting Time: Began-Ended	to	to
_____	Slump and Concrete Temp.		
_____	No. of Cylinders Made		

NOTES _____

_____

_____

STS CONSULTANTS LTD.

Figure D-22 Form for recording inspection and concreting of cast-in-place piles. (*Courtesy of STS Consultants Ltd.*)

INSPECTION OF AUGER-CAST PILES

PROJECT : _____ LOCATION: _____
OWNER : _____ STS JOB No. _____
ARCH / ENGINEER: _____ WEATHER: _____
PILING SUBCONTRACTOR : _____ AIR TEMP. : _____

A. PILE AND LOCATION : _____

B. DESIGN DIAMETER, in.: _____

C. DESIGN TOP ("CUT-OFF") EL. : _____

D. DESIGN LENGTH (BELOW CUT-OFF), ft.: _____

E. GROUND SURFACE ELEVATION : _____

F. TIME WHEN CEMENT WAS MIXED WITH WATER : _____

G. DEPTH, TOP OF TANK TO GROUT, BEFORE, in.: _____

H. DEPTH OF PILE BELOW "CUT-OFF", ft. : _____

I. GROUTING STARTED, TIME : _____

J. DEPTHS, PRESSURE BELOW 25 psi : _____

K. GROUTING FINISHED, TIME : _____

L. DEPTH, TOP OF TANK TO GROUT, AFTER, in. : _____

M. ACTUAL TOP ("CUT-OFF") EL. : _____

N. DISTANCE OFF-CENTER, N-S, in. : _____

O. DISTANCE OFF-CENTER, E-W, in. : _____

P. AGE OF GROUT (K-F), hr. and min.= _____

Q. NEAT VOLUME OF HOLE ($\frac{\pi B^2}{288} \times D$), ft^3 = _____

R. VOLUME OF GROUT PUMPED ($\frac{L-G}{12} \times 27$), ft^3 = _____

S. % OF HOLE FILLED (R ÷ Q) = _____

T. # OF CUBE SET, IF ANY : _____

U. REMARKS _____

_____

_____

_____

_____

_____

_____

INSP. BY : _____ RVD. BY _____

STS CONSULTANTS LTD.

Figure D-23 Form for recording inspection of auger-grout piles. (*Courtesy of STS Consultants Ltd.*)

D.5 PILE MONITORING REPORTS

PILE ANALYZER DATA RECORD			PILE No :		
			STATUS :		
PROJECT :			DATE :		
LOCATION :			PILE TYPE :		
OWNER :			X- SECTION :		
ENGINEERS :			LENGTH DRIVEN :		
PILING CONTRACTOR :			LENGTH AT GAGES :		
STS ANALYZER ENGINEER :			PENETRATION :		
STS CONSULTANTS LTD. JOB No :			BLOW COUNT :		
ANALYZER INPUT DATA			**ANALYZER OUTPUT DATA**		
MODEL : NUMBER :			TAPE REC. :	TAPE No :	
PILE DATA	MODULUS E	$KIPS/_{IN^2}$	PAPER TAPE	FORCE , F_M	KIPS
	AREA A	IN^2		VELOCITY V_I	$FT/_{SEC}$
	WAVE SPEED, C	$FT/_{M.SEC}$		CAPACITY , R_S	KIPS
	IMPEDANCE $\frac{EA}{C}$	$\frac{KIP-SEC}{FT}$		ENERGY , E_M	FT-KIPS
GAGE DATA	TYPE	No.	CALIBRATION	PICTURE	DIV. $\frac{VOLTS}{DIV}\frac{UNITS}{VOLT}$	UNITS
	STRAIN				F_M	KIPS
	STRAIN				V_I	$FT/_{SEC}$
	ACCEL.				$\frac{2L}{C}$	M SEC
	ACCEL				$\frac{VEA}{C}$	KIPS
SETTINGS	FORCE = K_ϵEAS			COMMENTS :	
	$\frac{MC}{L}$ DIAL = $\frac{10\ MC}{L}$				
	$L/_C$ DIAL = 60 $\frac{L}{C}$				
	TIME DELAY $\triangle$				
	DAMPING , J			HAMMER :	
	ACCEL. DIAL			RATED ENERGY :	FT-LBS

PICTURE

Figure D-24 Form for recording pile-monitoring data with the use of the pile-driving analyzer. (*Courtesy of STS Consultants Ltd.*)

PILE ANALYZER DATA SUMMARY

PROJECT : _____
LOCATION : _____
OWNER : _____
ARCH/ENGINEER : _____
PILING CONTRACTOR : _____

STS CONSULTANTS LTD. JOB No: _____
STS ANALYZER ENGINEER : _____
ANALYZER MODEL : _____ NUMBER : _____
TAPE RECORDER : _____ TAPE SPEED : _____
HAMMER : _____ RATED ENERGY : _____ RIG No : _____

STS TAPE NUMBER

| PILE DESIGNATION | STATUS | PILE TYPE | AREA | LENGTH DRIVEN | START DEPTH | FORCE: $K_eE AS$ | DAMPING J | C_{ASS} | START TIME | START LOCATION | CHANNEL 1 | 1st ACC GAGE # | 1st GAGE CALIBRAT | 1st STRAIN GAGE CALIBRAT |
DATE		CROSS SECTION	MODULUS	LENGTH BELOW GAGES	FINISH DEPTH	$\frac{MC\ DIAL}{L}$ ACC DIAL IO: $\frac{MC}{L}$	$\frac{L}{C}$ DIAL :60 $\frac{L}{C}$ ACC DIAL $\frac{L}{2}$ ACT AVG	$\frac{2L}{C}$ ACT $\frac{C_{ACT}}{2L/2L}$ ACT	FINISH TIME	FINISH LOCATION	CHANNEL 3	CHANNEL 4	INPUT RANGE	2nd ACC GAGE #	2nd GAGE CALIBRAT	2nd STRAIN GAGE CALIBRAT

Figure D-25 Summary form for recording pile-monitoring data with the use of the pile-driving analyzer. (*Courtesy of STS Consultants Ltd.*)

243

D.6 PILE SUMMARY RECORDS

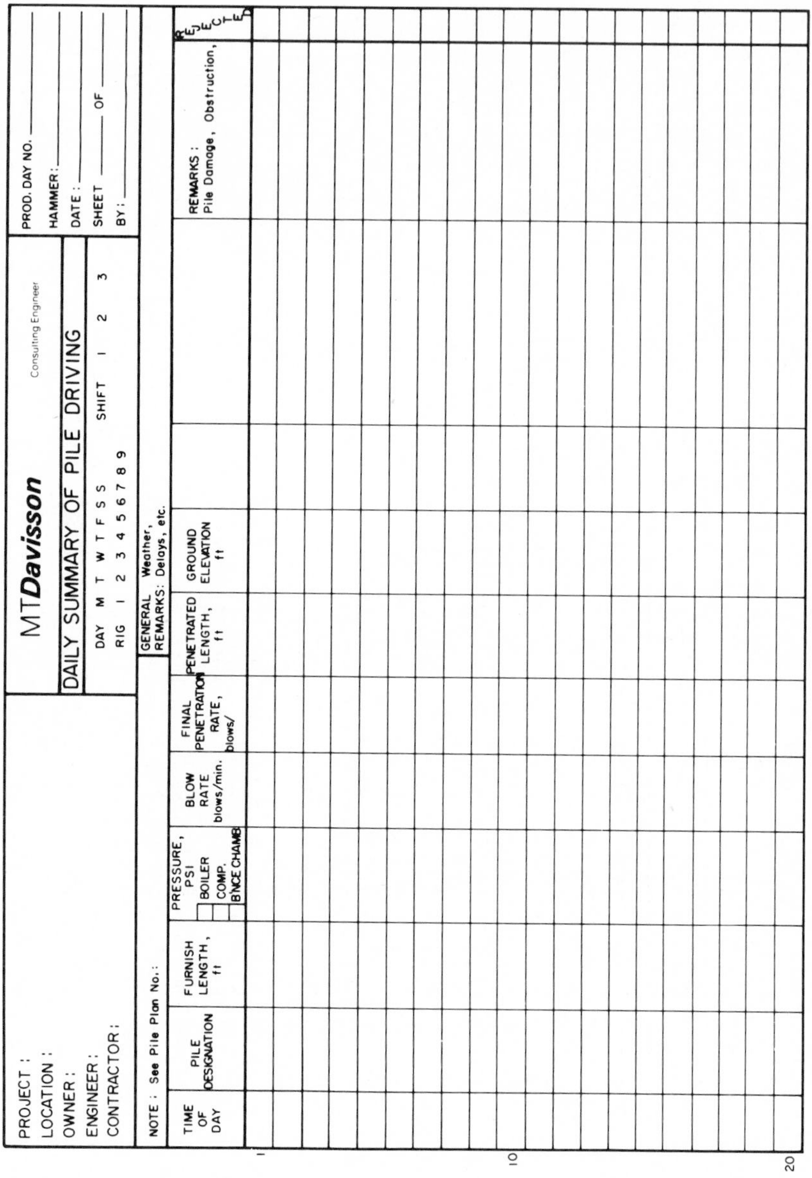

MT**Davisson** Consulting Engineer

DAILY SUMMARY OF PILE DRIVING

PROJECT:
LOCATION:
OWNER:
ENGINEER:
CONTRACTOR:

PROD. DAY NO. ____
HAMMER: ____
DATE: ____
SHEET ____ OF ____
BY: ____

DAY M T W T F S S
RIG 1 2 3 4 5 6 7 8 9
SHIFT 1 2 3

NOTE: See Pile Plan No.:

GENERAL REMARKS: Weather, Delays, etc.

	TIME OF DAY	PILE DESIGNATION	FURNISH LENGTH, ft	PRESSURE, PSI (BOILER / COMP. / B'NCE CHAMB)	BLOW RATE blows/min.	FINAL PENETRATION RATE, blows/	PENETRATED LENGTH, ft	GROUND ELEVATION ft			REMARKS: Pile Damage, Obstruction,	REJECTED
1												
10												
20												

Figure D-26 Form for daily summary of piles driven. (*Courtesy of M. T. Davisson.*)

PROJECT :
LOCATION :
OWNER :
ENGINEER :
CONTRACTOR :

MT**Davisson** Consulting Engineer

PILING PRODUCTION SUMMARY

PRODUCTION DAY NO.	DATE	SHIFT	RIG 1	RIG 2	RIG 3	RIG 4	RIG 5	RIG 6	RIG 7	TOTAL DRIVEN FOR DAY	CUMULATIVE TOTAL DRIVEN	TOTAL CONC. FOR DAY	CUMULATIVE TOTAL CONCRETED	REMARKS

Figure D-27 Form for summarizing daily summaries of pile production. (*Courtesy of M. T. Davisson.*)

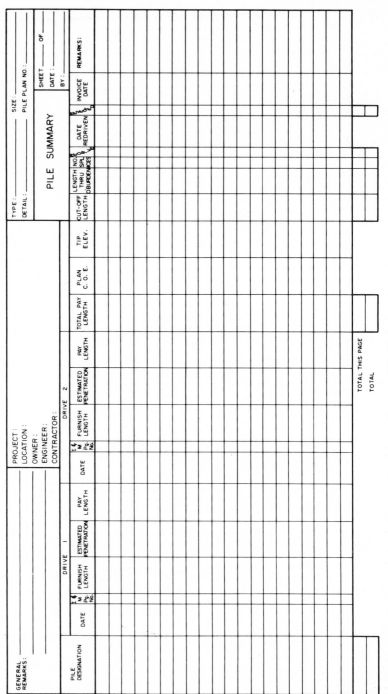

Figure D-28 Form for summarizing data on piles driven. (*Courtesy of M. T. Davisson.*)

246

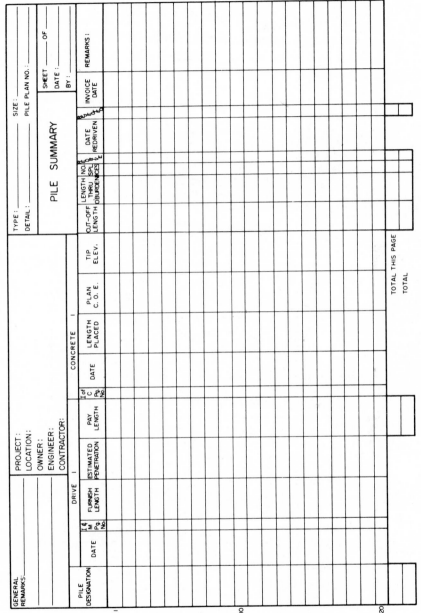

Figure D-29 Form for summarizing data on piles both driven and concreted. (*Courtesy of M. T. Davisson.*)

PILE DRIVING SUMMARY

Job No. _____   Project _____   Date _____

Contractor _____   Location _____   Inspector _____

Structure _____

Pile Type: ___ _____   Hammer Description: _____

Tip Diam. _____in. Butt Diam. _____in.   Rated Energy: _____ ft-lb/blow

Leads: Fixed/Swinging   Blows Per Minute: _____

Driving Cap: _____   Steam/Air Pressure: _____ psi

| Pile Designation | | Elevation | | | Blows Per Foot Last 5 Feet | | | | | Total Blows on Pile | Remarks |
Group	Number	Ground Surface	Predrilling or Prejetting	Pile Tip	1	2	3	4	5		alignment, plumbness, water, cleanness, concreting

MCCLELLAND ENGINEERS

Figure D-30 Form for summary of pile driving. (*Courtesy of McClelland Engineers, Inc.*)

RAYMOND INTERNATIONAL BUILDERS, INC.

PILE REPORT

NO. _____

JOB NO. _____   PILE TYPE _____   DATE _____

	NUMBER OF PILE							
	PIER #	PILE #						
1								
2								JOB LOCATION: _____
3								
4								
5								STRUCTURE: _____
6								
7								OWNER: _____
8								
9								WEATHER: _____
10								
11								FOREMAN: _____
12								
13								DRIVER NO. _____
14								
15								REMARKS: _____
16								
17								
18								
19								
20								
21								
22								
23								DELAYS (MEN AND/OR EQUIPMENT)
24								
25								
26								
27								
28								
29								
30								DURATION: _____
31								
32								
33								
34								
35								CAUSE: _____
36								
37								
38								
39								COVERED BY
40								
41								FORCE ACCOUNT SLIP NO. _____
42								
43								
44								RAYMOND INTERNATIONAL BUILDERS, INC.
45								
46								
47								Signature of Superintendent
48								
49								CLIENT: _____
50								
Totals								PER: _____

Figure D-31 Form for daily summary of piles installed. (*Courtesy of Raymond International Builders, Inc.*)

D.7 COMPARATIVE RECORDS

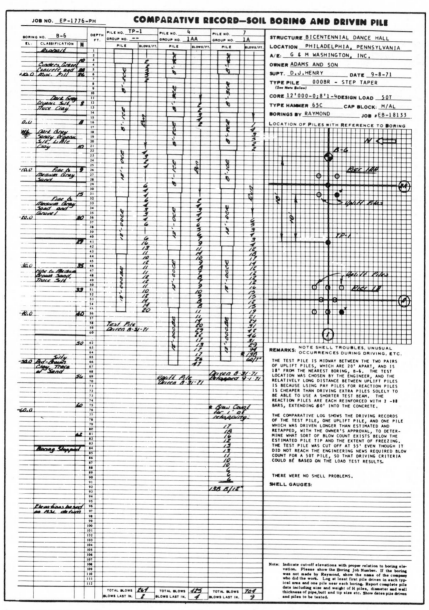

Figure D-32 Form for reporting pile-driving records versus boring log. (*Courtesy of Raymond International Builders, Inc.*)

D.8 LOAD-TEST REPORTS

PILE LOAD TEST DATA

Project : _____
Location : _____

	VIBRATORY	CONVENTIONAL
PILE LOCATION		
DATE DRIVEN		
DATE TESTED		
PILE JOB DESIGNATION		
PILE TYPE		
DIMENSIONS & WEIGHT		
TYPE OF MANDREL		
DIMENSIONS & WEIGHT		
EMBEDDED LENGTH, ft		
DISTANCE TO BORING		
LOAD SYSTEM		
DESIGN LOAD, tons		

VIBRATORY	CONVENTIONAL
DRIVER MODEL NO.	HAMMER MODEL NO.
PEAK FORCE/cps	RAM WEIGHT, lbs
TOTAL WEIGHT, lbs	STROKE, ft
NET HORSEPOWER (final)	RATED ENERGY, ft lb
FREQUENCY (final), cps	RATED SPEED, blows/min.
NET DRIVING TIME, min.	TYPE OF DRIVING HEAD
FINAL PENETRATION, in./sec	TYPE OF CUSHION
	FINAL PENETRATION, blows/in.
	NET DRIVING TIME, min.

LOAD   (tons)

SETTLEMENT OR UPLIFT (inches)

REMARKS : _____

*N = Std. Pen. Test, w = Water Content, q_u = Unconfined Strength , tsf

*SOIL DESCRIPTION
BORING NO.   Depth ft

PENETRATION RATE
secs / ft _____
blows/ft _ _ _ _ _ _

Figure D-33 Form for reporting load-test data and driving versus boring logs. (*Courtesy of M. T. Davisson.*)

PILE LOAD TEST DATA
PRESSURE INJECTED FOOTING

Project: _____
Location: _____

PILE DATA		PILE SKETCH	*SOIL DESCRIPTION BORING NO.	Depth ft	DRIVE CASING PENETRATION RATE blows/ft ———
Pile Location					
Date Driven					
Date Tested					
Pile Job Designation					
Pile Type					
Dimensions & Weight					
Type of Drive Casing					
Dimensions & Weight					
Embedded Length, ft					
Distance To Boring					
Load System					
Design Load, tons					
Test Load, tons					

HAMMER DATA

Ram Weight, lbs	
Ram Size	
Stroke, ft	
Rated Energy, ft-lb	
Rated Speed, blows/min.	
Net Driving Time, min.	

DRIVE CASING PENETRATION

Type of Plug Mat'l.:

Increments of Plug Mat'l.:

BULB FORMATION

Distance Casing Raised to Drive Out Plug:

Amount of Plug Mat'l. in Casing before Bulbing:

Type of Bulb Mat'l.:

Bulb Increment	1	2	3	4
Amount, cu. ft				
No. of Blows				
Hammer Drop				
Mat'l. in Casing while Bulbing				
Total Amt. of Bulb Mat'l.:				

SEAT SHAFT CASING

Type of Mat'l. to Seat Shaft Casing:

Amt. of Mat'l.:
No. of Hammer Blows:
Hammer Drop:
Movement of Shaft Casing after Hammer Drop on Shaft Plug: Drop: No.:
Movement of Shaft Casing while Pulling Drive Casing:

UNCASED SHAFT

*N = Sta. Pen. Test, w = Water Content, q$_u$ = Unconfined Strength, tsf

Type of Mat'l.:	
Charge Rate:	
Amount of Mat'l. in Casing while Forming Shaft:	
Hammer Drop:	

Remarks: _____

Figure D-34 Inspection and load-test report form for pressure injected footing. Sheet 1. (*Courtesy of M. T. Davisson.*)

PROJECT :	
LOCATION :	
OWNER :	
ENGINEER :	
GENERAL CONTRACTOR :	
PILE CONTRACTOR :	

ADDITIONAL PILE DATA

Pile Job Designation			
Pile Taper, in./ft			
Length Below Cut-off, ft			
Ground Surface Elevation, ft			
Type of Test			
Loading Device			
Load Measuring System			
Deflection Measuring System			
Maximum Load, tons			
Gross Settlement, inches			
Net Settlement, inches			
Yield Load/Settlement, tons/in.			
Ultimate Load/Settlement, tons/in.			
Type of Leads			
Type of Rig			
Bulb Material	Slump :	Aggregate Size & Type :	
Shaft Seat Material	Slump :	Aggregate Size & Type :	
Shaft Material	Type :	Slump :	Aggregate Size :
	Concrete Strength :		
Shaft Reinforcement			

PILE LOAD TEST

LOAD (tons)

SETTLEMENT (inches)

REMARKS : _____

SOIL DATA REFERENCE : _____

Figure D-34 *(continued)*   Sheet 2. (*Courtesy of M. T. Davisson.*)

PILE TEST LOADING LOG

PILE PROPERTIES

NOTES _____

PAGE NO. _____

PROJECT _____
PROJECT NO. _____
PILE NO. _____

DATE: DRIVEN _____
RESTRUCK _____
TESTED _____

FIELD ENGR _____

DIAMETER _____
WALL THICK. _____
STL. AREA _____
CONCR. AREA _____
COMB. MODULUS _____
LENGTH IN SOIL _____
TOTAL LENGTH _____
AE/L _____

Test Time	Incr No	Incr Min	JACK		LOAD CELL		1		2		3 (Tip)		4		HEAD MOVEMENT				Tip			Remarks
			Pres	Load	Read	Load	Read	Defl	Read	Defl	Read	Comp	Read	Comp	Defl	$\triangle$	$\triangle'$	Tilt	Mvmt	Chin	
																					Zero Reading

Figure D-35 Load-test report form. (*Courtesy of Bengt H. Fellenius.*)

254

Figure D-36 Load-test report form. (*Courtesy of Raamot Associates, P. C.*)

LOAD TEST REPORT

RAYMOND INTERNATIONAL BUILDERS, INC.
2801 Post Oak Blvd · P.O. Box 22718 · Houston Texas 77027

DATE **9-9-71**

PROJECT **BICENTENNIAL DANCE HALL** JOB NO. **EP-1776-PH**

LOCATION **PHILADELPHIA, PENNSYLVANIA**

TEST NO. **1** PILE DESIGNATION **TP-1** TYPE TEST **JACK AGAINST REACTION PILES**

PILE TYPE STEP TAPER DESCRIPTION **0Q00-0 @ 12'; 1-4 @ 8'** LENGTH (Tip to G.S.) **55.08'**

DESIGN LOAD **50T** TEST LOAD **100T** BUTT DEFLECTIONS GROSS **0.328"** NET **0.175"**

Dates Driven **8-31-71** Concreted **9-1-71** Tested **9-7-71** THROUGH **9-9-71**

Hammer Type and Size **STEAM, 65C** Total Blows **264** Final Set **2** Blows/in.

Pre-excavation Depth **NONE** Description **--**

Special Test Procedures and Instrumentation **REACTION BEAM WITH 4 UPLIFT PILES.**
SETTLEMENT RECORDED USING 2 DIAL INDICATORS AND A WIRE-MIRROR-SCALE SETUP.

Boring by **RAYMOND** Job No. **EB-18133** Nearest Boring No. **B-6** Distance **18'**
Owner **ADAMS AND SON** General Contractor **JEFFERSON COMPANY**
Str. Engr. **G & M WASHINGTON, INC.** Foundation Engr. **FRANKLIN ASSOCIATES**

REMARKS **ON 9-7-71, BEFORE THE 11:10 READING, GAUGE NO.1 WAS JARRED SLIGHTLY. GAUGE NO. 2 REMAINED UNCHANGED. THE AVERAGE DIAL READING CONSEQUENTLY CHANGED, CREATING A NEW REFERENCE FROM WHICH TO CALCULATE THE BUTT DEFLECTION.**

Load test report is certified to be correct:

Signature _____ For FRANKLIN ASSOCIATES

Signature _____ For RAYMOND INTERNATIONAL INC.

*Attach Comparative Soil Boring and Pile Driving Logs.

LOAD-TEST REPORT — TABULATION OF DATA — SHEET 1

TEST NO. **1** PILE NO. **TP-1** JOB NO. **EP-1776-PH**

DATE	HOUR	TEST LOAD INCREMENT	TEST LOAD TOTAL	GAUGE NO 1	GAUGE NO 2	GAUGE AVG	SECONDARY READINGS	BUTT DEFL INCREMENT	BUTT DEFL TOTAL
9-7-71	8:55	0T	OT	.000	.000	.000	0	.000	.000
	9:00	25T	25T	.014	.000	.007	0	.007	.007
	02			.018	.002	.010	0	.003	.010
	05			.020	.004	.012	0	.002	.012
	15			.022	.004	.013	0	.001	.013
	15			.022	.005	.013	0	.000	.013
	30			.023	.005	.014	0	.000	.013
	59			.023	.005	.014	0	.001	.014
	10:00	25T	50T	.063	.045	.054	4/64	.040	.054
	02			.063	.047	.055	"	.001	.055
	05			.064	.048	.056	5/64	.001	.056
	10			.065	.048	.056	6/64	.000	.056
	15			.065	.049	.057	"	.001	.057
	30			.070	.050	.060	7/64	.003	.060
	59			.074	.052	.063	8/64	.003	.063
	11:00	25T	75T	.182	.080	.131	12/64	.068	.131
	02			.183	.081	.132	"	.001	.132
	05			.185	.081	.133	"	.001	.133
	10			.195	.081	.138	"	.000	.133 (X)
	15			.198	.082	.140	"	.002	.135
	30			.208	.084	.146	"	.006	.141
	12:55	25T	100T	.213	.085	.149	13/64	.003	.144
	1:00			.325	.153	.239	18/64	.090	.234
	2:00			.345	.167	.256	19/64	.017	.251
	3:00			.358	.176	.267	21/64	.011	.262
	4:00			.376	.198	.287	22/64	.020	.282
	6:00			.417	.223	.320	23/64	.033	.315
	8:00			.431	.235	.333	24/64	.013	.328
	10:00			.428	.230	.329	23/64	.004	.324
9-8-71	12:00			.426	.228	.327	"	.002	.322
	2:00			.424	.232	.327	"	.003	.319
	4:00			.401	.192	.297	"	.027	.292
	6:00			.398	.188	.293	"	.004	.288
	8:00			.396	.184	.290	"	.003	.285
	10:00			.403	.183	.293	"	.003	.288
	11:00			.413	.187	.300	"	.007	.295
	11:59			.433	.209	.316	24/64	.016	.311
	12:00	-25T	75T	.464	.216	.320	23/64	.004	.315
	2:59			.462	.212	.317	22/64	.003	.312
	12:59			.457	.201	.309	"	.008	.304
	1:00	-25T	50T	.445	.191	.300	"	.009	.295
	1:59			.381	.115	.248	19/64	.052	.243
	2:00	-25T	25T	.364	.102	.238	18/64	.010	.233
	2:59			.309	.097	.203	14/64	.035	.198
	3:00	-25T	OT	.238	.084	.161	11/64	.042	.156
9-9-71	3:00			.261	.099	.180	"	.019	.175

*Attach supplementary sheets as necessary for additional data, tell tale readings, other instrumentation data. Explain all delays, resetting of gauges etc.

Figure D-37 Load-test report form. *(Courtesy of Raymond International Builders, Inc.)*

PILE LOAD TEST DATA

SHEET ____1____ OF _____
DATE : _____
PROJECT :_____
LOCATION :_____
OWNER : _____
ENGINEER :
PILE NO._____
BY : _____
WEATHER :_____
TEMP.   °F

HYDRAULIC JACK CALIBRATION :_____
SR-4 LOAD CELL CALIBRATION :_____

DRIVING RECORDS : SEE SHEET NO'S. :_____
DRIVING EQUIPMENT : SEE SHEET NO. :_____
PILE AND BORING LOCATIONS : SEE _____
SOIL DATA REFERENCE : _____
NOTES :_____
_____
_____
_____

Show Sketches Below for (I) TEST SETUP, and (2) PLAN of PILE LOCATIONS with respect to NEAREST
BORING. Use back or second sheet if necessary.

Figure D-38 Load-test report form.   Sheet 1. *(Courtesy of M. T. Davisson.)*

PILE LOAD TEST DATA

(See Sheet No. I For Plan)

PROJECT : ______

LOCATION : ______

OWNER : ______

ENGINEER : ______

BY: ______ DATE : ______ PILE NO. ______ SHEET ______ OF ______

TIME	NOMINAL LOAD, TONS	BOURDON GAGE PSI	SR-4 INDICATOR	LOAD TONS	AVERAGE SETTLE- MENT, IN.	DIAL INDICATORS				OTHER SETTLEMENT OBSERVATIONS			
						1	2	3	4				

Figure D-38 *(continued)* Sheet 2. (*Courtesy of M. T. Davisson.*)

RECORD OF FOUNDATION TEST LOAD

Loading No. ____

TEXAS QUICK TEST LOAD METHOD

County _____ Control _____ Structure _____

Highway No. _____ Project _____ Structure No. _____

Bent No. _____ Foundation No. _____ Sta. _____ Rt. _____ Lt. _____

Foundation Size & Type _____ Total Length _____ Design Load _____

Foundation Tip Elevation _____ Effective Penetration _____ Ground Elevation _____

Hammer Type & Size _____ Dynamic Resistance _____

Time Test Began _____ Date _____ Resident Engineer _____

Time	Time Inter-val	Load Added	Total Load	Extensometer Readings		Total Gross Settlement - Inches		
Min.	Min.	Tons	Tons	Dial 1	Dial 2	Dial 1	Dial 2	Average

Remarks: _____ District _____

_____ Date _____

_____ By _____

Figure D-39 Load-test report form—quick-test method. (*Courtesy of The Bridge Division, Texas State Department of Highways and Public Transportation.*)

```
                        SUMMARY OF DATA

                       PILE TEST LOADING

                 TEXAS QUICK TEST LOAD METHOD


County____Gale_____Structure__Intracoastal Canal Bridge____

Highway No._State 124_Control_376-3-48__Project__BRF 729(6)__


Date of Test Load                   Aug. 6, 1976
Bent No.                            Bent 29
Location (Station)                  187+84
Description of Pile                 18" Sq. Prestr. Conc.
     Total Length                   65'
     Ground Elevation               0.0'
     Btm. of Ftg. Elev.             -1.0'
     Pilot Hole Elev.               0.0'
     Pile Tip Elev.                 -59.0'
     Effective Pen.                 59'
Soil Type (General)                 Silt, Sand & Clay
Design Load per Pile                60 Tons
Type & Size of Hammer               Delmag D46-02
Dynamic Resistance (ENR)            28.9 Tons
Penetration per Blow                2.00"
Description of Cushion              Cap Block
     Type            Green Oak        Pine Plywood
     Size            24" sq.          24"∅
     Thickness       6"               3"


                                    7 Day Test
Duration of Quick Test Load         57.5 Min.
Maximum Load on Pile                160 Tons
     Gross Settlement               1.843"
     Net Settlement                 1.680"

Plunging Failure Load               160 Tons
Ultimate Static Bearing Capacity    150 Tons
Maximum Safe Static Load (Proven)    75 Tons
"K" Factor (Proven)                 2.6

Remarks:


                             State Department of Highways
                             and Public Transportation
                             District____21_____
                             Date_____8/7/76_____
```

Figure D-40 Example of summary of load-test data—quick-test method. (*Courtesy of The Bridge Division, Texas State Department of Highways and Public Transportation.*)

Appendix

Examples of Principal-Sum Payment Methods

E.1 AGGREGATE PILE LENGTH

Typical contract wording would be as follows:

1. The price for _____ piles having a base aggregate length of _____ lineal feet shall be the principal sum of $_____.
2. Should the base aggregate length of piling as set forth in paragraph 1 be increased or decreased by the addition or omission of piles or by a variation in the estimated length of piles, the principal sum shall be adjusted as follows:

   Additional Footage: Add the sum of $_____ per lineal foot.
   Omitted Footage: Deduct the sum of $_____ per lineal foot.

EXAMPLE

Bid Quantities

Number of piles	500
Base aggregate length, ft	50,000
Principal sum, $	500,000
Price of added footage, $/ft	8.00
Credit for omitted footage, $/ft	4.00

ACTUAL

	Case I	Case II
Number of piles	520	480
Average length, ft	110	80
Driven aggregate length, ft	57,200	38,400
Additional footage, ft	7,200	—
Omitted footage, ft	—	11,600
Adjustment for added footage, $	+57,600*	—
Adjustment for omitted footage, $	—	−46,400†
Final payment, $	557,600	453,600

*7200 ft × $8.00/ft.
†11,600 ft × $4.00/ft.

E.2 INDIVIDUAL PILE LENGTH

Typical contract wording would be as follows:

1. The price for _____ piles having an estimated individual length of _____ feet shall be the principal sum of $_____.

2. Should more or fewer piles be installed than stated in paragraph 1, the principal sum shall be adjusted on the basis of such piles having an individual length stated in paragraph 1 and as follows:

    Additional Piles: Add $_____ per pile.
    Omitted Piles: Deduct $_____ per pile.

3. For piles installed longer or shorter than the individual length stated in paragraph 1, the principal sum shall be further adjusted for each such pile as follows:

    Additional Footage: Add $_____ per lineal foot.
    Omitted Footage: Deduct $_____ per lineal foot.

EXAMPLE

Bid Quantities

Number of piles	500
Individual length, ft	100
Principal sum, $	500,000
Price of added piles, $ each	950
Credit for omitted piles, $ each	700
Price of added footage, $/ft	8.00
Credit for omitted footage, $/ft	4.00

ACTUAL

	Case I	Case II
Number of piles	520	480
Individual length, ft	Varies	Varies
Adjustment for added piles, $	+ 19,000*	—
Adjustment for omitted piles, $	—	− 14,000†
Adjusted principal sum, $	519,000	486,000
Adjustment for added footage	‡	‡
Adjustment for omitted footage	¶	¶
Final payment, $	§	§

*20 × $950.

†20 × $700.

‡For each pile installed longer than 100 ft, the additional footage would be paid for at the rate of $8.00 per foot.

¶For each pile installed shorter than 100 ft, the omitted footage would be credited at the rate of $4.00 per foot.

§The final payment sum depends on the additions or deductions for added or omitted footage, as applied to the adjusted principal sum.

E.3 AGGREGATE AND INDIVIDUAL PILE LENGTHS

Typical contract wording would be as follows:

1. The price for _____ piles having an estimated individual length of _____ feet and a base aggregate length of _____ lineal feet shall be the principal sum of $_____.

2. Should more or fewer piles be installed than stated in paragraph 1, both the principal sum and base aggregate length shall be adjusted on the basis of such piles having an individual length stated in paragraph 1 and as follows:

   Additional Piles: Add $_____ per pile.
   Omitted Piles: Deduct $_____ per pile.

3. After the principal sum and base aggregate length are adjusted per paragraph 2, the principal sum shall be further adjusted for any differences between the adjusted base aggregate length and the actual driven aggregate length as follows:

   Additional Footage: Add $_____ per lineal foot.
   Omitted Footage: Deduct $_____ per lineal foot.

EXAMPLE

Bid Quantities

Number of piles	500
Individual length, ft	100
Base aggregate length, ft	50,000
Principal sum, $	500,000
Price of added piles, $ each	950
Credit for omitted piles, $ each	700
Price of added footage, $/ft	8.00
Credit for omitted footage, $/ft	4.00

ACTUAL

	Case I	Case II
Number of piles	520	480
Average length, ft	110	80
Adjustment for added piles, $	+19,000[a]	—
Adjustment for omitted piles, $	—	−14,000[b]
Adjusted principal sum, $	519,000	486,000
Adjustment for added piles, ft	+2,000[c]	—
Adjustment for omitted piles, ft	—	−2,000[d]
Adjusted aggregate length, ft	52,000	48,000
Driven aggregate length, ft	57,200[e]	38,400[f]
Additional footage, ft	5,200	—
Omitted footage, ft	—	9,600
Adjustment for added footage, $	+41,600[g]	—
Adjustment for omitted footage, $	—	−38,400[h]
Final payment sum, $	560,600	447,600

[a] 20 × $950.
[b] 20 × $700.
[c] 20 × 100 ft.
[d] 20 × 100 ft.
[e] 520 × 110 ft.
[f] 480 × 80 ft.
[g] 5200 ft × $8.00/ft.
[h] 9600 ft × $4.00/ft.

Appendix **F**

Miscellaneous

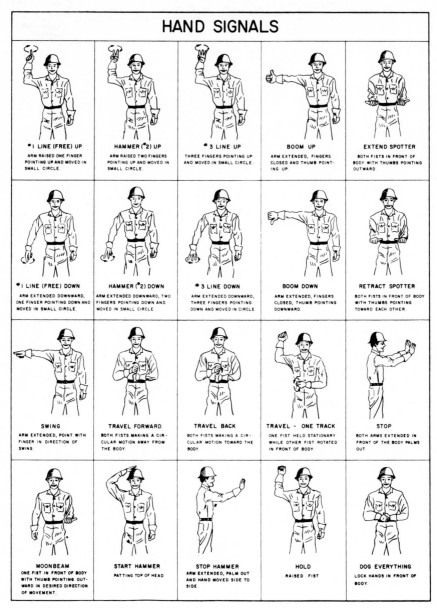

Figure F-1 Hand signals for directing the operation of a typical pile-driving rig. (*Courtesy of Raymond International Builders, Inc.*)

Table F-1   SI CONVERSION DATA

To Convert from	To	Multiply by*
bar	pascal (Pa)	1.000 000 E + 05
foot (ft)	meter (m)	3.048 000 E − 01
ft^2	square meter (m^2)	9.290 304 E − 02
ft^3	cubic meter (m^3)	2.831 685 E − 02
ft^3/min	cubic meter per second (m^3/s)	4.719 474 E − 04
ft · lbf	joule (J)	1.355 818 E + 00
ft · lbf/s	watt (W)	1.355 818 E + 00
free fall, acceleration of (g)	meter per second squared (m/s^2)	9.806 650 E + 00
horsepower (hp, 550 ft · lbf/s)	watt (W)	7.456 999 E + 02
hp (boiler)	watt (W)	9.809 500 E + 03
hp (electric)	watt (W)	7.460 000 E + 02
inch (in)	meter (m)	2.540 000 E − 02
in^2	square meter (m^2)	6.451 600 E − 04
in^3	cubic meter (m^3)	1.638 706 E − 05
kilogram-force (kgf)	newton (N)	9.806 650 E + 00
kgf · m	newton meter (N · m)	9.806 650 E + 00
kgf · s^2/m (mass)	kilogram (kg)	9.806 650 E + 00
kgf/cm^2	pascal (Pa)	9.806 650 E + 04
kgf/m^2	pascal (Pa)	9.806 650 E + 00
kgf/mm^2	pascal (Pa)	9.806 650 E + 06
kip (1000 lbf)	newton (N)	4.448 222 E + 03
kip/in^2 (ksi)	pascal (Pa)	6.894 757 E + 06
pound (lb)	kilogram (kg)	4.535 924 E − 01
lb · ft^2 (moment of inertia)	kilogram square meter (kg · m^2)	4.214 011 E − 02
lb · in^2	kilogram square meter (kg · m^2)	2.926 397 E − 04
lb/ft^2	kilogram per square meter (kg/m^2)	4.882 428 E + 00
lb/ft^3	kilogram per cubic meter (kg/m^3)	1.601 846 E + 01
lb/in^3	kilogram per cubic meter (kg/m^3)	2.767 990 E + 04
lb/yd^3	kilogram per cubic meter (kg/m^3)	5.932 764 E − 01
pound-force (lbf)	newton (N)	4.448 222 E + 00
lbf · ft	newton meter (N · m)	1.355 818 E + 00
lbf · in	newton meter (N · m)	1.129 848 E − 01
lbf/ft	newton per meter (N/m)	1.459 390 E + 01
lbf/ft^2	pascal (Pa)	4.788 026 E + 01
lbf/in	newton per meter (N/m)	1.751 268 E + 02
lbf/in^2 (psi)	pascal (Pa)	6.894 757 E + 03
ton (long, 2240 lb)	kilogram (kg)	1.016 047 E + 03
ton (metric)	kilogram (kg)	1.000 000 E + 03
ton (short, 2000 lb)	kilogram (kg)	9.071 847 E + 02
ton-force (2000 lbf)	newton (N)	8.896 444 E + 03
tonne	kilogram (kg)	1.000 000 E + 03
yard (yd)	meter (m)	9.144 000 E − 01
yd^2	square meter (m^2)	8.361 274 E − 01
yd^3	cubic meter (m^3)	7.645 549 E − 01
yd^3/min	cubic meters per second (m^3/s)	1.274 258 E − 02

Table F-1   SI CONVERSION DATA *(Continued)*

Some Derived SI Units

Quantity	Unit	Symbol	Formula
Force	newton	N	$kg \cdot m/s^2$
Pressure, stress	pascal	Pa	N/m^2
Energy	joule	J	$N \cdot m$
Power	watt	W	J/s

Other Units in Use with SI

Quantity	Unit	Symbol	Definition
Volume	liter	L	$1 \text{ L} = 10^{-3} \text{ m}^3$
Mass	metric ton	t	$1 \text{ t} = 10^3 \text{ kg}$
Cross section	barn	b	$1 \text{ b} = 10^{-28} \text{ m}^2$
Pressure	bar	bar	$1 \text{ bar} = 10^5 \text{ Pa}$

Some SI Prefixes

Multiplication Factor	Prefix	Symbol
10^6	mega	M
10^3	kilo	k
10^2	hecto	h
10^1	deka	da
10^{-1}	deci	d
10^{-2}	centi	c
10^{-3}	milli	m

*Conversion factors are written as a number equal to or greater than 1 and less than 10. This number is followed by the letter E (for "exponent"), a plus or minus symbol, and two digits which indicate the power of 10 by which the number must be multiplied to obtain the correct value.

SOURCE: Adapted from *Standard for Metric Practice*, ASTM E 380-79, American Society for Testing and Materials, Philadelphia, 1980.

Table F-2

DECIMALS OF AN INCH
For each 64th of an inch
With Millimeter Equivalents

Fraction	1/64ths	Decimal	Millimeters (Approx.)	Fraction	1/64ths	Decimal	Millimeters (Approx.)
...	1	.015625	0.397	...	33	.515625	13.097
1/32	2	.03125	0.794	17/32	34	.53125	13.494
...	3	.046875	1.191	...	35	.546875	13.891
1/16	4	.0625	1.588	9/16	36	.5625	14.288
...	5	.078125	1.984	...	37	.578125	14.684
3/32	6	.09375	2.381	19/32	38	.59375	15.081
...	7	.109375	2.778	...	39	.609375	15.478
1/8	8	.125	3.175	5/8	40	.625	15.875
...	9	.140625	3.572	...	41	.640625	16.272
5/32	10	.15625	3.969	21/32	42	.65625	16.669
...	11	.171875	4.366	...	43	.671875	17.066
3/16	12	.1875	4.763	11/16	44	.6875	17.463
...	13	.203125	5.159	...	45	.703125	17.859
7/32	14	.21875	5.556	23/32	46	.71875	18.256
...	15	.234375	5.953	...	47	.734375	18.653
1/4	16	.250	6.350	3/4	48	.750	19.050
...	17	.265625	6.747	...	49	.765625	19.447
9/32	18	.28125	7.144	25/32	50	.78125	19.844
...	19	.296875	7.541	...	51	.796875	20.241
5/16	20	.3125	7.938	13/16	52	.8125	20.638
...	21	.328125	8.334	...	53	.828125	21.034
11/32	22	.34375	8.731	27/32	54	.84375	21.431
...	23	.359375	9.128	...	55	.859375	21.828
3/8	24	.375	9.525	7/8	56	.875	22.225
...	25	.390625	9.922	...	57	.890625	22.622
13/32	26	.40625	10.319	29/32	58	.90625	23.019
...	27	.421875	10.716	...	59	.921875	23.416
7/16	28	.4375	11.113	15/16	60	.9375	23.813
...	29	.453125	11.509	...	61	.953125	24.209
15/32	30	.46875	11.906	31/32	62	.96875	24.606
...	31	.484375	12.303	...	63	.984375	25.003
1/2	32	.500	12.700	1	64	1.000	25.400

SOURCE: Courtesy of American Institute of Steel Construction.

Table F-3

DECIMALS OF A FOOT
For each 32nd of an inch

Inch	0	1	2	3	4	5
0	0	.0833	.1667	.2500	.3333	.4167
1/32	.0026	.0859	.1693	.2526	.3359	.4193
1/16	.0052	.0885	.1719	.2552	.3385	.4219
3/32	.0078	.0911	.1745	.2578	.3411	.4245
1/8	.0104	.0938	.1771	.2604	.3438	.4271
5/32	.0130	.0964	.1797	.2630	.3464	.4297
3/16	.0156	.0990	.1823	.2656	.3490	.4323
7/32	.0182	.1016	.1849	.2682	.3516	.4349
1/4	.0208	.1042	.1875	.2708	.3542	.4375
9/32	.0234	.1068	.1901	.2734	.3568	.4401
5/16	.0260	.1094	.1927	.2760	.3594	.4427
11/32	.0286	.1120	.1953	.2786	.3620	.4453
3/8	.0313	.1146	.1979	.2812	.3646	.4479
13/32	.0339	.1172	.2005	.2839	.3672	.4505
7/16	.0365	.1198	.2031	.2865	.3698	.4531
15/32	.0391	.1224	.2057	.2891	.3724	.4557
1/2	.0417	.1250	.2083	.2917	.3750	.4583
17/32	.0443	.1276	.2109	.2943	.3776	.4609
9/16	.0469	.1302	.2135	.2969	.3802	.4635
19/32	.0495	.1328	.2161	.2995	.3828	.4661
5/8	.0521	.1354	.2188	.3021	.3854	.4688
21/32	.0547	.1380	.2214	.3047	.3880	.4714
11/16	.0573	.1406	.2240	.3073	.3906	.4740
23/32	.0599	.1432	.2266	.3099	.3932	.4766
3/4	.0625	.1458	.2292	.3125	.3958	.4792
25/32	.0651	.1484	.2318	.3151	.3984	.4818
13/16	.0677	.1510	.2344	.3177	.4010	.4844
27/32	.0703	.1536	.2370	.3203	.4036	.4870
7/8	.0729	.1563	.2396	.3229	.4063	.4896
29/32	.0755	.1589	.2422	.3255	.4089	.4922
15/16	.0781	.1615	.2448	.3281	.4115	.4948
31/32	.0807	.1641	.2474	.3307	.4141	.4974

Table F-3 *(Continued)*

DECIMALS OF A FOOT
For each 32nd of an inch

Inch	6	7	8	9	10	11
0	.5000	.5833	.6667	.7500	.8333	.9167
1/32	.5026	.5859	.6693	.7526	.8359	.9193
1/16	.5052	.5885	.6719	.7552	.8385	.9219
3/32	.5078	.5911	.6745	.7578	.8411	.9245
1/8	.5104	.5938	.6771	.7604	.8438	.9271
5/32	.5130	.5964	.6797	.7630	.8464	.9297
3/16	.5156	.5990	.6823	.7656	.8490	.9323
7/32	.5182	.6016	.6849	.7682	.8516	.9349
1/4	.5208	.6042	.6875	.7708	.8542	.9375
9/32	.5234	.6068	.6901	.7734	.8568	.9401
5/16	.5260	.6094	.6927	.7760	.8594	.9427
11/32	.5286	.6120	.6953	.7786	.8620	.9453
3/8	.5313	.6146	.6979	.7813	.8646	.9479
13/32	.5339	.6172	.7005	.7839	.8672	.9505
7/16	.5365	.6198	.7031	.7865	.8698	.9531
15/32	.5391	.6224	.7057	.7891	.8724	.9557
1/2	.5417	.6250	.7083	.7917	.8750	.9583
17/32	.5443	.6276	.7109	.7943	.8776	.9609
9/16	.5469	.6302	.7135	.7969	.8802	.9635
19/32	.5495	.6328	.7161	.7995	.8828	.9661
5/8	.5521	.6354	.7188	.8021	.8854	.9688
21/32	.5547	.6380	.7214	.8047	.8880	.9714
11/16	.5573	.6406	.7240	.8073	.8906	.9740
23/32	.5599	.6432	.7266	.8099	.8932	.9766
3/4	.5625	.6458	.7292	.8125	.8958	.9792
25/32	.5651	.6484	.7318	.8151	.8984	.9818
13/16	.5677	.6510	.7344	.8177	.9010	.9844
27/32	.5703	.6536	.7370	.8203	.9036	.9870
7/8	.5729	.6563	.7396	.8229	.9063	.9896
29/32	.5755	.6589	.7422	.8255	.9089	.9922
15/16	.5781	.6615	.7448	.8281	.9115	.9948
31/32	.5807	.6641	.7474	.8307	.9141	.9974

SOURCE: Courtesy of American Institute of Steel Construction.

Index

About the Author

Frank M. Fuller is a registered professional engineer and has had a career of over 30 years with Raymond International Builders, Inc. (originally Raymond Concrete Pile Company), devoted entirely to pile foundation design and construction. Currently he serves as assistant vice president and manager of technical sales. During his career, Mr. Fuller has worked with many technical committees on the preparation of codes and standards relating to pile foundations. Founder, principal writer, and editor of the technical magazine *Foundation Facts*, he is also the author of numerous published papers, a contributor to various textbooks, and the technical adviser on several motion pictures, and he has been issued nine patents relating to pile foundations. He is a member of various professional and technical organizations, including the American Society of Civil Engineers (of which he is a life fellow), the American Concrete Institute, and the American Society for Testing and Materials.